PARALLELS

A Broad Look at Nature's Fascinating Ways

V.S.SURY

Notion Press

Old No. 38, New No. 6
McNichols Road, Chetpet
Chennai - 600 031

First Published by Notion Press 2020
Copyright © V.S.Sury 2020
All Rights Reserved.

ISBN 978-1-64850-885-1

DEDICATED TO

The sweet memory of
Sri S. Sankara Sastry, who was my collegemate,
friend, and brother: in that order of increasing affection.

CONTENTS

INTRODUCTION

It was announced recently that the English language crossed the million words landmark. A language containing a million words is vast indeed. One can only despair of ever knowing all the million words it contains. And then, proceed to think of how many *books* have been (and are being, even as these words are being typed) written in that language. I said, proceed to think, only, because I am sure you will give up very soon after you make a few valiant attempts.

That, as they say, was for starters. We began with the English language. There must be at least a dozen languages in the world that are nearly as rich (don't focus on the exact number one million), if not as pervasive. And then proceed–just make an attempt–to think of all the books that have been written in all those languages. Just so as not to overstrain your brain, I am not going to raise the topic of how many languages there are in the world and the number of books mankind has produced. The mind cannot conceive of such a humongous number. You can only ask a computer to compute that number and stare at it, without comprehending.

The situation appears to be hopeless when looked at in the above manner. Out of these mindboggling numbers, would there be a way to tackle the subject and find graspable, simplified order? A moment's patient consideration opens up an avenue of approach. Take, for example, the English language, and all the books (and printed matter too) that have been published so far. We can recognize that this humongous number (yes, we repeat the word) is the outcome of only the million words that the language contains. We can sigh in relief; that was a good reduction of an ungraspable number. Can we dare to go further? Oh, yes; the next line of reasoning is already beckoning us. *All the million and odd words of the language are produced just by using the 26 letters of the alphabet!* Think of it. Just by using the 26 letters of the alphabet, we have been producing for more than a thousand years an unimaginable number of sentences and phrases, and we will continue to do so. The same reasoning applies to all the other languages of the world.

We can proceed in the same vein and consider the sounds we produce: spoken words, poetry, music, and even plain noise–again, an infinite variety. All that can be boiled down to the variations in the frequency of sound waves, roughly between 100 and 30,000 cycles. This too can further be simplified and perceived as the manipulation of a laughably few items– throat, vocal cords, lips, tongue, and teeth. Man indeed is an ingenious animal.

Having used that word animal, my mind immediately conjures up the images of all the birds and animals; more–all things animate and inanimate. Put in other words, it is Nature. We can qualify the last sentence of the previous paragraph and say that Nature is ingenious. It has to be, one supposes, considering the unimaginable vastness of Nature. If we observe the endless phenomena of Nature, a pattern gradually emerges. The most striking is the phenomenon of parallels. In a small and limited field, Nature utilizes a particular program or way of functioning. And then it uses the same or similar template–to use an engineering term–to create a wide variety of other phenomena, to expand its kingdom of creation.

This theme of parallels has been fascinating me for a long time, and I would like to share that fascination with my readers.

Special Note: The personal pronouns I, we, and you are freely interchanged in these essays. This has been done so deliberately with a view to involve all (of us!). There is a subtler reasoning too behind this. The theme, the burden of this book, is to highlight the parallel phenomena occurring without limits, across diverse fields in Nature. Nothing is more obvious than that of thinking; it is happening incessantly all the time in the minds of all the human beings: us, you, I, and they. Seen from that perspective, the act of thinking is a common phenomenon for humans. Hence, to reflect this spirit, he, the narrator, jumps freely across all these pronouns. (The 'we' used in the pages below is not at all the royal 'we' employed by the kings and princes of yore! It is the exoteric I and you and all of us. The three pronouns have been deliberately used in these pages, in free exchange.) While reading these pages, imagine that you yourself are thinking and writing them down. It is your book, it is your universe. This book is only a door. Your walk inside is limited only by your imagination and energy.

There are a few concepts and examples which the reader will encounter repeatedly at random in these pages. It is quite natural in a subject like this, since all things in the world are interconnected. This is a book of parallels, so a fitting parallel is offered here. In the course of our daily lives, we meet many persons (friends or otherwise) almost every day, or at least quite often. It is part of life. This book too is an attempt at having a glimpse of life, and thus you are bound to meet, bump into some familiar ideas and sayings again and again. *Greet them as you would your familiar friend.*

Taste of things to come – Main Menu

How It All Unfolds

As above so below: This is a famous saying which crops up in a couple of Eastern philosophical systems. I am sure that many of my readers are familiar with the phrase. Not only above and below, but everywhere can you find surprising similarities in function or structure or other qualities. This fact is the main burden of the songs (in prose, why not?) in this book. Brief mention will be made of an interesting example as an introduction, and the rest will be elaborated upon as we proceed at a calm, leisurely pace.

The most interesting, unmissable similarity for what is happening above being (faithfully?) reflected below is this one. Going 'below' dives into the depths of matter, says the atom. Soaring 'above' goes up to the solar system. The meaning is obvious to any student of science at the school level. Let us fill up the dotted lines anyway. In the standard model for the structure of an atom, there is a center called nucleus deep, deep inside. Around this nucleus, electrons orbit continuously at various distances. This is astonishingly similar to the structure and functioning of the solar system! Replace the nucleus with the sun, and the electrons with the planets. Just as the planets unceasingly orbit around the sun, (being held in its grip) electrons orbit around the nucleus (being held in its grip).

Along somewhat similar lines, we see that our earth spins on its axis. Looks like everything spins everywhere! (Just a wee bit of poetic exaggeration, only a tiny bit.) Go below once again. Science buffs speak nonchalantly of the spin of electrons and other particles as a matter of routine. It does not much matter here if their definition of spin and yours (and ours) do not match fully. A spin is a spin. (Every cricket player agrees with that. Baseball players agree with that, though may call it a curve.) From the depths of the atom, come up to the familiar surface. A gyroscope spins, often at fantastic speeds; there are a good many gadgets and technical instruments which utilize that principle of the gyroscope. Rise up, as before, to greater heights into space itself. We and our solar system are a part (tiny) of the great Milky Way galaxy. The galaxy also is spinning, astronomers assure us. So do many galaxies, neutron star-couples, and so on. If you observe the range from that of the electrons to the locations (and sizes) of the galaxies, it is mindboggling. (An irreverent, if not irrelevant comment by The Brat, whom you are going to meet quite often in these mental peregrinations. Brat enquires with false sympathy, "Does your head reel?" and then proceeds without waiting for a retort, "That reminds me of vertigo. It is a kind of spin. Either physical or mental or neurological. It is a spin and spinning exhibits are not only up there in the skies, but inside our skulls too!" Better be acquainted with him.) We reluctantly have to admit that he has got a point there.

Strings: Strings hold up or keep things from falling down. That clothesline in your backyard is an everyday example. Strings bring things together. Look at a garland of flowers or a necklace. Strings can hold things in check and can manipulate them too. You only have to look at a harness and witness a puppet show. Strings can vibrate and give out music. (Quiz: How many stringed musical instruments can you name? Hurdy-gurdy, bouzouki, rebab, komuz, ghaychak, huobosi…) Already a parallel here: the poet insists that hearts too have strings and can be pulled to induce a variety of emotions.

Recall that a person in a tight emotional condition is said to be highly strung, or keyed up. How apt the description is!

Strings hold things in check. That is what the harness does to the horse. That is what the string does to the paper kite rising and falling and dancing in the sky.

Jump to another metaphor. People wielding power control those under them by pulling the proper strings.

In quite a different context, if the strings are made of metal (usually copper or silver), they can be used to carry electricity and the receiving machine can be controlled from a distance, through push-buttons and dials.

Do not underestimate those strings. We saw above that properly activated, they can enact an enchanting puppet drama out of inanimate objects. They can also–rhetorically–induce or control emotions in living beings. There is more. Nature enjoys playing many kinds of games (we are going to repeat this on every possible occasion; better brace yourself), play on words also being one of them. Okay, come back to that word and imagine long strings embracing each other, going around and around.

There, you have the DNA strands entwined in an intimate embrace, the very basis of all living forms.

The intimate embrace of the DNA strands is reflected in other ways in life forms and our lives. That embrace represents love, support, and inseparability (parallels, parallels everywhere) acting across the full stretch of Life itself. Witness the tight embraces of lovers all over the world, and nod your head in sympathetic agreement. It happens not only among creatures (snakes do it), but also among creepers! Go to your backyard and watch that tender creeper going up and around the tree trunk. What Nature is doing there, it is doing here and elsewhere also! (This too, is the burden of our pet song, and the lines will be sung again and again across these pages. Brace yourself.)

Up there we had a peep at the level of the basis of life. The same parallel phenomenon is hidden still deeper, at the level of the creation of the universe itself. We need not look askance at the mystics and theosophists for an answer. Scientists themselves are here to encourage us. It is the String Theory we are talking about. (A whisper; notice the play on the word String. We did not make it up–Nature did it!) The topic is very arcane and crammed with lots of the toughest mathematics. Better leave the details to the boffins, geeks, and nerds. Put in plain words, the String Theory posits that the creation of the world occurs due to the vibrations of strings in many dimensions. Hectic research has been going on on this hot topic and most scientists are confident that the String Theory will offer the final solution to everything in the universe. For our purpose, the metaphor of the String is enough.

What was offered above is an appetizer for an elaborate feast to come. You can pick on any concept, idea, fancy, natural phenomenon, scientific law, even words from the dictionary, and then you will be surprised to see that those ideas have analogies in diverse fields. That is not really much of a surprise if you see that all things in the universe are richly interconnected. This is the main menu, a gist so to say, of this book. We will leisurely examine whatever comes into our reach, link it up with the next item or perhaps with another one far down the list and come back, and so on. There is no particular preference or sequence. To say in another metaphor, this is like a walk in an immense park with innumerable roads and crossroads, and roundabouts. The visitor can saunter as (s)he likes, where (s)he wills.

CHAPTER 1

STATES

Three states: *srushti, sthiti, laya*

This is a beaut; in fact, it is grand and profound also. In some of the ancient Eastern philosophical systems, this is the core idea, the foundation for all the manifestations of Creation. Even when seen from the 'scientific' way of thinking, the idea holds good, being interwoven with faultless, seamless logic. Innumerable books have been written about the above concept by both ancient and modern thinkers. I am sure the diligent (and intelligent) readers can also find books offering even mathematical treatment on this profound concept.

The words in italics (in the title of the chapter), *srushti, sthiti,* and *laya* are of Sanskrit, an ancient language of India. Put very briefly, the concept runs like this. Creation (call it Nature, World, Universe, what you like) always and everywhere exists/runs in three states. The first one is *srushti,* creation; the essential connotation of creation is that 'something' comes into being–a state of existence–out of 'something.' (That 'something' can be anything! Yeah, it has been called nothing, nonexistence, zero, the Ground, the Source, the origin, 'breaking of symmetry!' Energy, the Tau: the list is long indeed. If you are so inclined, you may even add word, mind, and God to the list!) In fact, if you peep behind the back of that word, you will naturally intuit that creation implies that there was nothing

15

(or something else!) before the act, the manifestation. Let us keep it simple and stop it there; it serves our purpose well and that is enough. The next word of the mantra is *sthiti*. It roughly connotes maintenance or a state of continuance. This concept is easy enough to need little or no explanation. Once something comes into being, it is simple to accept that it continues to be (to exist). But, alas, philosophers and thinkers will not allow you to live peacefully in a simple way. They will shout at you that nothing is permanent in the world. They (at least the majority of them) insist that what (ever) comes into being must inevitably dissolve–sooner or later. The theosophical, teleological explanations are too erudite and abstract and involuted and recondite for innocent folk like you and me! But we can use our common sense and *observe* the world all around us; we can see that what those scholarly folks are trying to prove does not need wordy explanations. The common sense adage expresses it well, "Nothing is permanent." That is what our word *laya* is trying to tell us. *Laya* means *dissolution*. Theosophically, it connotes that that which came into being and was in a state of existence for a brief time (do not worry; brief, in the Indian system of thought may mean a period of time that may literally knock the breath out of you. We will mention it at an appropriate moment) merges eventually ("inevitably") into that from which it arose in the beginning.

In theosophical circles, the above profound idea refers directly to the world/universe as a whole. Now, reflecting back on our theme of parallels, we can apply the concept to many phenomena in life around us at many levels, and appreciate the simplicity and beauty of it. (Hey, remember the apothegm, "as above, so below!") There is no point in elaborately dwelling on the many similes that we can observe. We will give brief notes as we go along, allowing the reader to savor the beauty of it all.

States, daily: The above paragraphs dealt the topic at the most fundamental and universal level. Nature plays the same drama at a different level and in far greater frequencies. The states here refer to the state of a person's awareness, its clarity, brightness, and extension.

In the wake of the above idea of states of existence, we can immediately find a very beautiful parallel in what, again the Eastern philosophy calls, the states of *jagruti, swapna, sushupti*. Actually, the terms are used in discussing deep philosophy, but we will take the literal interpretation and proceed along those lines. These Sanskrit terms mean wakefulness, dreaming, and deep (dreamless) slumber, in that order. The states are common to all human beings. Wakefulness (to be aware) is a beautiful, poetic parallel to the act of creation. Creation has no meaning unless the act is witnessed—which, in essence, is the faculty of awareness. The second state, that of dreaming, can be interpreted as the state of continuing and maintaining awareness (in all its various shades). In the next state, that of deep dreamless slumber, there is no awareness of any mental or physical activity. This state, astonishingly, resembles the state of death! If you do not like that term, you can say dissolution of erstwhile 'normal' states. To repeat, the high drama of Creation and Dissolution is being played daily on the canvass of individual consciousness! In justified poetical rapture, one can say (exclaim) that Nature first conceived Creation and Dissolution. The time span was too long. Nature got impatient, because the act was fraught with delight (bliss, *ananda*) that only it could appreciate, and Nature wanted more and more of it again and again—forever! That is why it is enacting that drama every day, on a different scale and with less intensity (so that fragile humans may not burst) on the mental screens of human beings. Note the subtlety too. (This may be considered as wild speculation by some, but it is worth the exercise!) The act of creation and dissolution, we said, is a delight itself. The potion enjoyed by one human being during the three daily states is small, it was said. Then consider the number of humans that are undergoing such states daily across the surface of planet Earth—seven billion something. Add it all up and see how much that 'potion' totals up to. That is what Nature is enjoying through all of us combined. Nay, there is more. Add the (countless) number of animals and other creatures that sleep and wake up daily. Can you sum up the 'delight potion' of all such creatures? It is almost impossible—unless you go to a mathematical nerd;

and *he* goes to his *computer* to compute! Nay, there is still more. Consider the numbers of all the creatures that have been sleeping and waking up from time immemorial. Now add that sum up. We bet even your computer throws up its hands! (Meditate on this for some time and leisurely savor the delight before proceeding further.)

P.S. The foregoing paragraph refers you to the signpost reading 'ranges.' What Nature does once in so many billion years, it is also doing, in its own inimitable way, every day. Compare the range of one day and billions of years. If you want to rush to the chapter on ranges, we have no objection.

*In the description of the above paragraph we can notice that the different states are of a single object, the object being consciousness or awareness—which grows bright, dim, or goes into hibernation (as in a state of unconsciousness, or in deep sleep). Harping on the theme of parallels, we can see that Nature mirrors this property of being in different states, in the realm of matter also. Take the most common matter on earth—water. Water can exist in three different states. In its normal state, it is a liquid. When heated, it becomes steam. When cooled down below zero degrees, it becomes ice, a solid. Many metals and gasses too exhibit similar changes of states; not necessarily all the three, but at least two. Under very low temperatures, gasses can turn into liquids. As opposed to this, metals turn to liquid form when heated to high temperatures. Not only metals, but even rock too can melt and become a fluid—go and peer into a live volcano. (Suggestion only, please do not do it literally unless you are seated in a helicopter at a safe altitude!) By way of mentioning, liquids can also be in special states called colloidal form which is a special mixture of fine solid particles and liquid. Some solids too can exist with special structural identity, being defined as crystals. This does not affect what was said about the states of matter, but only adds further refinement in classification (in which Nature excels and seems to enjoy it).

There is another way of looking at the states of matter described above. Matter can be in a state of movement and can be also fixed. Liquids and gasses move constantly–like rivers and air. The rigid, fixed state is best illustrated by the mountains (and buildings!). Once more, Nature exhibits its special taste for nuances. There are solid objects that do not move, but yet move. And, as if mirroring the act, there are liquids that do not move but yet move! Does this sound like a contradiction? Not really, when you hear the word vibration. A solid, like a long pole, appears to be rigid but it is vibrating due to the effect of the surrounding air. Even tall buildings do so. Similarly, water exhibits this kind of property by way of waves. The water in a lake is unmoving. Waves on its surface mirror the quality of movement. As a humorous parallel, a person can also imitate this kind of act by standing fixed on a spot, but by waving his arms. (Smiling is permitted if you see a pun here! You can stretch the smile a bit more if you are willing to consider a person in deep slumber. That person is at rest, to use the term from physics. Yet he is moving, because you forgot to observe where the person is sleeping–like a log, as the idiom claims. The person is inside a transatlantic jet liner cruising at a steady high speed! For god's sake, don't bring in the Theory of Relativity and spoil the fun.) By the way, the topic of states deserves a haiku-tribute. Jump to the chapter on haikus if you cannot contain your curiosity, and come back here after your thirst is quenched.

CHAPTER 2

WHEELS WITHIN WHEELS; ALL THE WAY

The other day, you read in the newspaper about the death of a well-known person. The paper said that the person died due to the failure of multiple organs. That set you thinking in a kind of wondering-wandering mode. Multiple organs—that was the triggering phrase.

Let us take a look at the body of a living person. Normally, we think of the body as a single, whole unit; naturally, for the person is a single whole unit. Now go back to your school days and remember the basic biology lessons you were taught. You will remember that the body has many internal organs: brain, heart, liver, lungs, pancreas, and so on. Right? Each organ is a separate unit and *functions* beautifully as an organized living body. True, the units are mutually interdependent and interlinked functionally. But for our insight here, the point to be underlined is that there are several units functioning independently, in the sense that they have specific "assignments" and are marvelously capable of carrying on those assignments. (Of course, in terms of functionality, there are the external units like the arms, legs, etc. But we are focusing on the internal organs as they are more 'refined' and almost autonomous.)

Put aside the strictly scientific way and look at the above-mentioned human body from a marveling poetic view. There is one living body out

20

there, and then there are many living bodies inside that outer body. Bodies within bodies (wheels within wheels?).

Once you start a series, the temptation to extrapolate (as the mathematicians would fondly say) cannot be resisted. If there be bodies within bodies, then why not bodies be within bodies within bodies? Despite sounding slightly facetious, the question has an answer in an affirmative assertion. Take the 'heart' in the previously stated list of internal organs. Along the lines of the outer body, the heart too is structured (constructed) employing muscles and membranes and arteries and so on. The muscles have their own unique shapes and functions; they live like 'individual' independent entities in their own territory—see, wheels within wheels!

Can we go further, draw further parallels? Sure. Look at one of the structural units of the heart, like the muscle. The muscle too has been 'structured.' We do not need a deep knowledge of biology. Our basic-level knowledge is enough to tell us that the muscles are made up of cells—*living cells*. See the wonder of it. Each cell is a *living* unit. Each cell is a complete *functioning* unit. I am not ashamed to whisper, "Wheels within wheels." (I am thrilled, in fact.) An aside: see, we already have two parallels running along. One is that of structures within structures. The other is of living units within living units. ("A great wonder, my Lord. Please don't laugh my Lord, nothing less than Poetry can do justice to your creation!")

The universe—life, whatever—is densely packed with the ganglia of these parallels and parallels, parallels running along with parallels, and parallels within parallels in its every nook and corner. The only limit is our capacity to observe. Consider this book as a small park, and that you are invited to have a leisurely stroll. After you leave, you will realize that there are no boundaries to the park. The 'leisurely stroll' is going to be a lifelong affair. Just as we do in a park we will pace through the pages of this book unhurriedly, often looking back at a scene we have passed in order to appreciate its beauty again. We will perchance stop now and then, and take a 360-degree view of the panorama, inhaling the beauty and wondrous atmosphere before going further, and things of that sort.

Ah, where were we? Cells–life. Stop, look around and go to the 'Biology' chapter. Tarry, better have a second look at the plot 'structures and units of structure' before you proceed.

*Human world: This core concept is probably going to reappear several times in these pages. So, I will make a brief presentation.

(The nature of the theme of this book itself is such that repetitions cannot be avoided–since everything is connected with everything else. Do I detect an incipient sneer on the face of the dear reader? The sneer is unwarranted. Look back at your last month. Try to make a ballpark estimate of how much you must have talked during that period–the number of words that you have spoken. If you are the average extrovert type, the number could be quite big. Now, diligently write down all the words. Then, count those words which you have repeated, and strike them off. Look at the remaining words. I assure you that you will be aghast at how little the number of words there are on that paper, *which have not been repeated*. Probably it may even be zero! That is so even with the most original novels or books. Recently, I got hold of a bestseller book on popular science containing around twelve hundred thousand printed words. After I struck down all repeated words, there remained roughly only seven thousand words! Repetition is the essence of life. More on this in the chapter on cycles.)

Back to the human world and structures within structures. A straightforward enumeration will suffice to bring home the point. The earth, our human world, contains about 195 nations. Structurally, the nations contain many numbers of administrative units like states (Russia, USA, India, etc. for example). Moving further inside, we see that the states are again divided into districts. Wheels within wheels–the districts in turn contain a good number of units called *zillas* and *hoblis*, as in India. Other countries too, follow similar divisions, with different nomenclature.

Those units again contain many smaller units such as cities and towns. The division does not stop there. Cities and towns also are divided into smaller areas like boroughs, precincts, wards, and so on. Oh, and then there are streets and lastly, streets contain buildings and homes. If you want to continue the links further and claim that buildings contain families, we will not object. But the classification will change from the inanimate to the animate, that is all. Further, the family as a group contains individual persons. That appears to be the bottom line. But following the concept that a big unit is made of smaller units, we can again look inside the individual person's body and discover that it too is an assembly of many smaller units (working together and supporting the bigger, parent unit) like the brain, the heart, sensing organs, organs of movement like limbs, digestive organs, excretory organs, and above all, a protective organ enclosing all these; there are many more units left out here! Quite an elaborate mechanism, is it not? Not yet. Nature goes still deeper down. These working organs are further assembled out of yet smaller units–again, working units. Working by themselves, but more importantly, supporting the main parental organ. These marvelous units are the cells.

Things do not stop here. The process of breaking up into smaller units can be continued into the land of the inanimate, that of matter. It is quite elaborate, and we will be leisurely taking up these classifications at regular intervals as we proceed.

Wheels within wheels. Creation itself is referred to as a wheel by many old philosophies. Recall the familiar phrase 'wheel of creation' here. The wheel rolls and every point on it comes back to its original position in each revolution. This symbolizes what the ancient theologies describe as the eternally repeating cycles of creation and destruction.

Cycle–that word should remind you of all the bicycles (merrily and facilely running on wheels) that throng the streets of the world. That is why we feel (nay, we are sure) that *Nature inspired man to invent the wheel!* It wants to remind us that everything is cyclical. *That* should remind you this time of Time itself! And thereby man invented wheels with teeth (gears) and the wheels ran and rolled and gave us clocks–one of the grandest metaphors abundantly occurring in Nature. It may appear as trivial, but is not, that all the clocks had wheels with interlinked wheels. (Are you objecting here that we have now electronic, digital clocks? No worries. *It is again a metaphor indicating that times have changed!*)

A counterargument on that score. Times have changed, but not. What does it mean? The inner core theme, that of wheels with interconnected wheels, has not changed. Your best and unimaginably complex digital programs invariably have innumerable smaller routines and sub-routines interlinked with one another. Indeed, the phrase wheels within wheels, does not sound like a metaphor at all; it reflects a necessary mechanism by which machineries (all kinds, in all fields) run.

CHAPTER 3

CYCLES GALORE (OR WHO IS AFRAID OF INFINITY?)

Infinity is awesome, whether it be of time or space or matter. In non-mathematical terms, it can be designated as the immeasurable.

Yet, the human mind manages to grasp it in quite a different way. Take a minute quantity of the infinite, designate it as a unit. And keep on adding up that unit as long as you need or like, or forever! The first two options are the most practical, down-to-earth methods, useful in all our affairs. That is why Nature has filled our lives with cyclical acts and events.

At the most fundamental level, the universe can be seen as made up of three items: space, matter, and time. All the three are of unimaginable magnitude. Immeasurable. Yet, the strange part of it is that the human mind attempts (and manages to succeed for all practical purposes) to measure the immeasurable. How does it achieve it? Simple, or simply beautiful, as you prefer. We invent a small, manageable measuring unit and keep on measuring using such a unit as long as the units add up to the whole of that which is to be measured. Depending on the size of the item to be measured, the units can be as small as a millimeter or as big as a light-year. In this section, we are mainly interested in time and things which happen in it, like actions.

We can start measuring time by seconds.

Time by itself has not much relevance unless it is linked with action, which connotes change in position, or change in conditions of existence of an object. Just as time can be seen as an addition of seconds, change can be seen in many circumstances as consisting of cycles, repetitive acts. The beauty is that there are plenty of cyclical acts wherever we look. Almost all events of long duration can be broken up as cumulation of small cycles. Where time is not involved, the entities can be seen as cumulation of small bits and bytes! (The signpost reads bits and bytes at this crossroad. If feeling curious, the reader may saunter along that road in the spirit of a flaneur, and come back later. The crossroads and signposts are going to become a familiar sight. Better, the reader fills up his backpack with plenty of foodstuff and drinks!) A few examples will suffice here to highlight the phenomenon.

Begin with the beginning of our lives. One's whole life, seen from a purely biological angle, is a continuous, yes, nonstop workout; that of the heartbeats! The whole, awesome lifespan is a relentless repetitive act of small duration, one pulse, of roughly one-seventieth of a minute. Additional biological acts follow the same pattern of different durations. Like heartbeats, breathing keeps up without a break for an entire lifespan. Again, it is a cumulation of small cycles of inhalation and exhalation– repetitive acts. Digestion of food, sleep, regeneration of the body's cells, discharge of certain waste products, etc. are the other kinds of cyclical acts.

This naturally reminds us of the most familiar cycle of days and nights. That, of course, is due to the cyclical act of the earth spinning on its axis. The earth also keeps on going around the sun, adding up (and counting down at the same time!) years to our lives. The phrase 'circadian rhythm' is familiar to all of us in this context.

You start measuring infinity by counting just one. Hold on. But you go on repeating the act as long as you need it, or like it; that is all. (Bright, brilliant boy Brat–whom you are going to meet often from now on–says, "Now, you have a firm grip on infinity. The only thing needed is not to let go of it.") Do not ridicule the power of the number one. All your supercomputing, all your digital wonder-gizmos are built on the mysterious power of one (and none, if one is allowed to run one pun). An entertaining philosophical contemplation may well run as follows. One is the One, in the sense that it is all inclusive. It is also the countless individual entities as being separate. See, it is like this. Out there, there are guys: John, Ford, Bill, Will, and so on. They are all single persons only in their own right. If you count them, the count comes to ten. But, Zeno, ten does not exist, Zeno. Ten is a convenient number used in dealing with practical (or commercial) matters. Thus, only one exists. (Brat – "As one in each of those ten. Or a million, or a zillion.") Again, if you take the ten trees in a garden together as a group, that ten becomes then one. If you take all the billions and billions of trees on earth as representing a group of plant life, then those billions represent one only! Extending this sequence to everything that exists in the universe, we will see that all the zillion things in the universe become One only. ('O' has been put in caps because of the awe being inspired here.) Enow for now.

*The railway train on its tracks, travels hundreds and even thousands of miles at a stretch. Its wheels keep up the repetitive act of turning round and round. The automobile follows a parallel act—on the roads. (The signpost reads Haiku here. The road there stretches along similar themes and loops back here!)

CHAPTER 4

OPPOSITES

This topic deserves a separate book by itself. But that is for the scholarly; we are going to touch the subject lightly, giving a broad overall perspective.

There is simply no way you can escape from the ubiquitous occurrence of the opposites. They fill every nook and corner of the world. You will be stumbling on them at every step. In fact, you can safely declaim (imitating deep philosophers or a pure scientist) that there cannot be Creation without the opposites. We brought in scientists too, because the broad syllogism runs like this: Knowledge is information. At the most fundamental level, information is something new or a change from uniformity. If everything is totally uniform (homogeneous), technically such a 'field' possesses no information. So, for knowledge to occur, there shall be (Nature decreed) a difference in the homogeneity of the field. This can be brought about in two ways: by a *change* or by the *opposite* of what exists.

There are two signposts at this spot: change and opposites. If you are excited about change, take a turn and rush to that chapter, or if the post 'opposite' lures you more, continue to proceed straight ahead. Nature likes proliferation; it is not stingy. What we mean is this. Apart from those opposites which are strictly necessary for the act(s) of creation, you can find endless examples of opposites everywhere. Simply go to a dictionary of synonyms and antonyms–it will keep you busy for a good length of time.

*The most famous concept in terms of two is 'duality,' especially as in mysticism where it qualifies the nature of our perception of the world–reality and illusion. And then, there is the ancient Chinese concept of Yin and Yang, which stands for an elaborate system of all kinds of opposites in creation. Let us not dare to rush into that debatable area where even angels fear to… yes, you guessed the elision.

*There are plenty of websites which offer you considerable lists of antonyms; it could go on and on. Hence, a small list of opposites for the fun of it, reflecting the main theme of parallels. The obvious start is with God and the Devil! And then we have good-evil (add o to the first, remove d from the second). Beauty-ugliness. White-black. Near-far. Spirit-matter. And then to the sciences…

*In mathematics, we have the most fundamental, indispensable signs: plus and minus, and the signs for multiplication and division apart from other oodles and oodles of recondite symbols). Nature expresses this duality so beautifully and symbolically in the branch of physics (as we classify it) as what are called charges, poles, fields, etc. The result is attraction or repulsion, depending on which kinds of charge react with each other. Like charges (plus and plus, or minus and minus) repel each other and opposite charges (plus and minus) attract each other. As we are never tired of repeating, Nature diversifies in all possible ways. So it has created something unique among these so called 'attracting and repulsing' fields. Electric forces can attract or repulse, magnetic forces can attract and repulse one another. But Nature–as if to baffle us–has created one force which always attracts only. We are sure you have already guessed it. It is the force of universal gravity! Unlike the other two forces, gravity always attracts. There must be a deep and fundamental mystery behind this phenomenon, a complete understanding of which may someday reveal the ultimate secret of the creation of the universe.

(Said, with due respect, to Einstein and the guys who found the God Particle recently.)

*The two opposites, plus and minus, offer beautiful parallels to us. In mathematics (as well as in many other human commercial activities), when the two signs plus and minus come together, the result is zero. If the loss in a business venture equals the profit in that venture, then the net result is zero. If you put three steps forward and come three steps backward, the net result is zero. Now, that zero can also be termed as 'nil.' If you verbify (sorry there, just a wee bit. Twenty-first century English is unbelievably user-friendly. Friendly, in the sense that you can do anything to it and it is still your friend. After all, if you can alter any photo on earth through Photoshop, why can't we do the same with dear old English? See there, another parallel again—we are offering another neologism, 'Photoshopping!' Enough of the digression, *revenons á nos moutons*), yes, verbify 'nil' you have the word 'annihilation.' (We are not deliberately performing acrobatics with words. We are gently, leisurely leading you to a small bend around the corner.) In the previous paragraphs, spirit was shown to be the opposite of matter. But there is another surprising opposite in physics. Yes, antimatter is the opposite of matter. The funny thing is that just as plus and minus cancel/destroy each other in mathematics, matter and antimatter destroy each other if they combine; that is, if they come together! Scientists suspect that there is plenty of antimatter hidden in our universe. If ever we come to meet it, total *annihilation* will be the terrible result. God forbid. The microscopic kind of mutual destruction can occur quite often, and we need not lose sleep over *that*. For example, if an electron (negative) encounters its opposite, the positron (positive) particles destruct each other.

That straightaway brings us to an anomaly (it deserves a separate chapter for itself. You can follow that signpost and come back. Think there are too many parentheses and diverting signposts? That is life for you! Sit in front of your favorite laptop and start browsing. You will open with one single topic and lo, soon you are lost in a quagmire of ads, and ads within ads, and tempting links, and links within links. This book is all about parallels, and we are thus, offering an eminently suitable modus of browsing–*double entendre* there). The anomaly referred to here is that while opposites destroy or cancel each other, opposites also stay and work together in many ways! (Again, for the umpteenth time, an admiring salute to Nature.)

Combining the lines of our two favorite authors, if you are thinking of what we are thinking, that makes two of us! Mention of two opposites staying together should definitely make you think of man and woman! (You can reverse the order and say woman and man; that is fine.) That was for starters. There are plenty of examples in many fields.

A magnet has two opposite kinds of poles, south and north. Almost every kind of magnet comes with these two poles. There is a double parallel here. The north and south poles are situated at the opposite ends of a magnet. The magnet lines of force of the magnet's magnetic field *enter* through one end (pole) and *exit* through the other pole. Similarly, a battery has two opposite kinds of terminals, positive and negative. The plus and minus terminals are electric in nature. Both are necessary for the functioning of a battery. Here too, as in the case of the magnet, electricity leaves the battery through one end (terminal) and enters through the other. Entry and exit also reflect two other technical terms, namely, input and output.

Input and output are reflected in machines of all types. ("Opposites existing together are necessary for the functioning many things.") Even our human bodies are biological machines taking (needing) input at one end and giving output at other end, the input being necessary to produce energy. The output is of the nature of work, of the various organs of the body. If you focus on the words, entry and exit, there too you will get the obvious answers. For energy to be produced, the body needs an inlet for food, an entry point–you have your mouth there. Only a *part* of the total food is converted into energy, and the remaining matter (waste, as we call it) is ejected out of the exit point. Look at that word, part, in italics. There is a beautiful parallel from the point of view of engineering too. In engineering, they use the term efficiency of a machine to denote how much of the input (fuel) is actually converted into energy (output). No machine achieves a hundred percent efficiency; always, only a *part* of the input is converted into energy. Heat engines are famous for their low efficiency. Do not grumble. Psychologists and physiologists assure us that we are all using only a small percentage of the full capacity of our brains. One more parallel for you.

*Before we forget. It is our duty to record man and woman first in the list of opposites; rather, male and female of all life forms. After all, this is the biggest glory of Nature's creative acts. If that is so in the realm of life, then the old Chinese system posits the most sweeping (and equally popular nowadays) concepts of Yin and Yang, roughly equivalent to the male and female principles, and encompassing almost all categories of opposites. The symbol can be found these days wherever you go, or whatever topic you browse.

The parallels spread infinitely from thereon. We will be meeting a few of them as we proceed, in other chapters, inevitably. (The signpost reads haiku. Want to go there and come back?)

CHAPTER 5

INTERACTION, ESSENCE OF CREATION

Nature did not want to create just one simplest of the simple items and keep quiet. To show its infinite joy in the act of creation, it created millions of various things, besides creating trillions of quadrillions of things of the same type.

Next, it did not feel satisfied with that also. Imagine a world filled with, cramped with inert things, trillions and trillions of them, all stiff and cold and dead silent, totally unresponsive. Such a world would be most horrible. That is why Nature made things to react with and respond to other things. That is the essence of creation. All the libraries of the world are nothing but continuous paeons to this Grand Drama of Nature.

Humans are not humans if they do not react with one another. All other creatures do the same. This extends to the world of inanimate matter too. The reactions among particles of matter are also astonishingly extensive and no less varied than those of the living beings. It is not necessary to go on listing all of them; that is the business of textbooks. Mention of a few chosen examples is enough to savor the enchanting grandness of the phenomena.

Reaction can be of two kinds: attractive and repulsive. It is impossible in this context to ignore the fascinating parallels between human world and the world of physics, chemistry, and biology. The attraction between the

33

male and female species of all kinds of life-forms needs no mention at all. In physics, negatively charged and positively charged particles are attracted toward each other. Apart from the gender issue, it is the general characteristic of humans to avidly seek and mingle with their fellow beings. Two persons often develop a strong bond of friendship. Nature exhibits it in the realm of (so called) inert matter too, often in a more explicit way. The elements hydrogen and oxygen form a bond (and help all of us to live,) by becoming water. Three and more persons also often form a close, strong bond. It is reflected in chemistry also. There are innumerable instances where three or more elements combine to form stable compounds. Sulfuric acid and nitric acid, and your famous cyanides are such examples of 'triads.' Most proteins are made of a complex assembly of many elements. Generally, one person interacts with many other persons—a normal phenomenon. In chemistry too, there are elements which easily mix and interact with plenty of other elements. Oxygen, hydrogen, carbon, and nitrogen are good examples of gregariousness!

Interestingly, repulsion too has its parallels in both spheres. In physics, like poles and particles of the same charge repel each other. Among humans too, mysteriously, enmity (repulsion) develops between two persons (and groups, more often)! Among humans, there are those rare anchorites and thinkers who prefer to stay alone, dislike mixing with their fellow beings. In chemistry, there are a few 'neutral' elements which normally do not mix with other elements. Among atomic particles, there are neutrons (with no charge) which do not normally react, or bond with other particles. A few more random samples of the universal phenomenon of interaction are given in the Haiku section.

CHAPTER 6

DIVERSITY IN UNITY

Variations ("We are all same, but I am different." "If God wanted to just create, he would have created one electron, placed it at the center of the universe, and called it a day." – Jestus, a fictional Indian mystic. See footnotes, later.)

I want to start this topic with a grand, prolonged salute to Nature–with two hands, and if I had had a dozen more hands, I would lift all of them simultaneously. Secondly, in our opinion, those two quotes above say it all; they contain the condensed wisdom of a hundred books. We regret that our pen is not puissant enough to scribe a hundred books, but we will try to put forth at least a hundred words on the topic much dear to our heart. We very much want you to see what we are seeing, to feel what we are feeling. Here we (I, you, they) go!

*Trees and trees

There is a road here, in this city, whose sidewalk is filled with neem trees. It is very pleasant to walk under the cool shadows of the trees. As you walk along, one random ripe leaf detaches itself from a branch and lazily lands on your head. You pick it up and once, for a change, instead of being annoyed you become curious and admiringly look at the ripe leaf. You then throw it down on the sidewalk. That is when you notice one more leaf on the sidewalk. You bend down and pick it up; this leaf is a bit bigger in size.

And the color (of the leaf) is not as yellow as the first mellow one. (You are not ashamed of the rhyme. Nor are we. Nor also is the writer. And I am not too. (When we say, we, you, he, I, or writer, or reader, it all means the same. We are contemplating universal ideas in the midst of the vast heart of grand Nature. So, all such personal pronouns meld into one person.)) After that, you notice that there are plenty of neem leaves adorning the ground all around you. This is the end of the description of your physical journey for the day. You take off mentally at this point. You soon realize that the individual leaves are different from one another. There is always some (however slight) difference either in shape or size or weight, or color, etc. But they *are all neem leaves*! ("We are all same, but I am different.") You look up at the tree and realize next that even the stalks that hold the leaves are different from one another. But they all grow out of the same tree. ("We are all same, but I am different.") As your eyes dilate in wonder, gazing up at the tree, you also observe that, eh mon there, oh, even the branches too are different from one another. But they all grow out of the same tree. ("We are all same, but I am different.") It is a real wonder if we look at this in the proper spirit. A small diversion—but a relevant one.

You know why we said it is a wonder? Look at it this way. Suppose you are asked to build a small, compact house. There will be many walls, even if it is a simple house. You have been asked to put up brick walls. So, there will be plenty of bricks that make up your house. Right, okay? Now, all those bricks are identical, confess it! In fact, the factory which manufactures those bricks uses what is called a mould—a model into which the raw materials of the brick are cast again and again, to ensure that all the bricks are identical. More important and to the point is that *this method of manufacturing is easier and consumes the least effort in producing a huge quantity of bricks*. Suppose your proposed building needs, say 50,000 bricks. It will be ridiculous if you ask the supplier to give you 50,000 bricks of different sizes and shapes! (Insane. The supplier will look at you as if you have gone off the rocker. Even a writer of extreme sci-fi books will not touch on such an idea with a barge pole.) Hope we have made the point clear. When you are creating something involving a huge quantity of similar parts, it makes supreme sense to prepare all of them identically. Law of minimum labor, see. But Nature seems to take delight in squandering her energies! She must be having an infinite supply of it–that's why.

Let us come back to the neem tree and have another look. The tree should, following the law of minimum effort (this is a famous law in theoretical physics), produce all leaves with the same identical look, shape, size, weight, color, and so on. You (he, she, it, they, all) will probably laugh reading these lines. But if you look at the concept non-emotionally, without prejudice–say like a robot–you have to agree that the idea makes sense. (Unbelievable economy in production, see? If you print a 10-dollar note, *all the 10-dollar notes will be identical*. Agree?) So, it seems that Nature, apart from having infinite energy, also possesses an infinite supply of time (true, true) and more than that, patience. (Doubt it? Then you can jump to the chapter on Patience, read it patiently, and return here.) What was said about the leaves applies equally well to the fruits and branches and trunks and roots of trees. Trees of all kinds and species.

*Thinking deeply on this, a great unsung and unknown (untraceable, alas) professor, Professor Bagdenborg, has put forward his postulate (among many such). Kindly think again of the syllogism of the tree. All the leaves in a single tree should be identical from the angle of empirical ease of reproduction. But they are not. Yet they have the same name, belong to the same category. Bagdenborg extrapolated this phenomenon to the field of subatomic particles–like protons, neutrons and electrons. Bagdenborg's postulate states that each electron in the universe is different from the other by a slight margin, however slight that margin be. Truly a mindboggling hypothesis when you think of the infinite number of electrons that exist in the universe. "Think of all the human beings that were born on earth from the beginning. Everyone is different from another! The same logic applies in the case of electrons, protons, and neutrons," he persuades us.

(A forthcoming book "Fentoscience" by this author is dedicated to the exclusive insights of this great professor.)

*Numbers: Nature likes diversity, besides many other things. It does not leave numbers too alone! Some of you may murmur, "Numbers are simply numbers, that is all." But tarry. What you murmured is like saying that stones are stones. Ask a geologist; he will throw you a long list of Latinized technical names at you. Numbers too are like that. Ask a mathematician. In an even tone he will describe for your benefit, the characteristics of odd numbers. He does not stop there. Do you know that there are numbers called integers and fractions? That is good. Then you must have surely heard of prime numbers. How about divine numbers? (Ask Pythagoras) There are real numbers and unreal (imaginary) numbers too! (The square root of a negative number, like that of minus one is one such. It forms the fundamental base of what are called complex numbers, using which extraordinary calculations and manipulations and problem-solving procedures are done.) To boot all these names there exist as what are called transcendental numbers. Had enough? If not, there are things called surds (nothing to do with the absurd). You have to ask that mathematician again, to explain what they are. If you still want to continue, he will place before you a line of continued fractions.

*Fruits: Why limit variety to numbers only? Take fruits (as one instance among a million). In India, the mango is called the king of fruits. Do not sneer that a mango is a mango. There are plenty of varieties of mango varying in taste, content, color, and size. Badam, Raspuri, Malgoba, Neelam, and so on. All are mangoes, but each variety comes with a clear, distinctive characteristic of its own.

*Milk. Any subject will do. Even milk. There are milks and milks. Begin with the milk with which we all were brought up, mother's milk, and proceed along. You can have the milk produced by a cow, a buffalo, a goat, a sheep, a camel, and even an ass! Outdoing them (perhaps outnumbering?), there are innumerable companies selling milk powders and products of dizzying varieties. Plants and trees too jump into the fray, so to say, and give out their own brands of 'milk' when scratched or cut. Latex is the most famous and familiar among such kinds. In the end, if you want non-material milk, why, yes, that is also available. It is called the milk of human kindness.

*Water. You will start with the expected exclamation, "Well, water is water. Just as they say a rose is a rose." To that our friend of these pages, the Inner Child, aka Brazen Brat, would promptly respond, "Not well, well-water is well different from tank water. There are waters and waters." Now, you are lured to his way of talking. Well, there is sea water, gravid with minerals and solvents, but alas, unpotable. There are lake waters, both salty and sweet. In the polar regions, it floats on itself, apart from sinking too into itself *at the same time*! (The explanation that it is called an iceberg, is meant only for the moron. Is it not a beautiful irony–something sinking into itself and floating on itself at the same time? We may indulge in figures of speech through words, but Nature shows it to us by actions.) Further, Nature's thirst for variety–pun notwithstanding–is not quenched by turning into ice. For god's sake, do not begin the litany that ice is ice. Ice forms into crystals. Everybody from time immemorial knows that each ice crystal is different from another. And just keep in mind that there are countless ice crystals. (The word prolific in this context, appears too poor and dry. You have to tag together all its synonyms and form a new word.) Water resides deep in the ground and gushes out through geysers, or it can be pumped up by drilling borewells. Water resides not only inside the earth, but also inside our bodies. Just as it comes out of the skin of the earth, it comes out of our skins: as tears and saliva, sweat, sneeze, phlegm, and micturition. Rising up above, the same water goes as vapor, will spread as mist, will also rise higher and transform itself into clouds, and when it comes down it changes its name into rain.

*Tidbit: Standing tall. Humans may like walking tall and standing erect. But plants and trees outdo them when it comes to growing tall. Take the next term, standing erect. There, Nature shows its hand. We may like to stand erect—and even practice it diligently. (Else, we will break our spines.) Not so, the plant life. Technically, from the angle of engineering, it is most efficient and convenient for tall structures to be plumb-erect, to withstand the effect of gravity. But Nature delights in variety (and in taunting us). While some kind of trees trunks may grow (almost) vertically up, there are innumerable trees that do not like a rigid straight line. Some trees will appear as if they are dancing when you look at all the beautiful curves their trunks and branches take up as they grow. Especially, the coconut trees seem to take pleasure in rebelling against gravity. Some trees bend and twist so much that they appear to be almost parallel to the surface of the earth. Only architects and engineers can appreciate how much strength is needed for such a feat. (To get an idea, simply stretch your hand horizontally and try to keep it in that position for 10 minutes and see how you feel. Then remember that the coconut tree is 50 to 60 feet in length!)

*Faces: All humans have faces. Yet, each face is different from another one. You may be tempted to remark that it has to be so, so that each person can be distinguished from another one. If so, why does Nature bother to imprint unique fingerprints on every individual? That is an unnecessary luxury or exuberance of spirit! Apart from external appearances, even if you enter inside, the bodies show variety. Take blood. Why need it come in classified groups? We will not ask you to go deeper and enter the cells, because then you will encounter DNA and probably there does not exist anybody who has not heard of it.

A little of chinwag, a bit of an LOL moment. Man prides himself/ herself that she/he is very inventive and all that. At that, Nature does bother to laugh in its sleeves; it is guffawing. The joke runs like this. Grammar-wise, face is a common noun. That is not enough for humans. They had to give names for the faces, and thus invented proper names. This is in a way, a kind of mimicking Nature. The challenge falls flat right there on its face. (Gash! We seem to be serendipitously stumbling across plenty of puns.) Consider the present population of humans on earth–slightly more than seven billion. We do not have as many proper names to match each human representative of this population. Obvious, if you open any *one* telephone directory of any *one* city and notice how many Johns and Smiths and Georges repeat in those pages! A further cause for an LOL mood is that the population of the world keeps on increasing, and each newly born face is unique. *Nature does it so effortlessly and nonchalantly, whereas we sweat and think and scratch our heads and still come up with the same old names!* Do you agree, or do you agree? Of course, you guys of the present era are digital-soaked. So, how do you like to be called by your phone number, hello 1234567890? Our grammar pun-*dit* says that it is not a proper way of assigning a proper name. (There it pops up its merry head again.)

*Gait: Just as you said water is water, you can say that walking is walking. All of us walk, don't we? Walking is walking, but a subtle something (not even subtle, if you look at a few guys) called gait attaches and imbues itself into a person when he walks. Result–there are as many gaits as there are persons on earth.

*Voice: You talk, he talks, they talk. All talk. But the voice imprint of each person is different. ("We are all same. But I am a bit more of the same.")

*Handwriting is handwriting. Yet, the handwriting of every person is unique.

The expansive vista of Nature's varieties is truly mindboggling. If one attempts to compile a list, one can only begin and never end. Hills, rivers, forests, continents, clouds, leaves, bodies, even cities and roads (though manmade), stars, planets, galaxies, light: it goes on and on. Let us end this with a funny observation. That humans are inventive and do not like uniformity, is understandable. You need a chair to sit in. Just a need. Still, hundreds and thousands of models of every imaginable shape and size are being regularly manufactured. OKAY. But, why should Nature bother to go to lengths (often unimaginable) to create so much variety? Words like natural selection, struggle for existence, adaptability, pure chance, etc. are poor explanations indeed. See the joke; the explanations themselves come in droves! On the second level of this joke, it is worthwhile to observe that we humans who contemplate and are clever and inventive are also a part of Nature. After all, Nature created us and we live and exist in its vast folds…

This list can go up to an infinite length since anything that exists in Nature exhibits the property of variation. To sum up, take anything; that is the bottom line. Nature is so prolific and so exuberant in creation, that it produces varieties in every bloody blessed object (note, it is varieties within varieties) it creates. "Otherwise, there is no point in creating," it seems to be proclaiming as loud as possible (silently, as the oxymoron says).

CHAPTER 7

BREATHING

Let us start from the most basic thing we observe in our bodies–breathing. (We cannot live without breathing.) Of course, this is common to innumerable living forms like animals, apes, etc. But here, let us have a look at the act of breathing from a different angle. Breathing involves a repetitive rhythm–inhalation and exhalation. A cycle, in other words. Just mention that word cycle, and you will start wondering at the profoundly simple methods Nature adopts in enacting long, extended performances. A human body ideally lives a hundred years, say. It keeps on breathing for those hundred years. That statement may sound inane or puerile. But look at it from the wondrous mind of a curious, inquisitive child; genius lies dormant in the minds of all children. As a game, just imagine you are explaining the phenomenon of breathing to your own child. The child is listening to you with total attention. Then you notice that its eyes are gazing at infinity. The child is silent for what seems to be a long time to you. (Do not worry; it is experiencing what you just called a hundred years.) Then, it asks you a most innocent question, which in fact is truly a genius-laden one, "Dad, why can't we just breathe just one time only for that hundred years?" (!!) Try to answer that one seriously. It is a very valid and pertinent question if you are either a 4-year-old child or a genius in the making.

You see, Nature could very well have designed us to *take just only one breath in one hundred years; a long drawn out inhalation lasting fifty years and a long drawn out exhalation of fifty more years, if it wanted to.* No, we are not being unnecessarily perverse or facetious. On the contrary, we allow you the freedom to ask the perverse-or-puerile question, "If Nature asked us to inhale continuously for fifty years at one single stretch, OMG, to what size will our lungs expand?! Will not our lungs surely burst?" In spite of the risk of a digression, we will answer that—since you raised a question.

"Give some credit to Nature; it is far more inventive, creative, and productive than you think. Just remember the unimaginable variety and vastness of creation… May we draw your attention to that cylinder of cooking gas in your kitchen which the delivery man dumped at your doorstep this morning? Size-wise it is not such a big one. Imagine it, for our purposes of illustration, to be almost comparable to our chest—the thing where our lungs are ensconced. Now, if you open the valve of that gas cylinder and let out all the gas into the open, that quantity of gas will spread into the surrounding space, in its free/unbound state. *In such a state, it will occupy a space hundreds of thousands of times larger than that of yon cylinder.* Repeat that. You got the point? If the cylinder were made of a tougher material, it would hold even more gas. If you look along those lines, you will have to agree that Nature could have designed our chest and lungs in such a way that they would be able to contain all the air that we would inhale continuously—at a stretch—for fifty years. No big deal if you firmly believe in evolution. But Nature did not deign to do that. So, obviously, Nature must have other ideas on the subject.

Enough of light talk (if you feel that way). Let us ponder the matter a bit more seriously.

Nature had a more subtle idea. Leave aside breathing for now and think of *time*. That child genius of ours can say—á la breathing—this more reasonable sounding question, "I was joking and yet not joking when I asked of that single mega breathing act. In fact, I was thinking of time at the back of my mind. All you grown up people know quite obviously that there is only one single block of time (somewhat like a huge iceberg).

Only, unlike the iceberg, this time-block of mine stretches up and down up to infinity. You, I, and the universe are immersed in it. How wonderful!" Let us leave our precocious child there; it is difficult to stop him once he starts his harangue. The point of relevance for us is that Time is one huge undivided entity—the child called us sagacious grownups, and we accept it—and Nature enjoys breaking up such a huge one in terms of minute repeatable (identical) acts/units. Turning (ineptly) poetic, we can also say that Nature enjoys the process of adding up things interminably. The converse, that of breaking up/dividing is also true. We will take it up later; let us focus on breathing, that is, time.

CHAPTER 8

EXTREMES (RANGES)

This is a slight variation on the theme of opposites. Blow hot blow cold. Consider the variation range of temperature. The average body temperature of human beings is 98 degrees Fahrenheit. Yet, human beings manage to live in surroundings of temperatures varying between 55 degrees Celsius (Equatorial Regions) to -70 (Polar Regions). The surface temperature of the earth varies from place to place roughly in the above range, give or take a few degrees. The upper range of temperature goes far higher if you consider the volcanoes (about 1,800 degrees). The interior of the earth, as everybody knows, gets hotter and hotter as we go deeper and deeper. The temperature of the core is estimated to be around 13,000 degrees. (Of course, man has not been able to reach the center of the earth, except in Jules Verne's novel.) Notice that the range has already widened. Add to this the heat created by human enterprise—those of nuclear fission and fusion. 14,000,000 degrees for fusion!

Move away from the earth. The temperature of the interiors of stars would be around 70,000 degrees Fahrenheit, the maximum found so far. Even so, the range from -120 to +70,000 is tremendous. You can appreciate the degree of the range when you consider the span in which life exists, which is quite small indeed.

As we said, Nature enjoys manifesting wider and wider ranges. You may be wondering that 70,000 is quite a high temperature, and so, where in the universe could still higher ones be. Just hold your breath and go back a little in time. Well, a little back is a euphemism, but it serves us well. Just go back to the beginning of the creation of our universe–about 14 billion years; that is all! The universe, the scientists say, began with the Big Bang. And they say the temperature at that time was billions of degrees! It opened up grandly with a hundred million trillion trillion degrees!! Within a fraction of a second, it cooled down to 10^{14} degrees Kelvin! It is difficult even to imagine such an enormous temperature.

We have to thank God, or Nature if you prefer, that the Big-bang-temperature cooled down gradually (what are a few billions of years to Nature, anyway?), allowing us to be here now to comfortably contemplate that era… An aside here: Nature seems to have a peculiar sense of humor, or to nurse serendipitous partialities, in some fields. What we mean is this. Did you notice that there was a limit to the "coldness" of temperature? The zero, absolute zero, as it is called is set at -273.15 degrees. The minus sign means that the temperature is below our normal 'zero,' which is the temperature at which water freezes into ice. There is a lower limit (absolute zero; nothing can get lower than that), but apparently there does not seem to be an upper limit. Or, at least, it is so huge as to be unimaginable. (A hundred million trillion trillion is not easy to visualize.) Does it suggest that Nature likes it hot? Well, that reminds us of time, and if you are in a hurry or so inclined, you may jump to the topic on time-range.

8b. Range of time (Section a)

There is no need to paint an elaborate picture of time's range at all. From a layperson's perspective, it stretches to infinity in both directions, starting from here and now. A few facts and figures are enough to bring home the unimaginably vast range of time, since it is impossible to visualize the infinity of time.

Since we are human beings, we will look at time from our perspective. Time can be scrutinized along two venues; it can be scanned along directions, it can be measured in terms of quantity. By direction, we mean that time has got the peculiar property of being able to be viewed toward the past and toward the future. Quantity-wise, time can be measured in terms of seconds, minutes, hours: of which we are all too familiar.

Direction: Naturally, we start from the present and look *back*, which we call the past. (Yesterday, today, tomorrow.) The usual unit of measurement is a year. Sometimes the years become too big to handle, or can be arranged into groups, in which case we use the term ages. Stone age, iron age, and bronze age are some examples while describing the stretch of civilization (usually the past). Pleistocene, Neocene, etc. are other examples. Here too, we can observe a general increase in gradation of time as we peep back into the past of the earth.

Begin with our normal yardstick, one year. From the view point of a single human being, a stretch of one hundred years denotes a man's full existence. From there, the reckoning back is usually in terms of generations. Then come the eras. Even with all this, the (scientifically, archaeologically) recordable range of man's history of civilization goes to around 8,000-10,000 years. From the point of view of a single human being, a period of one hundred years seems to be quite long; 10,000 is thus a hefty figure since with all the recorded words, the ages of the Grecian, the Egyptian, Chinese civilizations appear to be extremely old to us. But even that period of time (10,000) is small when compared to the period of time that man, in the biological, evolutionary terms, has existed on the face of the planet Earth. Man, as per science, is supposed to have evolved from the apes. The evolution occurred over a very long period, as modern man (*Homo sapiens*) evolved through many stages starting from that of *Homo erectus* etc. Just skip over the scientific jargon like Australopithecus, Africanus, and Neanderthal as we are more concerned here about the time span of their evolution. Thus, this period (age) would be roughly a few hundred thousand years. See, already, we have moved back across a vast span of time.

As we noticed earlier, the time span increases at every stage. The next stage, naturally, will be that of the advent (birth) and evolution of the other kind of life-forms, like those of animals, the birds, the aquatic-life-forms, etc. Their journey of evolution probably took more time than that of the human arrival. We can wander back still further as we consider the next (natural) stage down the evolutionary ladder: the genesis and evolution of cellular organisms; multicellular and down that, the unicellular. Already, at this stage, it appears as if we are seeing an immense panorama of time stretching back.

Yet, there is more. For, what we considered so far was the time span that was needed for the evolution of life—in all its diversity. The next logical and obvious step for us is to step further back, beyond life's appearance. The time spans again are huge; they use the GSC, geological time scale, mya (million years ago), to demark various stages of the history of earth. We have to think in terms of geological formations and upheavals: the formations of mountains, rivers, seas, forests, deserts, and so on. (We are skipping technical terms; our aim is to look at the broad picture of the vast stretches of denotable/markable time.) And lastly, there is the period when the earth's tectonic plates were formed, and further before that, the era when the earth was a big globe of burning, molten liquid. Just imagine how much time it must have taken for the burning, boiling earth to cool down. Thus, the earth was formed 4.5 billion years ago—just try to imagine such a span of time!

8c. Range of time (Section b)

The range of time can also be viewed from another perspective too. We can look at individual entities, things, phenomena, etc. and note how long they last. We can confidently expect Nature to flaunt her bounteous expression in these fields too, and we will not be disappointed. To begin with, we are taking the case of the elements (as in chemistry and physics), which are the fundamental constituents of matter. The same element can exist in slightly modified forms called isotopes. Normally, we expect 'matter' to be permanent; we feel that matter should go on existing forever. But you will be surprised to see that even matter decays! Decay, here, is a scientific term. It means that the element/particle concerned changes into something else. Some particles decay quite fast and some stay for quite a long time. Please scan the list given below at a leisurely pace to appreciate the true flavor of the life spans of various things in the universe. Just as in the cases of distances, mass, and sizes, the range from the lowest quantity to the highest is enormous beyond belief. Look at the last item in the list, Tellurium, and go on staring at it–till you slip into a blue funk of non-comprehension. Same goes for the first one, hydrogen-7. It is impossible to imagine something living for such a short period, which is less than a trillionth of a trillionth of a second! Yet, these scientist guys have devised ways for measuring such minute quantities. (Note: Do not worry much about the word 'half-life' shown in the list. It indicates the period in which a given amount of matter decays to half of its initial mass.) As before, look at the numbers for the first item and the last one–10 raised to the power of -24 and -30. So the full range contains a number with 1, followed by 54 zeros. It is just impossible to conceive of such a humongous number. Once again, that is Nature's way of sportive play. Exuberance beyond the comprehension of human minds.

List showing lifespan of various particles (half-life):

Hydrogen-7.........2.3×10^{-24} seconds

Helium-10...........1.52×10^{-21} seconds

Beryllium-8.........81.9×10^{-18} seconds

Boron-16............190×10^{-12} seconds

Oxygen-13..........8.58×10^{-3} seconds

Oxygen-22...........2.25×10^{0} seconds(that is 2.25 seconds)

Carbon-11...........1.22×10^{3} seconds (20.334 minutes)

Vanadium-48.......1.38011x10^6 seconds (15.9735 days)

Titanium-44........2.0x10^9 seconds (63 years)

Nickel-63..........3.16x10^9 seconds (100 years)

Plutonium-239.....761x10^9 seconds (24,110 years!)

Uranium-233..........5.02x10^{12} seconds (159.2x10^3 years)

Uranium-235..........22.21x10^{15} seconds (703.8x10^6 years)

Osmium-186..........63x10^{21} seconds (2.0x10^{15} years)

Xenon-136...........75x10^{27} seconds (2.38x10^{21} years)

Tellurium-128.......69.4x10^{30} seconds (2.2x10^{24} years)

Tidbit: a) The half-life of the last element in the list, Tellurium-128, is over 166 trillion times longer than the amount of time the universe has been in existence! b) There is a fundamental's fundamental quark, called top quark. Its life span is less than a billionth of a trillionth of a second.

Our sun has been in existence for about 4.6 billion years. Our universe is about 14 billion years old.

8d. Range Speed

We are not quite done with this fascinating topic of ranges. After observing masses and distances, we are naturally reminded of speeds. Here too, there exists an astonishingly wide range in the speeds with which various objects in Nature travel. (If you are literature-inclined, you will think of the hare and the tortoise. If you are a science buff, you will naturally gloat over the famous Zeno's paradox of Achilles and the tortoise. In either case, we are with you.) The running speeds of the hare and the tortoise might have served well to highlight a good contrast in the good old days of Aesop. But nowadays, we have plenty of examples of things moving at diverse speeds. A short list as below will make the point.

Tortoise.......3-4 km/h

Hare...........60 km/h

Cheetah.......100-120 km/h

Sound..........340.29 meters/sec or 1235 km/h

Cyclone.......about 120 km/h

Bullet..........about 2500 feet/s or 1700 m/h

ICBM...........18,000-20,000 m/h

Earth, around the sun.....18.5 miles/s or 30 km/sec

Galaxies (at 2 mly-2 million light-years away)....60 km/sec

Galaxies (at 10 mly-10 million light-years away)....300 km/sec

Galaxies (at 20 mly-20million light-years away)....600 km/sec

Rotational spin of neutron stars....716 times per second! (Remember, our Earth spins *once in 24 hours*!)

Light..........186,273 miles/h (Nothing can move faster than light.)

8e. Range: Force

Without going into too much of scientific jargon, we can say that force comes into play when two objects interact. The interaction can be direct, as in physical contact of two (or more) objects, or it can be from a distance too; what is generally described as 'action at a distance.' For example, the earth is many millions of kilometers away from the sun. Yet, the sun attracts the earth, the earth is being pulled continuously around the sun and orbits around the sun. This kind of force is called gravitational force. Gravity is universal and comes into play wherever an object/mass exists. Nearer home, the raindrops and the flowers of a tree fall on your head because of the force of gravity exerted by the earth on them. There is another kind of action at a distance. When a piece of iron is brought sufficiently near to a magnet, the magnet attracts the piece and 'grabs' it. This kind of force is called the magnetic force. The magnetism is due to a particular kind of arrangement/alignment of electrons inside the atoms of the magnetized material. So, usually this force is termed electromagnetic force. There are two other forces called the 'strong' and the 'weak' force. These exist deep inside the nucleus of the atom (any atom). They are too technical in nature; we will just mention them here at the end of the list, to illustrate once again the vast range that exists between the weakest force and the strongest force. (A range of 1 followed by 39 zeros!) A tidbit again. Usually, we think that gravity is actually a very 'strong' force. It is naturally ingrained in our lives from birth, since our whole lives are spent on earth, and the earth is relentlessly pulling us and everything else toward its surface all the time. From the time we are babies, we stumble and fall and our brains automatically register the impact and the consequences. People slip and fall down from buildings and windows, and get their bodies broken, and die. Heavy things occasionally fall down on unprotected heads, and crack open skulls. There are countless examples of this kind. Even we see a meteor streaking down toward earth and getting burned in the process, in the atmosphere itself. On very rare occasions, quite a few manage to reach the surface of the earth, with terrible impact, creating huge craters. Finally, we all are familiar with the imagined scenario of a good-sized asteroid striking the earth and wiping out all life. From the last example, you can understand how powerful the impact of an object falling down and striking the earth will be. It is due to the gravitational force. See this also: the earth is many millions of miles distant from the sun, and yet it is being pulled around the sun because of the gravitational force. Topping it all up, you have the black holes whose gravitational attraction is so strong that even light is swallowed up by them! (That is why we cannot see the black holes. Latest tip: scientists have finally managed to photograph a black hole for the first time in April 2019.) Their gravitational power is truly awesome.

We deliberately gave a somewhat long list illustrating the power of the gravitational force. In spite of all that, look at the figures in the list below and you will have to feel puzzled since gravity is shown as the weakest force in nature! Not to worry. The explanation is like this. Gravity is the property of mass, matter. So, as mass increases, the effect of gravity too adds up proportionately. The gravitational pull of a single molecule of earth is indeed so negligible as to appear non-existent. But the number of all the molecules on earth—the total content of matter—is immense, and so the accumulated force of gravity becomes correspondingly overwhelming. The earth (all its molecules acting in unison) is thus able to pull the moon, a hundred thousand miles away, into an orbit around it. The power of gravity is truly tremendous. Yet, at the level of its origin, it is too weak beyond comparison when tallied with the other three types of fundamental forces. We repeat, as usual—try to visualize a quantity which is a fraction, equal to 1 divided by a number equal to 1 followed by 39 zeros, accept your defeat and scarper from the scene, if you have not yet swooned! Notwithstanding such a minute quantity, you cannot jump from the top of Pisa and live to tell the tale. That is because of the number of molecules in your body and those that make up the earth. Yeah, we said that; Nature enjoys playing games with immense numbers, in immense ways.

The other kind of force, occurring from direct contact between objects, is most familiar in our daily lives. A small list of various kinds of forces in nature is given below.

(From relevant Wikipedia pages)

Gravitational attraction of the proton and the electron in a hydrogen atom...3.6×10^{-47} N

Weight of an electron...8.9×10^{-30} N

Force measured in a 2010 experiment by perturbing 60 beryllium-9 ions...170×10^{-22} N

Brownian motion force on an *E. coli* bacterium averaged over 1 second...10×10^{-15} N

Force to stretch double-stranded DNA to 50% relative extension...$\sim 100 \times 10^{-15}$ N

Force on an electron in a hydrogen atom...8.2×10^{-8} N

The weight of an average apple...1N

Average force of human bite, measured in molars...720 N

The estimated bite force of a large 6.7 m adult Saltwater Crocodile...25.5 to 34.5×10^3 N

The average force applied by seatbelt and airbag to a restrained passenger in a car which hits a stationary barrier at 100 km/h...10^5 N

Maximum pulling force (tractive effort) of a single large diesel-electric locomotive...890x105N

Thrust of Space Shuttle Main Engine at lift-off...1.8x106 N

Thrust of Saturn V rocket at lift-off...35×10^6 N

Simplistic estimate of force of sunlight on Earth...570×10^6N

Gravitational attraction between Earth and Moon...2.0×10^{20} N

Gravitational attraction between Earth and Sun...3.5×10^{22} N

Gravitational attraction between Sagittarius A and Sun...2.25×10^{32} N

The Planck force...1.2×10^{44} N

*Comparison of fundamental forces

Strong force...1 (Taken as 1, for comparing with the others, below)... range, 10^{-15} m

Electromagnetic...1/137...range, infinite

Weak force...10^{-6}...range, 10^{-18} m

Gravity...6x10^{-39}...range, infinite

There is an exquisite irony in the above table. Look at the ranges attributed to each of the four forces. Gravity is the weakest force, as we overstressed above, and the 'strong force,' the strongest is trillions of trillion times stronger. Okay? What about the ranges across which the forces are effective? Lo, the strongest force acts across the shortest–unimaginably (unreasonably?!)–distance, and the tentacles of the weakest one (poetically speaking) stretch to the ends of the universe! Can anything be more ironical? Pardon us, but we would like to illustrate this situation with a stretched, absurd analogy as follows. Imagine that lightning and thunder strike your house, while the thunderclap shatters your eardrums, the people on the opposite side of the same street do not even hear it! Some frightened soul in the same house farts (no, we are not being obscene), *that* sound carries all the way to the farthest galaxy in the universe! Hope you got the idea. This is only a facile analogy, but yet it underscores the most paradoxical and intriguing phenomenon in Nature. We can, of course, explain away the anomaly by saying that the nature of the four forces is different in each case. The strong and weak forces act within the nucleus of the atom, being properties of the inter-nuclear particles bla bla. But yet? Ah, better leave it to the boffins.

8f. Range of electromagnetic waves

Again, we look at another kind of range: that of frequencies. Frequency here refers to the rate at which things vibrate, or magnitudes (like force, density, etc.) change. (This is said with appropriate apologies to all those readers who already know this–and much more.) The list below, taken from the savant pages of Wikipedia, specifically pertains to the electromagnetic waves. Again, the term electromagnetic waves encompass a wide range of waves like radio, TV, radar, X-rays, and even light. Notice that as the frequencies of the waves decrease, the corresponding 'wavelengths' keep increasing. (Note for the laypersons: If you are reminded of the water waves along your favorite beach, you may probably mistake the visible length of the waves skirting all along the beach for the term wavelength. Wavelength in science means a different aspect. The upper portion of a wave is called a crest, and the lower dip is called a trough. 'Wavelength' means the distance between two consecutive crusts (or two consecutive troughs). For practical purposes, you can think of electromagnetic waves as being similar: replace water with the electromagnetic field. We are deliberately describing this in these terms so that you may appreciate what we are going to highlight soon.

Type Frequency Wavelength

Gamma rays…300 EHz…1 pm (pico meters)

Hard X-rays…30 EHz…10 pm

Extreme ultraviolet…30 PHz…10 nm (nano meters)

Near infrared….300 THz…1 µm (micro meters)

Far infrared….3 THz…100 µm

EHF, Extremely high frequency…300 GHz….1 mm

UHF, Ultra high frequency…3 GHz…dm

HF, High frequency…30 MHz…10 m

MF, Medium frequency…3 MHz…100 m

LF, Low frequency…300 kHz…1 km

VLF, Very low frequency…30 kHz…10 km

ULF, Ultra low frequency…3 kHz…100 km

SLF, Super low frequency…30 Hz…10 Mm

ELF, Extreme low frequency…3 Hz…100 Mm

Hz (named after Hertz), in the above table, denotes frequency, cycles per second. Cycle refers to the way a wave starts from zero value, rises to its maximum (crest), comes back to zero, goes down in the opposite direction to a maximum(trough) and comes back to the zero state. The term wavelength has been explained above. Note how the wavelength increases as the frequency decreases. So, our table shows two kinds of ranges. Starting from the bottom, kHz means 1000 Hz or cycles per second. Mhz is 1000 kHz, gHz is 1000 mHz, tHz is 1000 gHz, and so on up the ladder. Thus, gamma rays at the top 'vibrate' at unimaginable rates–millions and millions of times faster than the lowest waves, the ELF ones. The range (as usual with Nature) is breathtaking. An interesting tidbit here. Before beginning the table, we talked about the nature of wavelengths.

Recall how the wavelength was defined. Visualizing waves in water as at seacoast will give you a fair idea about the wavelength. (Once again, it is not measured along the coastline: rather between two wave-crests.) The interesting aspect we mentioned is that as the frequencies of the electromagnetic waves increase, their corresponding wavelengths decrease, and vice versa. So, naturally, we obtain another parallel *range* for the wavelengths. Observe, again, the immensity of the range. Gamma rays, at the top of the table, (the highest frequencies) have minute wavelengths— in picometers. A picometer is an extremely small fraction, less than a nanometer, indistinguishable to the naked eye. (That is, the 'gaps' between two successive waves are so small that 'waves' themselves seem to merge into one another.) As you proceed down the line, you can see that HF, High frequency waves (30 MHz) come in wavelengths of 10 meters! A 10-meter wavelength is not a joke. Already, the range has increased from that of a picometer by billions. Still, that is nothing. As you go down the list toward still lower frequencies, (as if ironically) the wavelengths begin to extend farther and farther. To give a commonplace graphic idea, you may imagine the wavelength in terms of the inside convex-shaped dome of an arch. (As the wavelength increases, imagine that the ends of the dome are stretching further and further. See the list again. When you come to what is termed 'low frequencies,' the wavelength stretches to one *kilometer*. (Your dome is now one kilometer wide!) Yet, even that is nothing compared to those at the bottom of the list. Hold your breath and look at the VLF, very low frequency range. The wavelength? 100 kilometers! (Visualize a dome of such size). At the very bottom, is the ELF, extreme low frequency wave with a value of 3 Hz. That is three cycles per second. To describe in terms of the man-in-the-street, you can say the wave is 'winking' at you three times in a second. (A little humorous digression is indicated here. To humans like us, three winks per one second may seem to be a bit on the fast side. But remember we are talking of electromagnetic waves. Winking a million times per second is normal to them.)

8g. Range, births

"The mountains were under labor and gave birth to a mouse." – A Roman saying.

By the bye, we can see this propinquity of Nature to manifest in ranges even in such a mundane occurrence as birth.

Begin with the lifeless form of matter. Wonder how matter can give birth to matter? It is not such a tough conundrum after all. Birth of matter occurs both in the fields of physics and chemistry, apart from biology. In physics, when fundamental particles collide, new particles (apart from the original ones that collide) are born as a matter of routine. This is being witnessed and recorded regularly in every particle-smashing laboratory around the world. The point of relevance here is the sizes of such particles. The sizes are comparable, more or less, with those of electrons etc. A list showing the sizes of electrons etc. has been given elsewhere in these pages, so you may refer back and recall the extremely small sizes of the subatomic particles. Forget it, you simply cannot see such particles with your naked eyes. (Nor can the best microscopes in the laboratories.)

The next, higher range of birth takes place in the field of chemistry. Atoms (two or more) can combine and give "birth" to new forms of matter. In chemistry, they are called molecules. Molecules can be created in nature itself, or can be deliberately produced in the laboratories. The simplest and most common molecule in nature is that of water, being obtained when two atoms of hydrogen and one atom of oxygen combine together. Laboratories can create more complex molecules; in the modern world there are hundreds of thousands of such molecules (chemicals) which did not exist freely in nature two centuries ago. (Yet, Nature does give a good run to those boffins. Nature's favorite, the DNA strand, if stretched, can reach from here up to the moon!)

We were surveying the range aspect of births. Already, at this small circle, the range has increased incredibly. Compare the size of one subatomic particle with that of a DNA molecule; the ratio is enormous, running into millions! Consider again the next single unit of life, a unicellular organism. The cell, again, is immensely huge, compared to its DNA strand. After that come the multicellular organisms, which are still many times larger. Since we are considering births of life-forms (single units), we may as well take a seed as a unit; it contains potential life as a new life-form sprouts out of it. This unit of birth, the seed, is now beyond doubt many mega-million times bigger than a simple multicellular organism. At this stage we have already traveled very far along the road of ranges. Metaphorically speaking, we have passed billions and billions of miles. We can still go further and think of eggs. Generally, with possible, anomalous exceptions, eggs are bigger than seeds. (A coconut is a seed, because it gives birth to the coconut tree. It is bigger than many kinds of eggs.) Can we think of still larger units of birth? Sure, we have human babies, freshly out of their wombs (remember 'unit of life') as everyday examples. Mass-wise, a human baby exceeds a coconut many times over. This is usually so with viviparous animals. Whew! What a distance, what range we have covered! On the bottommost level of the range we have the mass of an electron, and at the top we have a baby whale: compare the sizes and wonder. We have to gaze in wonder at the enormity of ranges in every field of Nature. The fields are vast and innumerable. We have given only a few examples. The diligent reader will surely find hundreds of ranges, no doubt. One thing is certain— Nature is not tight-fisted at all. A small list (culled from the pages of the world wide web) showing the various sizes/masses of what we discussed above, is given below:

Weight of the biggest seed (of coco de mer, palm tree) …40 pounds, 12 inches long

Weight of the biggest egg (of an ostrich)… above 5 pounds (2.589 kgs)

Weight of the egg of the kiwi bird, an anomaly…half the body weight of the bird!

Weight of a human baby (record weight)…23 pounds

Weight of a baby giraffe…165 pounds

Weight of a baby bear…2 pounds!

Weight of a baby hippo…100 pounds

Weight of a baby elephant…up to 250 pounds

Weight of a baby white whale…180 pounds, 5 feet long

Weight of a baby blue whale (highest among all life forms) …3 tons! (3000 kgs), 25 feet long

Postscript (or bon mot): A good raconteur will not stop at this; elephants and whales are nothing to him. That guy has a sense of humor too. Can you guess what he is alluding to? A hint–remember we are discussing births here. Okay, okay, we will not tease you further. The man avers that the birth of the universe itself is one heck of a super-mega-mega event. The mass and size of the universe (ours) is beyond the thinking capacity of ordinary mortals like you and me. Our man argues that the birth of the whole of the universe took place in one instant, as a single act. That act is most popularly known as the Big Bang.

No, no, do not knit your brows. The universe may have taken about 14 billion years to become as we see it today, but you have to agree that the *whole* of it (in whatever form) was conceived and delivered at one go. To adopt the popular saying, it was the mother of all births!

A second postscript to ranges. All through the previous pages, we saw Nature's exhibition of ranges in a wide variety of its manifestations. The list indeed is too huge and needs a separate book to enumerate all those fields. The wonder of the thing is that apart from ranges in species, Nature is so exuberantly promiscuous in its sport, that it exhibits exhaustive ranges in producing different samples (again infinite, especially where life forms are concerned) *of the same species.* To give one concrete example. Look at trees. In the first tier of manifestation of range, you can see that there are innumerable kinds of trees. You will need a very hefty book just to write down all their botanical names. OKAY. Now, take any single category of tree–say a mango tree. There must be uncountable mango trees in the world. Begin by comparing each tree with the next of its kin (if you have that kind of time and patience!). Each mango tree is different from another mango tree in terms of size and shape and many other factors like leaves, flowers, fruits, branches, and so on. The variations will almost be infinite. And Nature enjoys creating all those specimens. Wait, sir, wait: it enjoys doing that not only with mango trees, but with all other trees! Wait, sir, wait. It enjoys doing that not only with trees but also with animals and birds and human beings! *If you are in a truly proper mood, you will have to simply swoon in rapture!*

It does not end there by any means. This perception we had above applies to every bloody object created (ah, excuses solicited; *mais non,* the expletive is appropriate.) Why trees, take human beings. There are more than seven billion of them teeming around the globe. Each one of them is unique considering size, color, shape, voice, and ah, shucks! We almost forgot fingerprint and DNA. And then, you gotta add to those seven billion, all those that ever strode on the surface of the earth from time immemorial and all those to do so in the next quantum of future time incalculable!

After that, you have to do a similar computing in the case of all those tigers and lions and elephants and cats and… forget it, the scenario is beyond imagination.

Tell us, honestly, is this not a grand wonder? Nature is Nature–the incomparable.

CHAPTER 9

ORBITS

Nature seems to enjoy the act of going round and round. There are two modes, one is for an object to go around another object–orbiting. The other is for the object to go around itself–spinning, where the contents of the body orbit around the axis of spin. There are plenty of examples, comprising of even similes and metaphors!

The earth on which we live is itself a perfect and first example of both the kinds of motion mentioned above. It is spinning on itself, giving us days and nights. It is orbiting the sun, giving us years. Planets orbit a star, our own solar system being the best, nearest, and the most familiar example. In the field of toys, the spinning top is one of the oldest toys. The oldest manmade invention must be the wheel. (From here, the chapter spills over to that on the Haiku.)

CHAPTER 10

COMBINATIONS

This particular topic is something after my (remember, I, you, and us are interchangeable in this book) own heart, sort of a bee in my bonnet. So, you have to kindly excuse me if I unabashedly gush forth on the subject. The main 'theorem,' if one may use such a ponderous word, is that when things (things may be anything or many things!) come together or are held together in a particular space, they exhibit different properties depending on their combinatorial configuration. Just the combination of things creates a new thing! The statement may sound bald when put so blandly. But we will try to justify and elucidate it with plenty of examples. Combination is a trick which Nature employs deftly–and copiously–to flaunt its fantastic magic, for indeed what it (Nature) performs is beyond all human logic. Please savor the examples that follow leisurely, like connoisseurs.

Line: There is a line, say, a simple straight line. Friends, that is a line, a line by itself. Well, a line is a line just as a rose is a rose, you may sneer. Well, imagine then, a number of such identical lines–plenty of them. Your sneer does not fade yet. Yet, all you see is lines and lines. We are purposefully dinning that word 'lines' into your ears. Hold on a sec: now bring any two *lines* and place them together such that their tips touch each other at one end, and the other ends are visibly apart. You will immediately perceive that a *new figure* has emerged–that of an arrow head! Hide all the rest of the lines and show to your friends the new *configuration* that you have achieved. The chances are that almost all of them will invariably recognize your artistic achievement as an arrow head. A few may see the mathematical symbol denoting the meaning "greater than," and so on.

The point of the above elaborate charade is that almost none of your friends will see two straight lines in the new figure. *And yet the new figure, if you see honestly, is not new, but only a different arrangement of the old.* And therein lies the whole megillah of creation. (One can surely be pardoned for sounding bombastic, for once.)

Combination, dots: The effect of combinations is seen beautifully in the case of dots. About 80 years ago, most newspapers (especially here, in India) did not have the facility of color photography. There used to be only black and white photos. But the printing of the photos was very fine and life-like and we, as children, used to like many of them. Later on, sometime in our college days, we learned that all those beautiful photos were made up of dots, precisely aligned, density being suitably manipulated! If you are able to get hold of any old photo of those days, scan it under a good magnifying glass and you will see dots, dots, dots all over.

That was in the days when digital photography had not arrived. (People had not heard of the word digital even.) Now they use a similar technique. In the place of those dots, they use what are called pixels, which are very minute-sized squares. The computer codes each such micro-square with a special color code. The web page or the screen you are viewing (the picture, to be more precise), consists of these squares assembled horizontally and in specified rows. The result will give you a beautiful, clear picture. While viewing the photo, you will never see the actual squares at all, just as in the first instance you do not notice the dots. In this computer age, you can easily magnify any portion of the picture; they call it zooming in. If you go on zooming, the picture will get more and more blurred, until in the last stages of magnification, you will see only the squares, pixels. (To use a pardonable pun, you will see the true colors of the picture!)

10b. Combination, binary

In the above section, the effect of the combination of dots was seen. Mention was made of the computer age. Computers can do most mindboggling works (in a jiffy, that too). This brings us to the topic of one of the most marvelous kinds of combinations. The real wonder (miracle, no less) is that such an act of marvelous combination is also the simplest one! This, in fact, is also deeply linked to the concept of creation through opposites. At the most fundamental level, things can be said to be (or perceived) as either existing or not existing. There is a beautiful mathematical analogy for this, stripped of all bombast and fanfare. The numbers 1 and 0 represent these two states without much ado. A genius, Boole, invented a new kind of algebra, logic employing, and manipulating these two numbers. That was the precursor for the Rise of the Computer which was to occur far later. Ask any geek friend of yours. He will tell you that all programs (millions? trillions?) are, at their deepest roots, compiled out of clever manipulations of the numbers 1 and 0. (You have to tactfully stop him before he becomes excited and gushes eloquently about recondite intricacies.) The bottom line is that all our present-day technological advances, gadgets, and marvels owe their birth to zero and one. Philosophers, old and New Age alike, will be ecstatic while pondering this poignant point.

10c. Combination, words: A recreative tidbit. Since we are pursuing parallel themes and analogies across diverse areas, here is one for recreation. Even manmade things, apart from those of Nature, show a tendency to come together, to combine with one another. That the all-pervasive machines, gadgets, and toys are a result of many items being combined with skill and forethought needs no mentions at all; it is a part of modern life. We are hinting at something else—words! As mentioned at the beginning, most languages have stockpiles of plenty of words. In English (as is the case with almost all languages) there are abundant single words representing objects, ideas, actions, and so on. Like sun, sky, earth, hill, father, mother, son, daughter. Then, as our needs and moods begin to escalate, we combine two or more words, birthing new ones to satisfy those needs and moods. Two words, usually, if from Latin or Greek, combine to form a single word (in English). Any good dictionary will give you the etymology of such words. (Like philosophy, which is a combination of love and wisdom, the meanings of the original roots. Democracy and monarchy are other examples.) If the words are from the same language, they just sit side by side glued together, to mean a new word. If the lingual glue is weak, you bind them together using the grammatical all-purpose (see?) hyphen. Blackberry, whitewash, hogwash, brainwash are such examples of the former kind, while that 'what-was-that-again?' look on your friend's face represents the latter kind. Since this is a natural phenomenon of the human mind, we can find such compound words in all the languages of the world.

*The list of combinations is too long. Let us close it by looking at one of the most familiar and fundamental ones, existing from as long as history. Two persons (man and woman) combine and form a couple. (Oh, this word is so fundamental that it you come across it in the phraseologies of many disciplines like physics, chemistry, biology, engineering, machinery, and so on.) The couples become a family. Families combine to form a community. Communities join together becoming a village or a town. Towns combine to beget a district. They combine in suitable numbers to beget a state. States join together to grow into a nation. Nations combine to form the earth. (Do they call it the UNO? Or is it a fancy Utopia? At least physically, geographically, the statement is valid.)

Many other combinatorial analogies beckon us temptingly. We relent, but carry them over into the Haiku section.

CHAPTER 11

CONTROL FROM CENTER

Consider a purely imaginary, ideal human being; we mean one single human. We further imagine that such a human being is living alone, entirely isolated from any other person. The ideal person is able to take care of his/her needs. We say this with 'tongue in cheek' as they say. Most probably, a *single* human can take care of his bodily needs if he/she lives like an animal only, depending solely on the strength, agility, and skill of his/her body! Forget it; it was said just for argument's sake. Refurbish your knowledge of sociology you had gleaned in school. There are three basic needs without which humans cannot live or survive–food, clothing, and shelter; remember? To put it baldly, a human being needs, forgetting grammar for the present, basic clothes to protect himself from the inclement weather for one, ah, and that brings us back to the good old hat, the good old umbrella, oh, you forgot the soles of ur feet which are probably burning or paining or both so you need a pair of boots, no? And you are not finished with it yet for U need food first of all, for which you need tools like knife, bow, sword to hunt if you are so inclined or tools of agriculture called something like a plough (pother, U need to wait for a *looong* time to quell the damn hunger pangs if you adopt that route) and in any case, in both the alternatives, you gotta cook ur food and where is the time and who will do it for you, can't cook even if your life depended on it, and after all this razzmatazz, you gotta have shelter to sleep safely at night for one and to keep ur things in a safe place for another and for many more civilized reasons and so on and oh bother again, you need some other guy(s) to construct a minimally decent shelter for you for U can't build a house by yourself even if ur life depended on it and then uh, U remember clothes, dammit but dammit you need some or another guy to construct wearable clothes for you (who calls himself a gentleman's tailor (and you cannot mess with him) for you cannot stitch out clothing even if ur life depended on it and so on and so forth and also the tight situation applies regarding your footwear, and and and you... the list, like this grammatically monstrous sentence, seems never to end ever.

The bottom line, as the most worn out cliché says, is that a person cannot live an isolated life all by himself/herself. Out of sheer necessity we humans have to live in a group. This, of course, is not a brilliant discovery or a new idea; everybody knows it and is aware of it. Nature has seen to it. We take off from here. We see humans clustered around in groups–small or big (village, town, city, metropolis, etc. Ah, that arrow points toward the road 'clusters.' If you are curious, or distracted enough, you can take a diversion here and jump straight away to the chapter on clusters).

*Body of humans: What we are more interested in right now is about the organization, the functioning of the clusters. Two or three examples will amply illustrate our point. Take the case of a cluster of human beings, as in a small village. Let us assume arbitrarily that there are roughly about 200 people in the village. The village can be viewed as a viable, sustained organism consisting of various limbs, each limb efficiently performing its exclusive function/work so as to aid the existence of the organism as a whole. (Are you thinking of the human body as a multicellular organism, here? Right, we have mentioned it too, and you can jump to that paragraph and come down here, if you are so inclined!)

Now, each of the 200 people of the village has his own needs–essential needs. And as already pointed out earlier, if you count the total needs of the village, one particular individual cannot by himself cater to all those needs. (Here arises the division of labor). Thus, obviously (most) each task for catering to the needs of the cluster is apportioned to different persons. Like you know, there will be a farmer, a builder, a tailor, etc., to mention the most essential needs. And…here comes the subtler, but most important point. *Even if each individual is capable and an expert in his field, the village as a whole needs a central controlling/regulating body to oversee the overall functioning of the village.* Here (in India) we have what is called the village *panchayat*, a governing body (usually belonging to the government) which looks after the welfare and affairs of the village. Invariably, in any such unit (anywhere in the world), there will always be issues concerning crime, protection of the citizens, disposal of law, healthcare, continuous supply of food, and so on, to mention a few salient points. It is the duty of the governing body (cluster) to take care of these matters and it is the duty of the functioning (physically working) body/cluster to obey the instructions of the governing body. The words body and cluster have been deliberately used here in order to induce a mental picture of a diagram in the readers' minds. The diagram now facilitates us to abstract further; it can be applied not only to clusters of humans, but also to any union of clusters—either of living forms or of non-living forms. The best example of a non-living cluster is a machine! (If you are so inclined, you can take to the road marked 'machines,' or jump to the hyperlink, to say in digital language. See how abstraction and generalization help us in getting surprising insights; that is the beauty of the parallels.

The series of above clusters do not, of course, stop at the village. A bigger cluster forms with the town. The town grows in size and becomes a city. Clusters of cities (and towns and villages) form what is called a district, in old British parlance. Again, these clusters of districts combine to form a state, and finally a number of the state-clusters go into the making of a grand nation. Lastly, the nations *can* form—theoretically—a world, our world. Unfortunately, this is only an ideal utopia at present. (Yet, the spirit does not die; we have other kinds of organizations like the UNO, UNICEF, and so on.) Ah, one cannot resist the temptation of noting the further obvious parallel similarities here. See the beauty of it: each unit, starting from the village, is an organized unit with a head and a body, metaphorically speaking. When such a unit joins other more such units to form a new kind of cluster, it coalesces smoothly (and efficiently and beautifully) as a part of the higher organization, while at the same time it preserves its own identity too.

A small addendum

*One more simile, extending the above idea further–and farther–entices us to go ahead. Why limit the above clusters to earth only? Go ahead; take a gigantic leap outward into space itself! A simple listing is enough to give you a picture of the grand (limitless) vista. Planets can have satellites: the Earth and its satellite, the moon, form one cluster of the simplest type. There are planets in outer space which have more than one satellite revolving around them. Think of Jupiter and Saturn. There are innumerable such systems lurking in the depths of space. If we go to the next logically higher level, we obtain the sun, a star, and the solar system. Earlier, we saw the planets with their satellites. Now, the planets themselves (along with their satellites) revolve around the sun! Our Sun commands eight (officially accepted, so far) planets which obey him and revolve around him eternally. As with the planet clusters, there are, in the universe, innumerable stars having planetary systems. We have by now clusters and clusters of clusters. The sequence does not stop there. To speak poetically, Nature's thirst for play is not quenched yet. Solar systems are nothing–in terms of numbers–when Nature gets going. Note that the distances we are considering has already crossed our mind's grasping powers. The sweep of the solar system goes beyond millions and millions of miles. Yet, that distance is nothing but less than a speck when compared to the visible dimensions of the universe (ours). That is what we hinted at when we said, 'When Nature gets going!' This is related to the chapter on distances; go and have a peek and come back. Ah, everything is related to everything. That is what we meant when we used the descriptive term 'Nature's play.' Well, we next come to a cluster of star systems. That is a galaxy. And there are enough and more than enough of those galaxies in the universe (ours). And, yes, the distances between galaxies are also incredibly enormous! (The litany–Nature gets going.)

CHAPTER 12

EXPAND, EXPAND

A beautiful phenomenon of Nature is that things expand. First, start from where you are! As you look around, your vision expands–in all directions, and in depth in those directions. There are umpteen numbers of parallels here. Pick any subject at random and you will observe the scope.

*Fibonacci series: Somebody has associated (read "parallel!") the Fibonacci series with the way leaves in a tree proliferate. We are actually interested in this natural phenomenon than the name of the series here. The parallelism is connected with the previous paragraph where we saw how numbers proliferate astonishingly as we move further and further from a given point (source). Look at a well-foliated tree. Starting at the trunk, we get the number one. Depending on its genus, the tree branches off into two, after it reaches a certain height. Those branches too branch out after growing up to certain lengths, and so on, the process repeats. Again, depending on the kind of tree we get plenty of branches in the end. Again, we see that as we proceed farther and farther from the source, the *numbers* proliferate.

As we said, one thing invariably suggests another thing in a natural way. Does not the word 'tree' suggest the familiar phrase 'family tree?' Yes, and we will offer just a couple of sentences on it, before sauntering on toward other equally alluring images.

72

Consider a gentleman who lived roughly about a hundred years back. We are assuming that he was married–and was in good health. (Ah, and loved his dear wife!) Further, call him grandpa. Grandpa begat six children; all in good health. Naturally, they too got married, and loved their spouses. Each of those children begat four children. Permit us to repeat the litany about health once more. Those children begat only two children each, for they had heard of the Malthusian diatribe and family planning, and the government was issuing free condoms. (Oh, does this make grandpa a great grandpa? Never mind.) See what we said? Great grandpa was one (1) to begin with: the trunk of the tree. Then as we moved further and further from the source, one became six, six became twenty-four, and twenty-four became forty-eight. Just go on doubling the numbers, and within a few generations ("as we move further from the source") the numbers become stupendously large.

A small, tempting diversion here. We moved from grandpa to his great grandchildren. It is a tempting idea to move the other way, back into the past. The present population of the world is around seven billion (and rising). If we move back from grandpa to his grandpa, to his grandpa, etc. all the way back, is it not tempting to assume that all of the seven odd billion guys merrymaking on the surface of this planet sprang from one single father, the father of all fathers? (Remember Adam and Manu.)

*Distances: Concomitant with the perception we had with regard to expanding numbers, we naturally latch on to the word expansion and make the association with the expanding universe. That brings us to the topic of distances. Just as we saw the numbers expanding, we see that distances too expand. A few illustrations will suffice, and then we can saunter on into other fields.

It is not necessary for our purposes here to stick to too much scientific/ technical details or accuracies of measurements. Adopting the layman's stance, we can take the atom and its interior as the starting point of our journey of measurement of distances. The nucleus of the atom is our starting point. As everybody knows, the atom is made up of a tiny central point called nucleus, around which electrons (their number varies from the atom of one element to another's) revolve, much like satellites around a planet. (((Oh, excuse us, these abounding and ubiquitous parentheses seem to be unavoidable, as we *proved* earlier! We instantly got the image of the solar system when we talked of the electrons orbiting the nuclei of elements. ((In fact, we are direly tempted to ensconce the parentheses within deeper and deeper levels of embrace. But then, it may be almost impossible to properly audit (ha ha!) the numbers of the open and the closed.)) That is one more parallel/simile/image being generated automatically. In fact, the scientists who envisaged the model of electrons orbiting the nucleus must have definitely been inspired by the solar system—the planets going round and around the central sun.)))

It doesn't stop there! The image of things orbiting around a central object needs only to be changed slightly to get us another beautiful (*and universal*) image. Replace the central object with an imaginary straight line, what is called an axis. You get spin—an object going round and round itself. Plenty of images are now ready to march past your mind's retina. An aside again; it looks as if Nature does not like its subjects to be absolutely immobile. They have to be either moving or orbiting or spinning! There must be some mathematical necessity behind this phenomenon. We better leave such things to the geeks and nerds and content ourselves (wholeheartedly) with the more satisfying poetical visions.

*Another fascinating detail here, as a parallel to the phenomenon of increasing distances. It is that of numbers. Notice the beautiful (and breathtaking) way Nature enjoys in spreading itself in every conceivable way. What we mean is this: let us begin at the starting place of the series under purview—the satellites. The numbers of the satellites orbiting their planets are within easily countable range; one for our planet Earth, more for planets like Pluto (3), Neptune (13), Saturn (60), and Jupiter (67) and so on. That is nothing compared to the stars in a galaxy; the numbers run in millions! Think that is too big? Then you got another think coming, as my favorite author is fond of saying. How about the galaxies themselves? How many galaxies are there in the universe (ours)? (A parenthesis in a parenthesis in a...? Looks like we cannot avoid them. The topic we are discussing is like that; it is rich with associations of all sorts, and each association, at every stage, generates one more new offshoot! (Makes you think of the nuclear fission's chain reaction, does it not? See, there it goes again.)) Well, going back, the answer is, a hundred *billion* as estimated now; and it is likely to double with the advent of the latest telescopes! A billion, we need not remind you, is one thousand million! (Before the invention of modern gigantic telescopes, even scientists at the end of the 19th century guesstimated that the "star-studded" sky was populated with perhaps a couple of hundred thousand stars. The ordinary man in the street thought the number was highly exaggerated! This is how illusions are shattered again and again with the progress of knowledge.)

Spinning! What does not spin! Who does not spin? (Even the writers spin their yarns.) Spinning tops are one of the oldest gadgets or toys. The wheels of a carriage spin; so do the potters' wheels, so did the spinning Jennies of yesteryears. Electrons spin, whirlpools spin, water in centrifugal pumps spins, tornados spin, stars spin, and even whole galaxies spin. (And we darkly suspect that our universe itself is spinning. It just needs a genius like you to discover/prove it!)

Spinning bestows enormous stability to an object (the stability depending on the product of its mass and *speed*). So, even a small object can have extreme stability when it is spinning at high speeds. This property is ubiquitously leveraged in gyroscopes, which unerringly point their axes in a fixed direction. Gyroscopes are employed in umpteen numbers of machines, especially where one needs a reliable reference for direction. They are widely used in airplanes, in space vehicles (where up, down, east, west, etc. have no meaning), and now in your smart phones too.

(Simile, similarity–there we go again. Does this property of spin (and an unchanging axis) remind you of any very *heavy* object? Real heavy. Of course, you are standing on it all your life. It is the earth! The earth is spinning at a very good rate: more than a thousand miles per hour at the equator. That is why the position of the Polaris star does not change in the sky, while all other stars describe a full circle around it, from morning to next day morning–the axis of the earth is always pointing at the star.)

*Things expand II: As we look around us we observe that the millions and millions of 'things' surrounding us exhibit a peculiar property. They either expand in size or do not. Why things should expand at all is itself a mystery, if you look at it impartially (like with the mind of a child). Replace the word expand with grow; you will immediately think of life forms. Plants, animals, birds, humans–all of these grow ('expand in size') up to varying sizes. Look at the size of a flea and that of a huge elephant or whale. Or compare the volume of an alga with that of the giant sequoia tree. (Go and browse the sections, Ranges, The Big, and the Small. And don't forget to come back!)

The Big and the Small: Blackhole. (An irreverent, if not irrelevant 'aside' here. MS Word chides us if we write blackhole as a single word; it advises us to either insert a hyphen or write the two words separately. That is silly, you know why? Friends and all-country-men, the super-super density of a black hole, accompanied by the concomitant super-super gravitational force will, beyond all doubt–reasonable or unreasonable–compress the two words, black and hole into a single word, along with the hyphen beyond existence, if a hyphen is inserted. QED.)

With that well-deserved nose-thumbing at venerable MS Word, let us come back to our black hole. Our main interest here is in appreciating the enormous ranges that Nature takes delight in creating. Elsewhere we talked of ranges in distances and numbers. We will specifically look at the range in mass, of matter–a truly mindboggling phenomenon. Previously, we saw the gigantic difference in the mass between that of a flea and that of a whale. But that is nothing when we enter the arena of matter. Nature throws off the (apparent) restrictions it has imposed on itself in the case of living forms.

Let us start with the electron, the most familiar subatomic particle. We are also most familiar with the kilogram, the widely used unit of measurement of mass ("weight," if you want to visualize in terms of common, everyday experience). We have a fairly good idea of how much a kilogram weighs. Creation-wise, the electron is one of the smallest particles in nature and weighs unimaginably small. Please see the list below wherein the mass of various things are shown:

Electron ...$9.10938356 \times 10^{-30}$ kilograms (Neutrino...Previously this elusive particle was thought to be having no mass! Latest conjectures suggest that it could have a mass less than a billionth of that of a proton.)

Hydrogen *atom* ...1.66×10^{-24} gms

Tennis ball...58.5 gms

Cricket ball...163 gms

Shot put ball...7.260 kg

The pyramid (Khufu)...5,216,308,000 kg

Earth...5.972×10^{24} kg

Jupiter...1.898×10^{27} kg

Sun...1.989×10^{30} kg (this is the yardstick in space for measuring masses of stellar objects; called a solar mass)

Neutron stars...1.4 solar mass (Sometimes a giant star explodes and a neutron star forms. Though a neutron star contains just a comparable 1.4 times of a solar mass, it is unbelievably dense ('heavy,' in ordinary parlance).) It is so because all that mass is compressed incredibly tightly into a small volume. A neutron star is about 20 km across size-wise, but 'weighs' about one and a half times than a sun (does). Compare the diameters–that of the neutron star, which is 20 miles and that of the sun, which is 1.392 million kilometers! Another interesting fact is that neutron stars spin quite fast; about 43,000 times per minute! Black holes beat the neutron stars hands down. See the items down below.

Milky Way…5.8×10^{11} solar masses

Black hole (general)…Five to several tens of solar masses

SMBH…These are what are called super massive black holes. Their theorized masses could be–ah well, hold your breath–between *hundreds of thousands to billions* of solar masses!

Mass of the universe (observable, ours)… 3×10^{55} gms as calculated using the known uniform density of the universe and the radius of the universe as known at present. (That is equal to the mass of 25 *billion* galaxies, the size of our Milky Way! By the bye, the average density of matter in space is unimaginably minute: 3×10^{-30}! That indicates how vast space is. And by the same token, how much vast it must be so that the total quantity of mass has to work out to be as shown above.) (The astute reader–you, who else– might have observed that whenever we mention the universe, the qualifier 'ours' is being attached to it. We strongly believe that there must be other universes too, of which we are not aware at present. As usual, go to The Other Universes. And come back here. Ah, qualifier; if you go *there*, we are not sure if you can come back.)

Please go through the above list patiently. The range of the masses of different types of matter is more than (the usual) mindboggling. The human mind simply cannot grasp such microscopic and macroscopic quantities. Only bland numbers are to be employed while dealing with such super-super gargantuan quantities. Just a few words here to give you a general picture will suffice. Look at the superscripts of the number ten (10) in the list. The superscript indicates how big the number is in terms of the number 10. (Those numbers are normally referred to as the 'powers.') If the number 10 is multiplied by itself (100), the result is called '10 to the power of 2.' If that number is again multiplied by 10, it becomes 10 to the power of 3 (1000). 10 raised to the power of 6 is one followed by six zeros (1000000). In spite of the risk of over-exposition, we would like to draw your attention to the negative index for the number showing the mass of an electron–the minus sign before 30. It denotes a fraction. Imagine the number, 1 followed 30 zeros. (((Abject apologies to the readers; it is 1,00000000000000000000000000000!!! It is so huge that if you start continuously counting a number every second from the time you are born till you die, and assuming that you will live for a hundred fruitful years–God bless you–you will still not be able to reach that number! Such numbers are simply beyond our visualization, we repeat. ((Another aside–Nature wants to show us that the human mind too is limited.)) Now, *divide* the number 1 by that gargantuan number. The result is so infinitesimal that you can almost say it is zero. And that is the mass of an electron! (One more aside to an aside; you have obviously noticed that we have been using too many exclamatory marks. We are not inflicted with any kind of OCD. We are simply being amazed again and again by Nature's manifestations, and we are trying to convey our emotion to you, the empathetic reader, that is all.)))

Now, back to that fantastic fraction which nobody except God can see. Hope you appreciate how small it is. Okay? Then, look up another item in the same list above, the weight of the sun. The weight of the sun is indicated by a number involving 10 raised to the power of 30. This 30 again means that we have to place 30 zeros in front of the number 1. Only, the number is positive this time; that means that the mass we are considering (of the sun) is huge, very huge, not a fraction. Just try to imagine such a big number, and accept your defeat. Okay, so far? Ah, tarry, you ain't seen nothing yet, as the saying goes. That huge mass of the sun, our sun, is generally taken as a unit for measuring other huge masses in the universe–the way we take a foot or meter as a unit while measuring distances. The mass of the sun (don't forget the 30 zeros!) is dubbed as a solar mass, and we measure/compare other masses in terms of solar mass.

The next huge mass, dwarfing our sun's is naturally the Milky Way in which the sun stands (not exactly) in a corner. The mass of the Milky Way is about *6 followed by 11 zeros of solar mass*! If you want to exhale strongly (accompanied by audibles like OMG, Lo, whoa, whoosh, and so on), we do not object. But save all that for things yet to come.

Here, you may be tempted to indulge in hair-splitting. While comparing masses, we see that the sun, the star, is a single object, whereas the Milky Way and others galaxies are a group of objects. Considering in terms of single, standalone objects, you may still insist that the sun as an object is still the heaviest among the denizens of interstellar space. You are correct, if you think of the sun as a star. Yet, in space, there are millions and millions of stars, many having far greater mass than that of our sun. Even so, you are going to be disappointed–by a story. That story is written by gravity, the gravitational force. It briefly runs thus.

All matter, whether small or big, possesses gravity. Matter attracts matter, and thus grows in size (read mass). This is more so especially when matter in gaseous form is concerned. Space abounds in gaseous forms of matter. This is how stars are formed. Stars attract more matter and become more massive. Initially, let us think ingenuously and assume that such stars continue to grow in size (read volume). It is true, of course, but up to a certain point. Puzzled? Recall that matter possesses gravity. But it is to be noted that as matter accumulates more and more, the gravitational power (pull) also increases proportionately. So, what happens? When the star reaches a certain size, its gravitational power becomes so powerful that the size of the star shrinks, because gravity is pulling all matter (star contents, usually gasses like helium) *into itself*! Imagine a giant fist is compressing the 'ball' of the star. This repeating process of increase in mass, increase in gravitational pull, shrinking of the size of the star finally reaches a climax. It is a real 'climax,' drama-wise too. *The self-compression power of the enormous gravity makes the star shrink to hundreds of thousands of a fraction of its original size.* The power of gravity too becomes immense beyond credulity.

You know what we mean? The gravity of the new star is so strong that it traps even light into itself (let alone any other kind of matter) and does not let go! You see (pun intentional), we 'see' an object when light from it reaches us. So, when the stomach-heavy star does not let go of light, we will not be able to see the star! That is why such a monster is named a black hole. We infer its presence indirectly, by the effect its abnormal gravity produces on other surrounding objects. Apart from other technical details, our focus here is on the mass of such a black hole. From the list above, you can see that such a single black hole usually contains tens of solar masses; single object, we repeat.

The story is still not over. Not for nothing did we say that Nature takes pleasure in stunning the arrogance of the presumptuous human mind. There are black holes and black holes. What we saw just now is a black hole of the 'general' category. There are supposed to be what are called SMBHs–super massive black holes. Their masses? There is no point any longer in our asking you to hold your breath. This is something above all that. The SMBH is the mother of all objects in the universe. A single such black hole has been estimated to contain matter of *a billion solar masses*!! This is the ultimate in the masses of single objects in the universe.

Whew! Stand still for a second and glance back at the mass of the electron, one of the lightest of objects. And then as the shiver and thrill infuse your being, ponder the mass of the mother of all objects, if you can. The range is so huge that all words fail to do justice in describing it. We can only take recourse to enumerating all relevant data using numbers.

While we are at it, we can also consider the whole of our universe as a single object and try to guesstimate its mass. The exercise may appear to be daunting, but enterprising souls have found an easy but logical solution. The universe appears uniform to us, wherever we look and in all directions. The average density of the universe has already been calculated. So has been the extent (width, radius) of the universe. (Of course, limited for the present by the power of our technical instruments.) Thus, the total mass of the universe (ours) can be calculated. Look at the list given in the previous pages; the calculated mass of the universe is 3x10e55 gms! One final statistic, just to remind you what we were aiming at all along–the unimaginable vastness of range in Nature. The figure for the mass of the electron contains the number showing a *fraction* of 1 followed by 30 zeros. That of the universe has 1 followed by 55 zeros (positive). So the overall range stretches to 1 followed by 85 zeros. Neither you nor I, nor he, she, it, they can really grasp the size of such a number; forget it. In our mundane life, we are accustomed to thinking in terms of millions and billions, and in rare cases, of trillions (as in national budgets etc). Those numbers are less than specks of dust when compared to 1 followed by 85 zeros. Ah, forget it.

*Sizes, distances: That reminds us of another similar extravaganza indulged by Nature. The ranges of measurements size-wise, distance-wise too exhibit a similar phenomenon, though not on the humongous scale as seen in preceding paragraphs. Please peruse the list given below:

Range of sizes

Electron …2.82×10^{-15} m

Hydrogen nucleus …1.6×10^{-15} m

Hydrogen *atom,* radius…1.6×10^{-10} m

Tennis ball, radius…2.7 inches

The Giza pyramid…139 meters high Volume = 2.583 million cubic meters

Earth, radius…6,371 kilometers

Jupiter…69,911 kilometers

Sun, diameter…864,938 miles (1.392 million kilometers) 109 Earths can be lined *across* its surface

Milky Way…100,000 light-years! ((Not that you do not know: A light-year is a distance that light travels in one year. Just remember that light travels at 186,270 miles *per second*! Imagine light traveling at such an enormous speed for one hour, and then a day, a month, and a year. That distance is the usual yardstick for measuring distances in space. (Somewhat similar to a foot in comparison with the vastness of space.) Imagine again that it continues traveling at the same speed, with undiminished enthusiasm for 100,000 years! By that time it would have just finished crossing the Milky Way. (Our solar system is situated in the Milky Way, in a corner.) As we are not tired of repeating, these quantities are simply beyond our normal imagination.))

Universe (ours), diameter…93 *billion* light-years!! (As known so far) This is the ultimate in size/distance as far as our universe is concerned. Distance here means physical, not conceptual or imagined as can be derived in mathematics. (Maths has its own concept for such limits. The infinity.)

Just a brief comment on the list before we proceed to other topics. As with masses, we begin with the electron representing the smallest size. (No nitpicking please. This is not a scholarly treatise on science. The electron will do for our kind of speculative flights of ideas.) In the case of masses, the index representing the mass (of the electron) was the fraction, denoted by 10 raised to the power of minus 30. Here, it is half of that figure, minus 15. Do not be deceived, however: 10^{-15} is still so small a figure that you cannot see an individual electron. Next in order comes the nucleus (of a hydrogen atom), which is roughly two times bigger. Then we see the atom; the wonder begins at this stage itself.

(Notice that the size of the nucleus is in the order of 10^{-15} m and that of the simplest atom is at 10^{-10} m. Recall that the nucleus is inside the atom. This means that the size of the atom is 20,000 times more than that of its nucleus. *There is an enormous amount of empty space inside the atom!* There is a beautiful and breathtaking similarity between this and the universe. As of yore, if you like to be diverted, jump to the section 'empty space' and come back here, or bookmark it and proceed straight ahead. See another parallel here? It is that which you experience in the great www's webpages! You browse a topic and before you know it some other item and its link have goaded you to another page, and then in a jiffy you are lured to another page in another site by an irresistible link and so on, till you have forgotten the original first page, or don't have the time to revisit it.)

Back. What we notice is that sizes and distances are beginning to expand at this microscopic level itself. (Recall the image of the tree, branches, and leaves we have elsewhere studied.) The next item in the list is the tennis ball of 5.4 inches size. The minus sign attached to the power of 10 has gone by now. The atom was 20,000 times bigger than the nucleus. Compared to the size of the atom, our tennis ball is *billions* of times bigger! (Pardon us again for repeating. We are not afflicted with OCD; we are not unduly using the exclamatory sign. In fact, if you actually follow the workings of Nature with the zeal of a poet or philosopher, you will justify the employment of exclamations at the end of every sentence.) Our earth is 12,742 kilometers across. (A *small* percentage of the seven billion and odd human population might have traversed the earth. How many would have traveled to all the countries of the earth?) The sun is 1.392 million kilometers across. We have already commented on the sizes of the Milky Way and the universe. Just spend the rest of your life trying to figure out how long 93 billion light-years is, how small the size of an electron is and how huge the breathtaking difference between the two is. If you want to swoon, you have our sympathy.

Range of Joy: There is a wide range in terms of joy experienced by human beings. People doing what they love to do, people engaged in artistic expressions, etc. experience joy. Indeed, there are plenty of activities which bestow joy to humans. (Joy, pleasure, and happiness are all considered as synonymous here.) Reading, writing, playing sports (watching too), athletics, walking, running, talking (gossiping too), singing, sitting idly in silence: all these and many more activities give pleasure to humans. The list of such activities is endless. (A humorous aside. All verbs you can find in the dictionary, when indulged as actions, are sources of pleasure to some human or other.) Again, range is the operative word here. Nature is prolific and munificent.

An interesting tidbit here. The ancient Indian scriptures contemplated on this very phenomenon of joy. They proceeded to measure it and have put on record as a grand scale of comparison. After perusing it you will agree that the word 'joy' is not able to contain the full import of the description. (Bliss is a better word.) A succinct description of the mindboggling (no less) scale of bliss follows. Imagine a human being in the prime of life and in perfect health with no worries or burdens. All his needs of food, clothing, and shelter are fulfilled. Take him as representing the best human being enjoying the perfect measure of joy. The joy quotient of such a person is taken as one unit of joy. In a higher echelon of existence, there are beings above human level but less than God. (Don't worry whether such a supposition is factual or not. Follow the breathtaking scale—and swoon promptly!) The joy quotient of the second tier of beings is 100 times more than that of our ideal human! Ah, that is nothing. There is a third tier of beings on a higher stage whose capacity for joy is a 100 times more. Keep a diligent count; hundred hundreds are 10,000. Okay? Then a fourth tier of higher beings exist whose joy quotient is a further 100 times more. Add two more zeros to the previously obtained number; guess it is a million. Joy, which is a million times more than that of a (blessed) perfect human being, is impossible to imagine. Maybe there are some nerds (or drug junkies) out there who could *pretend* to conceive such a state. Further updates are awaiting them as follows! We are at the fourth rung of beings only. The breathtaking, beautiful, blessed books bound beyond that. They go up to the 11th, the highest tier. (Mercifully, no, most logically, there is only one being at that height, height that defies any description.) Now, our purpose was to view the vastness of range. Begin to compute. Even if you miss by a hundred or thousand, it does not matter. There are 11 stages, and so add two zeros after the number 1. That is 22 zeros!! (One exclamatory mark will not suffice). If you have heard of the word trillion, go and ask a mathematics teacher how many trillions there are in our blessed number. Assuming that you have not swooned, we will proceed to name that being. He is called Brahma, the Creator, in Indian scriptures. His bliss is called *brahmananda* in Sanskrit. Remember those 22 zeros again. (The suffix, *Ananda*, is attached to the names of many Indian saints and yogis.)

Okay, a wee bit of pardonable pontification. Even if you do not subscribe to theology, let us latch on to the word Creator. Don't like that word also? No worries, let us get back to our original nomenclature, Nature, which we adore. Drop creator but retain the essence, the act of creation. Contemplate for the last time on the joy quantified by 1 and 22 zeros, and attribute that joy to Nature. That means, creating this immense universe is an act of such immeasurable joy for Nature. Be poetic or prosaic, but you will agree with that!

Lastly, when we feel joyful in our myriad activities, *it is all just a tiny reflection of what Mother Nature has been doing all along*—every blessed minute of all these uncountable eons.

*Human body: When one mentions the above multicellular organism, the body of humans, the very first thing that comes to mind naturally is the image of the human body. Being humans, we can proudly proclaim that the human body is the ultimate creation of Nature in its endeavor of evolution. It (the human body) is an engineering and biological marvel. In an earlier paragraph, we talked of clusters of functioning organisms. You can go on and on enumerating the clusters that make up the body: brain, heart, stomach, lungs, limbs, sensory processing organs like eyes, ears, skin, tongue, nose, organs for movement like feet, legs, arms, the underlying organs responsible for these like muscles (quite a lot by themselves), and most importantly, organs/clusters for controlling these amazing mazes of organs, namely the brain and the nervous system. The above list is kept at a small size in order to provide the reader a fairly recognizable map of the hierarchy of the organ-clusters. The intention is to show that when a large number of clusters join together to act as one single unit, the master unit (the 'whole') beautifully organizes itself into two main bodies: the working, functioning body, and *an overall controlling console*. Mark the words in italics. It is such an efficient design, if seen from an engineer's point of view, and a beautiful one if seen with the eyes of a poet, and sublime if grasped with the heart of a philosopher. Verily, the greatest, the most profound designs–add, the most complicated too!–have been perfected by Nature itself.

Spreading: In nature, some things are immoveable; they stay put. Some things spread. You can enumerate plenty of things that move and spread. Technically, there is a difference between moving and spreading. Things that move need not necessarily spread. You move your limbs, you move from place to place. The branches of trees move. But that is not spreading. But liquids and gasses spread; their constituent molecules are not rigidly bound together. Fluids can spread in two ways. Air spreads, as in a breeze, or storm. Air spreads in a different way–by means of vibrating waves. Strictly speaking, it is the wave that is said to travel. They use the word propagate to denote it. There are more scientific nuances and definitions and jargon. We can safely ignore all that here. Propagation, spreading is the main idea to consider as a phenomenon occurring parallelly in various fields.

Terse PS–Ideas and rumors spread. Reputations spread. In olden days, kingdoms used to spread.

CHAPTER 13

NATURE'S PATIENCE

Just as we have the Game of Patience, Nature too has its own personalized version of the game, starting with a big, bold capital P. Since our angle of view (of Nature) is more poetic than academically scientific, let us for a few minutes pamper that Inner Child which resides in all our hearts.

"I want it now."

You are all too familiar with that booming shout issuing forth from the bulging throat of the fulgent boss. Actually, however mature ur (excuse us) boss may pretend to be, he is acting out the deeply-buried scenes from the drama of his trauma-filled childhood. Instant gratification: that is the theme. Probably, these old fashioned sapient sentences may serve well in an essay on papa Freud and his legions. Life has terribly changed from those days of somnolent pace. The TV and Internet-fed babes of today do not need those old-fashioned traumas to screech, "I want it now." Babes are born with ADS nowadays!

Now, fueled with the above background information, fire the rockets of your Inner Child's imagination into fantasy-filled (erratic?) orbits.

The justification for the IWIN syndrome can follow quite a convincing ratiocination. If you look at it objectively, there is nothing wrong in insisting that a thing be done immediately. It is in fact, super efficiency. (We warned you in advance that we are not nerdy-geeky science buffs. Do not confuse that everyday 'immediately' with 'instantly' of the scientific jargon. You cannot insist on going from here to the moon instantly, because nothing can move faster than light–as on this year, 2020!–and the moon is a couple of hundred thousand kilometers distant. We are not talking *that* kind of science here.) Just hold on a sec and we will show you what your Inner Child should gleefully be imagining about. Your Child is actually thinking on behalf of Nature. Thus, or along similar lines:

Seed of the tree: There is the seed, there is the tree and there is yon Nature brooding over it. (That description, 'brooding over it' is pregnant with deep meaning, pardon us, even if we are saying it.) Your Inner Child pours forth the following wacky catechism:

"The seed, the seed, where is the seed?"

"It is in the soil."

"Is it situated at the proper depth?"

"Yes, yes, yes."

"Has it been watered?"

"Yes, yes, yes."

"What is the destiny of the seed?"

"To grow into a tree."

"Is that the intention of Nature?"

"Yes, yes, yes."

"*When was the seed sown?*"

"Just a minute ago."

All of a sudden, the Child begins to throw a mighty tantrum. It begins to get wired. Its face is turning red, along with the eyes, hot drops dripping down from them. It is shouting, it is screaming. It stamps on the ground, it falls down and rolls, gets up and again stamps, shouting with tightly clenched fists. The shrill words are almost incoherent, but gradually, you can make out what it is demanding—it is your Child, after all.

"One minute! My god! One long frigging minute has passed and nothing is happening. *I want it now, I want it now.*"

You already have a growing sense of suspicion of what the *enfant terrible* is demanding. You ask anyhow, to make sure, "What do you want, my sweet child?"

Fresh bouts of stamping and rolling on the ground arise as a response. In between the cacophony, you are able to make out the lines, "I want it now. (Short pause) I want to see the seed becoming a plant. Now. I want the plant to become a tree. Now. Full-grown. Now, yes, a hyphen there, yes. I want the tree to bear flowers, and the flowers, fruits. Now. I want to eat those fruits. Ripe ones, instantly. I want it now." Stomp, stomp, holler.

We were able to understand what the IC (Inner Child) was trying to express, and hope so you were too. By pacifying and patiently throwing a couple of questions at our ET (*enfant terrible*), we can elicit somewhat cogent and coherent answers from the guy. (Our questions are under 'elision' as grammar geeks would call it.)

Why *should* it take time?

Tell your mother, sorry, I mean Mother Nature to speed it up.

So what? That is an excuse only.

Example? Instantly? Well, I bust your nose and blood and you can taste it immediately.

Offensive? Okay, sorry. Well, how about this? I pull the trigger and your brains…oh, so sorry again, my sincerely civilized apologies and all that. Well, I throw the burning matchstick into the gasoline tank, and you know what happens instantly. The flying plane nosedives and bites the ground, and you know what happens instantly. I can go on and on…

Yes, we can see that he can go on and on. Better shut him up and take the reins into our control. We have to point out to that brat that he is chattering about physical and chemical reactions, whereas the seed and tree (and his darned flowers and fruits) are biological entities. A fully grown tree is thousands and thousands of times bigger than its tiny seed. The molecules constituting the tree are millions and millions of times more numerous than those of the seed. The seed has to take in water, air, minerals from the soil, and sunlight too later, and so on. *It is the game of numbers, see?* After having said that, we have to bite our tongue at once. "Numbers mean nothing; we (here, The Brat is mimicking us) mean, do not count. (Good pun no? Ha ha)," would be his answer. The fellow will ask us politely sarcastically, if we have heard of some ancient thing called nuclear bomb! Ah, we remembered it just now, and that was why we bit our tongue. The nuclear bomb explodes because of atomic fission and *chain reaction*. First the nucleus of a suitable atom is made to break into two pieces ('fission'). (One atom, pl note.) The process yields certain kind of rays/particles which penetrate the nucleus of an adjacent second atom, initiating the breakup of that atom, which process releases more rays/ particles which penetrate the third adjacent atom and split it up, which process... See, this can go on endlessly, but the main point of interest to our (IC's) argument is that the extent of the action increases at a very terribly fast rate–almost instantaneously. You see, one (split-up) becomes two, two becomes four, four becomes eight. Recall what we said about the power of 1 being followed by a number of zeros. That is what happens in an atomic fission; the chain reaction. Its power is terrible–we need not have to remind you of that. More to the point is that the splitting of all those millions and millions of atoms happens very fast, almost instantaneously. That is what our spoiled brat is talking about: instantaneity. That is why kid said numbers don't count. Enough said.

We will just top up the remaining part of his tantrumatic (excuse me, please!) argument. We dive into the ground and go back to the seed for the last time. What is the destiny of the seed, we asked. It has to grow into a tree and bear fruits and flowers. If that is the only intention of Nature, then why let it take a cue from the chain reaction we just mentioned and do all the sequences it has to do (be it millions or billions, no worries; chain reaction will take care of it. If chain reaction is unsuitable or unavailable, Mother Nature can surely invent some another path, probably more productive and faster), and be done with it. Imagine the scene, gentle readers. You sow the seed in your backyard, water it, go into your bathroom, wash your hands, and come back to the backyard again. (By the bye, don't forget to take a big basket with you.) Lo, (truth to tell, if you follow our Brat's reasoning, that interjection 'lo' is unnecessary) there the full-grown tree is, all flowers and ripe fruits gloriously strewn on the ground all around the tree. "*Let what has to happen happen instantaneously and be finished.*"

The argument is not all that farfetched if you look at it purely from the angle of ratiocination. (We are trying to make this a bit lively, instead of following the dull academic route of facts and figures.) The most striking feature in the episode (of the seed to tree) is that of the enormous difference in the size between that of the tree and the seed. But, all it involves is the process of division/multiplication of cells. This is similar to that of the nuclear chain reaction, as the Inner Child argued. One becomes two, two becomes four, four begets eight, and so on. Actually, if this occurs flawlessly you will have an enormously unmanageable number (let alone a paltry thing like a tree) in your hands before you complete saying, 'Long live mathematics and the geometric progression.' If you have doubts, go to a computer geek; he can load you with the weight of all the numbers contained in the universe, just by pressing a key. That is all—the argument is clinched in favor of the Inner Child. (Shouts rise in the air, 'I want it now, I want it now!') The rest is a matter of filling up minor details. One powerful objection ('So called,' taunts The Brat!) is that, for the one cell to explode into a conglomeration of billion cells, an enormous amount of energy is required—from the outside of the cell. Air, water, nutrients, sunlight—all of these are required in measured proportions so that energy may be converted into the form of new and appropriate type of cells that constitute a tree. This objection, though appearing to be serious and cogent, does not carry much punch. The fact is that transformation of energy from one form into another can be almost instantaneous. (Solids, liquids, gases, rays, waves, all are forms of energy. Recall the atomic bomb!)

So, why does it take such a long time for the seed to grow into a tree? The only real explanation, according to us, is that Nature (mark, starting with a capital, as it should) is playing the Game of Patience. ("*Patience is the favorite child of Time*." – Professor Bagdenborg) Also, Nature seems to enjoy immensely, playing that game.

(A gentle whisper into your ears. In the ardent pursuit of science, there is no place for emotions–there are only equations there. In science, you say what you have to say with equations, and that is that. (Can't help pointing at a small joke, however insouciant it is. In science, there is a symbol used with all seriousness. It is the exclamatory symbol of grammar, '!'. Of course, scientists, being serious killjoys, ascribe a completely different meaning to that symbol)). Therefore, we prefer to look at Nature with a combination of a good many emotions: awe, joy, humor, appreciation, gratitude (yes), and so on.

As we remarked earlier, the enthusiastic reader (you, who else?) can find plenty of examples of Nature playing patience. (In fact, such a search will become a lifelong hobby once developed.) We will just offer a couple of brief descriptions and move on to further fields beckoning us enticingly.

Homo sapiens: Yes, we come next in the list of Nature's Patience naturally. We may assume that the acme of a human being's growth is represented by a full-grown adult. Including full development of the brain, we can put the age of such a being at roughly 22 to 24 years. That means Nature is taking its own sweet time (as the idiom says,'Whether it is sweet or not to the being being considered, we cannot avouch') to manifest its (proud) product. Add to it the traditional additional nine months the baby has to live ensconced in the womb of its mother. Adopting the same kind of arguments we employed in the case of the developing seed, we can again assert that there is really no valid reason for the final product (the full-fledged adult) to manifest itself instantly (well, almost) after conception. 'ASAP' as we say these days. Recall, "Transformation of energy is immediate" etc. Risking the intrusion of a burlesque comedy, we invite you to visualize our Inner Child in the previous example to come here and react, accompanied by its tantrums and all. The Child/Brat will insist that the embryo should begin gobbling up all the energy or food or whatever it needs to grow in a nuclear chain reaction fashion and come out of the womb instantaneously as a full-fledged baby. (It is the parent's responsibility to supply the necessary fuel.) That is not enough. The baby is a baby for name's sake only. For, as The Brat insists, before you ask the baby "What is your name darling?" there would no longer be a baby there. There would (should) be a full-grown adult there. In fact, the adult would no longer be there, because that 'there' is not a location where our adult would like to tarry. He would have walked out from the scene. (The parent/s would better be advised to keep a suitable size readymade dress at hand.) (Oh, one more aside; please excuse us. The hypothetical scene just imagined, has been described with great authority, aplomb, and seriousness in one of the ancient Indian mythologies written by Veda Vyasa, the original writer of mankind!)

Nature takes pleasure in leisurely sculpting for 24 years, what could have been potentially done in a jiffy. That is called the Game of Patience, in which it excels. And we strongly suspect that patience, here, is equivalent to Joy—the kind which only Nature can know and indulge in. The temptation to philosophize is strong here. Professional philosophy is a tough discipline which requires plenty of gray cells—and gray hairs. We will do a micro, man-in-the-street kind. You know why Nature is sportingly playing the Game of Patience? Because it takes time, naturally. Puzzled? Time is the operative word. You see, if the seed becomes a tree instantly, bearing further fruits and seeds, those seeds will immediately produce more trees and those trees... It is a mega-mega chain reaction with a vengeance.

The same kind of argument can be put forth in the case of humans too. Embryos will become adults will beget fresh embryos will become adults will beget...Before you notice it, the surface of the earth will be covered with human beings (and other life-forms)!

There is a flip side to this. As things stand in Nature (in the present universe), everything/one that is born will die. Our Inner Child, the young Brat, forgot this aspect when he demanded his I-want-it-now. So, what happens? Following the demand of The Brat, the embryo has to not only grow into a full-fledged adult, but it has to fulfill its final destiny and die too, instantly (well, almost)! The same rule (fate) applies to all other life-forms. Imagine such an awe-inspiring scenario. *Untold billions and billions of lives are being born instantly and dying immediately.* It is like a fantastic flashing of strobe lights on a universal scale!

Further, the same argument can (has to) be adduced for the other kind of existence, namely that of 'inanimate' matter. Science assures us that our universe is going to extinguish itself ultimately. It has got to do with some mysterious thing called entropy, which poor souls like you and I cannot understand. But rest assured that the universe will die a cold death ultimately. We still have got some billions of years to witness that fate, do not worry. But we have to worry seriously if we take our young Brat's demand seriously. Because (as you have already guessed), following the screaming *diktat* of The Brat ('I want it now.'), the entropy thing has to follow the ultimate course now itself and so, the universe has to shut down as soon as it is born! There will be nobody to witness anything, or write or blog anything. That is why, we, as armchair philosophers, conclude that Time (Patience) is the essence of Creation. *That is joy*, in other words. There is no formal proof for that statement, but we feel it in our bones, and are confident that you too do. Amen.

In Nature, everything is connected. The above chapter is also interconnected with that on ranges. (If you have not read it yet, better go there and come back here!) Nature manifests extreme ranges in Patience too, specifically in the evolution of things as we saw in two instances above. We will close the topic with further assorted comments, grumblings, and musing of the Brash Brat—sans quotation marks.

*They say it took millions of years for the first life-form to appear on earth. I don't understand the necessity of such a long time! (In the background, you can hear the music of "I want it now.") As an antiphon, you can hear the song and tunes of the fugue "Patience."

*Along the same lines is the story (yes, story, as far as I am concerned) that it took equally many more million years for man to finally evolve as the crown of creation. Too long a time, honestly speaking. And quite unnecessary in my, again, honest opinion. (In the background, you can hear the music of "I want it now.") As an antiphon, you can hear the song and tunes of the fugue, "Patience."

*That same song of Patience reminds you in its last lines that Nature has been playing many games of Patience, and that the *greatest game of them all is still being played and has not ended yet!* Guess what that game is. Simple. It is called the game of creation, the mother of all games; the game has been going on for the past 14 billion years, and you can rest assured it is not going to end soon. When the Brash Brat is asked to ponder this vast scenario, he is so dumbstruck that his favorite song 'I want it now' is stuck in his throat.

A lemma: There is a subtle difference here in what we are discussing above. There are any numbers of 'processes' which can be described in terms of physics and its equations. All these things too take time. These kinds of processes, besides being innumerable, are occurring all the time. (Otherwise the universe will be frozen and come to a standstill. These processes too exhibit an enormous range of time—that is the beauty and bounty of Nature. Let us have a brief look at a couple of such instances before proceeding to other topics.

*The simplest one: There is the fruit on the tree. You throw the stone at it. The fruit falls down etc. Throwing the stone is strictly governed by the laws of physics, by Newton's laws of motion. It takes some time for the stone to reach the fruit, the time being determined by the weight (mass, as they say in physics) of the stone, the power behind your throw, the resistance of the air to the movement of stone, and so on. The fruit too takes a certain time to reach the ground, the time depending on the height of the fruit, air resistance, etc.

*The same process can be 'extrapolated' as they say in mathematics, into many more similar situations, obtaining various ranges. Instead of the stone, you fire a bullet at the fruit. The bullet travels faster than the stone, of course, and hits the fruit far quickly. But the fruit still takes the same time as before to reach the ground.

*You are feeling whimsical and aim the bullet up into the sky. Depending on the power of your pistol (or rifle), the bullet travels up losing its initial speed steadily, until its speed becomes zero. Then it commences to fall down to the ground gaining speed every second (it is called acceleration) until it reaches the ground. This too is a kind of process that takes a definite time, following the laws of physics.

The same bullet ('projectile'), if fired at a calculated angle and speed, will, instead of falling down, begin to orbit around the Earth at a calculated height. (This is how all those busy, buzzing satellites are placed into various orbits by the technocrats of a handful of nations.) The act of that projectile completing one revolution around the earth can be dubbed as a process; this has a definite time schedule.

And the same projectile, if fired at what is called the 'escape velocity of the earth' will go away (hence, 'escape') from the clutches of earth's gravity and begin to travel in empty space. Theoretically, it can go on forever if it does not encounter another object in its path, or if a gravitational field does not gobble it up, to the edge of the universe, assuming also that the universe (ours) would be still there till such time. This destiny too can be dubbed as a process, and it will qualify for being crowned as the mother of all processes. Ranges, ranges, ranges… you can go into raptures over it.

*There are many other long-term processes, though not comparable to the 'mother' mentioned above. The formation of fuel oil like petrol is one such example. Geologists say it has taken a million years for the 'golden liquid,' as it is called, to form inside the womb of earth. That is what we meant when we talked of Nature's patience.

Radioactive decay is another instance. A given amount of a radioactive element decays gradually in mass by way of radiation. The time taken for such a mass to get reduced by half is called the half-life time of that element. Some elements have a short half-life span, and some have quite a long life. (You have surely heard of what is called carbon dating technique employed by archaeologists etc. The technique is based on the half-life period phenomenon of radioactive carbon.) Plutonium has a very long lifespan of 24,110 years(!), which is one more reason why everybody is afraid of nuclear bombs, since Uranium and Plutonium atoms are released in the explosions, and the deadly radioactive elements stay in the environment for thousands of years. Even the survivors of a direct explosion have no chance of living. (A small note: we said range. Nature, in keeping with its fantastic sense of frolic, displays its hand here too. Elsewhere, we have given a list of half-lives of elements. If you look up once more, you will see that the shortest span is of 23×10^{-24} *seconds* and the longest one is of 2.2×10^{24} *years*! We are not ashamed to sing the psalm of Nature's Range once again!)

A tag to the note! These tags and notes cannot be avoided. Our subject under study is like that. It shows that Nature's fabric is so richly and intricately interwoven. At every step, everything reminds you of an interconnection with every other thing. In this particular instance, the theme of the ranges in creation and dissolution is being reflected off the surface of the topic of elements and their life spans. The universe birthed itself with the Big Bang, which was of an extremely tiny duration. But then, the universe has been still living (existing) for the next 14 odd billion years. Nature is playing the same tune in the case of its constituents, the elementary particles. And everything else too; you can read it at leisure in another chapter.

*An appendix to the paragraph on human birth—just to show you how it pleases Nature to play at patience in intermediate stages too. We mentioned about the 24-year span of the human adult. But in a minor way, Nature deliberately broods even in the case of a baby coming out into the world. There is the usual gestation period of nine months. It looks as if, apart from the mother, Nature is enjoying that period of preparation. (The gestation period for baby elephants is more.)

*On the contrary, most seeds come up above the ground far more quickly. But here too, Nature shows its quirky sense of humor. How about this? It is said that there is a certain seed of a certain tree which lies in the soil for a period of 12 years before breaking the soil, sprouting up!

Tidbit: Recently, a seed of Judean date palm took the pride of place for lying dormant in the ground for nearly 2000 years! (It sprouted in the year 2015.) It was discovered when digging up was done in Israel at Herod The Great's palace. The same quirkiness occurs in the case of flowers also. Flowers of certain plants (Kurinji in the Nilgiris, South India) take 12 years to bloom. Those of the Sheep Eating Plant bloom once in 15-20 years. That is nothing. It is said that the Madagascar Palm blooms only once in 100 years!

A small table showing the gestation periods of some animals (culled from Wikipedia) is given below:

Opossum (Virginia) 12 days

Mouse (domestic white) 19 days

Squirrel (gray) 35 days

Alpaca 345 days

Zebra (Grant's) 375 days

Giraffe 430 days

Rhinoceros (black) 450 days

Whale (sperm) 535 days

Elephant (Asian) 617 days

Elephant (African) 645 days

*Patience, did we say? Well, how about this? Look at all those wonderful trees and plants out there. What is the most beautiful thing that trees and plants do? Produce flowers, no doubt. So, we (and you too) naturally expect that the trees would start blooming at the earliest. But no, Nature takes a fancy. Most of the trees produce flowers during a certain season only. It is a well-known fact, you may smirk. Tarry there. The whims of Nature are diverse! (As we are not tired of repeating, take any field and you can rest assured that Nature likes to explore innumerable possibilities there.) Nature thinks that blooming regularly once a year is dull and monotonous! There are some trees/plants that bloom after some years (of deliberation and contemplation?). There are even a few trees that bloom only once in a lifetime of their existence! Hope you now appreciate what we said about Nature's whim. Hope also that you are by now accustomed to look up lists on various subjects of interest that we have been presenting at regular intervals. (Sometimes, lists, objective facts convey the intended meaning more tellingly than whole paragraphs can.) Forward ho, then to one more small list, illustrating what we said above about blooming:

Night blooming Cereno takes 1 year to bloom

Sheep eating plant (Yes, that is its name. The plant traps sheep in its thorns, and digests the rotting body after the sheep dies of starvation, unable to escape!)…blooms after…15 years!

Kurunji plant…blooms after…12 years

Tail pot palm…blooms only once in…30-50 years

Madagascar palm…blooms once in…100 years

Queen of Andes…blooms after…80-150 years

Amazingly, some seeds can lie dormant for unimaginable lengths of time and grow again in a conducive environment. Archaeologists have dug up seeds which lay buried deep in the ground for 2000 years, and then were able to revive the seed; the seeds germinated! That, again, is nothing. There was one particular seed of a plant ('Narrow Leafed Campion') which was revived after 31,800 years! The time was, of course, determined by carbon dating.

CHAPTER 14

BORDERS

The universe consists of one thing and many things–a zillion things in fact. This is the most obvious observation. Yet it is amenable to lots of philosophical interpretations. As we said elsewhere, let us leave philosophy to the gray-celled-haired gents and look at dear Nature from the platform of plain common sense mixed with plenty of curiosity and wonder. And a bit of mental adventure that is not ashamed of itself. So...

To start simply, how do we know that a given thing is different/separate from another thing, or the rest of the world? Or, to put it differently, how does Nature tell us that two things are separate from one another? The obvious, immediate answer is that Nature simply *creates a border* for the object! So simple, yet so profound–and more mysterious. (If you are properly attuned mentally, you can also be deeply mystified.) Of course, there could be many other attributes too, but a border is the most primary, the most fundamental tool for creating a differentiation. Look everywhere in Nature; you will find borders all around you, for all objects. Borders can be of the solid type, or of shapes/curves/lines which close on themselves. (Words and definitions too are incomplete by themselves, and raise scope for plenty of quibbling! Curious? See it thus.)

A small list of borders before closing the chapter will suffice. (Small only, since the actual list will be as big as the universe.)

*Let us start with us, humans, the *embodied* beings. Each of us is distinguishable from the other beings (and objects) because of our bodies. That is the first stage of assessment. If you ponder a bit more, you will see the obvious thing. The body itself is bound by a border–the skin. The skin of humans and animals not only serves to demarcate and protect the body from the rest of the world, but it also acts as a medium through which the body can sense and react to the environment.

*Trees and plants have the bark as a border.

*For inanimate objects of Nature, their outer surfaces themselves constitute a border.

*All manmade objects too invariably obey the above rule. And borders can be passive or active too. Generally, artificial borders (manmade) are passive, in the sense that they do not react with the environment. Fences, dams, buildings, national borders, containers: things of that sort exemplify it. *Ironically, borders of living beings and many inert material objects respond to environment, even though the borders seem to have been created in order to keep them as distinct from the surrounding environment.* Skin is a very good example; it is acutely sensitive to everything that happens around and near it.

*If you are trying to be clever and thinking of liquids, then the answer is that they must have some kind of containers, and those containers form the requisite borders. Even lakes, rivers, and seas are not exceptions to this. Contemplating about gasses? They come in cylinders with tough metallic containers or in leather as in footballs, or plastic, nylon, etc. as in balloons.

*The borders are usually created in regular, recognizable or geometrical shapes. Of course, even those of irregular shapes serve the primary purpose of separating one object from another.

*In short, even the smallest unit of life, the cell, has a border.

*If you are pondering about gases in a free state without being contained, then there are two answers to that. 1. Gases (or fluids) consist of discrete particles–either of atoms or of molecules. Each of those atoms and molecules has its own individual border, configuration. 2. Secondly, we have to consider the action of gravity, which is universal. If the number of the free-floating particles is very large, then under the influence of gravity, the particles tend to congregate together into distinct groups. This is how stars and galaxies are formed.

*That should remind you of the border of the other kind–the virtual border. (Nature, variety, you see.) Wondering what the heck a virtual border is? It is a border that has been created by or suggested to our mind when we perceive a group of objects that stay put together into an invariable form–or an easily recognizable form. Examples of this kind are the innumerable galaxies.

*Nature loves to play another trick too. There can be borders that go on changing continuously! Yes, just look above at all those billowing clouds–and then, clap your hands in joy. (Try to imagine such a similar thing happening among the borders of the nations of the earth. The ensuing mayhem–apocalypse would be a better word–would be unthinkable.)

*We touched the subject of geographical borders among the nations of dear planet Earth. Permit us to stray into philosophical ponderings very briefly. Set aside the abstract and highly impractical treatises of Utopian thinkers and look at our human world with down-to-earth eyes. You will see that the creation of borders among its denizens is a Natural, unavoidable phenomenon. Capitalizing the word Natural was done deliberately in order to bring in the link with Mother Nature. The short syllogism runs thus. The physical national borders were created by humans. Humans have minds that work in immense varieties of ways. The minds, taken in the broadest perspective, are reflections of Nature (Mom, Mother) at work, at play. The syllogism concludes by saying that Nature creates borders not only of the physical kind, but also of the mind.

*We said that borders are of the fixed (shape) and changeable type. This is directly connected to Nature's immanent desire (read joy, oh, ye poetically inclined) to proliferate. There is no doubt about that. *Otherwise, Nature could have simply created one single electron in the whole universe and keep on narcissizing on her handiwork for a few billion years!* (Come on, how do you feel if you are asked to keep on looking at and admiring just one letter of the alphabet that you have managed to write on a sheet of paper, for, say, the entire lifespan of yours, and do nothing else? Let alone a billion years! Yeah, we intend to write a big book on this intuitive thesis one fine day.) Hope we have established our point. Nature's joy knows no bounds; its acts of proliferation know no bounds. That is how it creates both fixed and changing borders. Momentarily, you may feel that fixed borders are limited in scope. Not at all. Nature thinks otherwise. Fixed shapes too come in infinite ways. (Go and ask an artist). Apart from that, Nature reproduces the same shape in infinite *numbers (quantities),* as if it were not quite satisfied with its plenitude of manifestations!

*In one of the above paragraphs, it was said thus, "Words and definitions too are incomplete by themselves, and raise scope for plenty of quibbling! Feeling curious?" Come this way, please. We will indulge in a bit of quibbling just to see where it leads to. There we said that Nature draws or creates a border in order to distinguish one object from another—either of the same kind or different. Nature also takes delight in tantalizing us as to what exactly it is up to. What we mean is this. Take one concrete example, like that of the shell of an egg. The shell enclosing the contents of the egg serves as a border for the egg. Okay, thus far. But things can really get hazy if you try to dig deeper. (That is one more trick of Nature. Things appear to be clear when seen from a distance. As you approach them nearer and nearer, they become more and more hazy and blurred! The signpost here asks you to go to the chapter on 'clear vision.' Go, if you are so inclined; else, tarry and take the straight path.)

This is a beaut straight out of those old Greek boxes of paradoxes. One famous Hellenic conundrum runs thus – "Who will guard the guards themselves?" You got the photo? Well, if the shell (or whatever) is a border for the egg, what is the border for that blessed thing, the shell itself? What is the border for a border for a border for…! This is what is called an infinite regression. So, you have to eat your words and say that there are no borders. And then, if there are no borders, everything (that includes all the godzillion things in the universe) is one. Unity, you see. Some particular brand of philosophers will be highly pleased if they hear this conclusion!

We are not done with the eggshell yet. Let us accept the shell as a real border and proceed, or dig deeper. We ask you to go and perch on the surface of the shell first. Did you land there safely–we mean, without breaking the rather delicate shell? Now, take a deep breath, get inspired and begin to contemplate the shell. Okay? If you look at it from a scientific angle, the shell is a chemical containing a number of compounds, which are 'conglomerates' of a number of molecules. These molecules in turn are 'conglomerates' of a number of elements. From there, your next journey will be one of physics. Elements are nothing but various kinds of atoms, as they are called in physics. By now, we have already traveled very deep into the shell of the egg. In fact, at this stage itself, the image of the shell has become too blurred to be visible as an independent entity. Try to look around from this vantage point. In the previous exercise, you were asked to land on the top of the eggshell. Now, you are to stand on the surface of an atom and look around. What you will see from there will be almost like a small galaxy. You will be in the inside of a galaxy made out of an uncountable number of atoms (instead of stars) of various kinds. The shell, which you saw (or imagined to be so), is no longer there. You are seeing an immensely huge amorphous cloud of 'gasses.' (Incidentally, that is the favorite word of astronomers, used to denote particles in space.) Indulging in poetical fancy, we can say that shapelessness and befuddlement are the reigning terms in this empire. The journey does not yet end here. We ask you to plunge just one more level and survey the scene around. Now let us dive down and into the inner core of the atom itself. If you, by chance, are unfamiliar with the structure of the atom (the chances are almost nil, for nowadays everyone is familiar with the atom) you may belittle our use of the word 'dive' there, thinking that the distance between the outer surface of the atom and its core is so negligible as to be nil. But comparatively, your dive to that depth will be more than the hypothetical dive from the surface of the earth to its center! That indicates how tiny the nucleus (the core of the atom) is and how 'empty' the inside of an atom is. If the atom is a heavy one, like that of a metal like gold, or of Uranium or Plutonium, you will see a lot of electrons swirling furiously all around you. For one thing, your egg border has receded out of sight. For another thing, you thought the border was fixed and static, like a line, but alas, what you see now is a dizzying swirl of cloud! So much for your border. There is no recognizable (decent!) line anywhere in sight, nor any stable shape. Remember that the electrons are constantly, furiously swirling around. If you still want to cherish the dream of a decent border (there is a word, mumpsimus, if you can recognize it!), we ask you to take one final-fatal dive again. You are now standing on the top of the surface (Border? Whose border, gentlemen? What kinda border, Ladies?) of the nucleus. The nucleus too has a certain size and contains particles like protons and neutrons, the actual numbers of the particles being dependent on the atom of the particular element you choose. Inside here too, you will meet again many numbers of particles in frenzy. (The frenzy is due to the incessant 'exchange' that goes on happening among one kind of those particles, called protons. Protons are all positively charged and so they furiously repel one another. Left to themselves, they cannot stay grouped together in one place. How such mutually fighting particles are kept tightly bunched within the tiny space of the nucleus is a mystery by itself, known only to Nature and, of course, the boffins. That aspect is not relevant to the topics we are pursuing. What is of interest to our angle of enquiry is that once again there are no visible (decent, we said), 'solid' borders here too. To be naively explicit, you cannot see the kind of shell you saw long back when you were staring at the egg on your palm before this bizarre inner journey began.

Actually, if you are still adamant and want to find the borders of those protons and neutrons and electrons, you only have to ask one of those physics boffins. The gent will enthusiastically explain to you that there is nothing certain in those ultramicroscopic areas you are exploring. There is that revered (in hushed tones) Heisenberg's Uncertainty Principle, you know? You do not know? Never mind, the thing means just that. Our consolation to you: do not worry. Something more hazy is in the offing. They call it probability. Probability is itself a huge subject and there are mindboggling mathematical equations at every turn. But the bloody thing is that the equations give you *practical results of extreme accuracy!* Apart from the ghosts of probability, in those mysterious depths of the atom, even matter (think solid) loses its materialness. There are entities which behave like particles when you examine them from a certain angle (say, in the morning), but behave like waves when you examine them from another angle (say, in the evening). For example, light can be both a particle and a wave–there are famous experiments to 'prove' it has both the qualities.

There are plenty of such-like puzzles and mysteries deep down there in the bowels of atoms. So, the bottom line as relevant to our line of enquiry in these essays is that what we first perceived as a 'solid' border is not so solid after all. It may not even exist! (Do not worry, we are not going to prove it. It is a highly romantic-cum-nevertheless-scientific idea we are putting forth for your inner bliss. We started this small digression with a view to show how quibbling about words and definitions can confound you if it is carried out to extreme limits. We hope we have made the point. Let us get back to our refreshing look of poets and philosophers.)

*Ah, after floating up from those terror-filled depths of the subatomic zones, we are back to the normal, comforting areas of the mundane world, where we can clearly see and recognize borders. Skins, barks, shells, coatings, cocoons, and so on: there can be many kinds of borders. Again, one more example of Nature's bounty. Since we are describing the vast and ubiquitous phenomenon of parallelism, we can as well have a swift glance across many other kinds of borders too. The above examples are of the kind that show demarcation between two entities. The principle can be extended to include multiple things/entities–in fact, we may even include abstract ideas too. (Why not? In for a penny, in for a pound.) Let us reel off a few examples to satisfy our penchant for making lists. (List-mania is uncurbable. Search Google and your brain will start reeling if you go on counting all those never-ending lists of all imaginable and unimaginable kinds.)

*The most common (and indisputable) boundary is that brick compound which separates your house from your pesky neighbor's. Note: We can analyze that same solid boundary, again, like the way we analyzed the eggshell and come to the (cofounding) conclusion that the boundary does not appear to exist. Neither you nor your neighbor will be pleased with that. So, let us drop the idea and follow the decent path of mundane affairs. Then, entering your house, you will notice that it has many rooms, which again have boundaries called walls. Roam about freely (it is your house, after all) and try to espy as many boundaries or borders/demarcations as possible. You will be surprised to find quite a large number of them. The door, the floor, ceiling, even each wall, the windows, ventilators, cupboards, niches, the sink in the kitchen, and so on. Then there is again a very long list of things, all the articles you possess. We are back to the basic observation: every distinct object has a border–which serves to proclaim its separateness from *its* immediate neighbor.

When asked to give an example for a solid border, we can immediately offer that of a shell–the shell of an egg. The outer shell of the egg defines an egg and differentiates it from not only other eggs, but also from the rest of the universe. Here too, Nature exhibits its propinquity for diverse ranges. These borders come in a vast range of shapes and sizes and types. Human skins, animal hides, plates (for tortoises, rhinos), membranes of internal organs, arterial walls are some of the many types of borders nature gleefully creates. (Ah, one signpost on the road at this junction points toward ranges.

Divert your walk toward that road, go to the chapter on Ranges, and come back here.)

Addendum: This is directly related to the chapter on opposites. As we said there, no sooner do you think of one quality or attribute, than Nature immediately points at another object possessing an opposite quality. Thus, when you forget yourself counting endless numbers of borders, Nature smiles and gently diverts your focus. There are also many things without a clear-cut demarcation. You only have to recollect the popular saying that there are many shades of gray between black and white. This is true, especially in the case of all colors, even though only three or four 'fundamental' colors have been defined (RGB, RYB, or CYMK). You can follow the signpost 'Blends of Opposites' and come back here, as usual.

CHAPTER 15

BLENDS

As you might have noticed, we are not tired of repeating that Nature has an inbuilt sense of joy. Well, it has a lively sense of humor too. One of its ubiquitous pranks is that the moment you make a serious statement about something, it will remind you of an existing opposite. This leads to a hilarious situation; many paradoxes are born this way...

You – "There are plenty of white things here."

Nature – "No, look there. There are equal, if not more numbers of black things there."

You (abashed) – "Yes, that is correct. There are both black and white things."

Nature (smiling mischievously) – "No, look yonder. Those things are neither totally white nor totally black. They are blends, shades!"

You (taken aback, stammering) – "Er, ah, er, yes."

Nature (still smiling, but approvingly) – "Thank you. You human guys told me somewhere there that your TV screens boast of a million colors. But there are only three fundamental colors, and all those million colors are but clever blends of the primary three. Do you remember?"

You (taken aback, stammering) – "Er, ah, er, yes."

You are stammering because you are not sure whether Mom Nature is going to contradict you once again! That is the way Nature enjoys interacting with us, tiny humans who think of ourselves as being very smart.

*Remember also that our main theme here is one of parallels. You can see a parallel in another field—that of acoustics, the study of sound waves. Especially in the field of sound, the phenomenon of blending (mixing) is the most common. Be it a matter of music or just plain conversation, they (waves) cannot exist without a vast amount of blending. Please recall that we have mentioned earlier that waves and frequencies are inevitably joined together. When you carry on a conversation with somebody, the words are actually a product of innumerable numbers of sound waves of varying frequencies—all smoothly blending and coexisting together. A small but interesting and relevant digression here. We have to simply stand amazed, dumbfounded at the two 'instruments' which Nature has endowed us with. You guessed it correctly—they are the mouth and the ears! Please follow the ensuing short explanation of what the human ear does when it hears, and you will agree that the adverbs we used are very mild and inadequate indeed. The mouth is, leaving aside the biological functions, a simple structure as seen from the mechanical angle—that is, like a kind of machine. Yet, it (the mouth in combination with the throat and tongue) is able to produce huge combinations of sounds of all types, besides serving its owner faithfully every day for a hundred years. You may still feel like grumbling, "No big deal." But you will be able to appreciate it truly when we come to the mysterious (mystic is a better word) capability of the ears. To begin with, we have to keep in mind that what we call a normal, routine conversation is in essence a continuous output of sound *waves*. Waves, as we explained often, have *frequencies*. The normal, audible/recognizable frequencies of sound for humans stretch up to an upper limit of 30,000 cycles per second. When we talk, we produce plenty of sound waves with plenty of frequencies along this range. Okay? Now, here comes the beauty part of it.

There is a technique by which you can see the waveform of the sounds you utter on a computer screen. (The technique is quite old by now. Even persons with average knowledge of computers/cellphones can see such waveforms, choosing from a slew of apps.) So, when you see the actual shape of the sounds on the screen, *that shape shows up as a summing up, a blend of all the various frequencies that are required to produce the sounds uttered by you.* There is a branch of mathematics which enables us to break down a composite waveform into its various individual frequencies–and vice versa. The wonder is that your mouth/throat does that much-complicated mathematical operation quite easily and completely naturally. This is a real wonder of Nature, if you ponder it in an appropriate mood. Next comes the rivaling wonder–that of the ears. Let us begin this with a small image. Drop a pebble into a smooth pond. You will see circular rings of waves forming and spreading outwards. The shapes of those waves differ if you throw pebbles of different sizes at different speeds into the water. If you throw two pebbles into the water, two independent sets of waves will be produced. But the two waves will interact with each other, and a new kind of wave-shape will be generated. If you throw a hundred pebbles of different types, the interaction in water will generate quite a complicated set of waves. The point to keep in mind is that even though each of the pebbles can produce its own signature wave, *you cannot spot it in the combined waveform.* If the complicated, combined wave shape is presented to a mathematician, he can competently break down the wave and give you back the original signals of the individual pebbles. That is the power of mathematics! If that is the power of mathematics, Nature challenges to consider this! The scenario: You are in a party thrown by your pal and there are about 30 people in the hall. All the 30 people are talking. (Simultaneously, what else, of course.) And there is soft music in the background. At the same time, you are engaged in a conversation with your friend. Now, inside that hall, while all those persons are talking, they are all (each of the persons present) producing innumerable, person-specific waveforms of sound. This scene is equivalent to the one in our above example where pebbles of various sizes were being dropped in the pond. Thus, the innumerable sound waves inside the hall interact and *a common, combined waveform is being continuously created. It is this extremely complicated waveform (of sound) that impinges on the eardrums of your friend and you all the while during your conversation.* Here occurs the magic and miracle of Nature. From out of those garbled sonic waveforms, your ears (brain) filter out only those sounds that belong to your friend and you! This is super wizardry if you look at it from the perspective of mathematics; and mathematics should feel ashamed and astonished at what your ears (Nature) are accomplishing so unerringly and effortlessly! Of course, as you have already guessed, there is a bit more to it. Suppose you want to listen to the background music from out of that jumbled complex form. You can, effortlessly. You have to only focus your attention on the music; as simple as that. Are you curious to know what the person sitting behind you is talking? No problem. You have to only focus your attention on his words; as simple as that. You have to appreciate the extraordinary power of the brain. Sorry there, we are talking about Nature (Mom), and so we appreciate the extraordinary power and felicity of Nature, since, you see, Nature has deigned to take pleasure in creating a fantastic instrument that is the brain. Do you suspect that we are almost personifying Nature in these pages? To ease your discomfort, we suggest that you can look at Nature as a kind of super-coordinating-controlling force. Anyway, defining the nature of Nature does not matter much here, since we are more interested in what Nature has done (and is doing) than in what or who Nature is; leave that to the professional quibblers of words. In these pages, the focus is more on joy, romance, admiration, awe, and such things.

*Blend, radio waves: A similar phenomenon occurs in the case of the other waves—the electromagnetic waves (your radio, TV, Internet waves, etc.). In space, unbelievably huge and different kinds of these waves exist constantly. The beauty (and great wonder) is that they all exist together in the same space; blend, we said. Just as your ears can tune in and listen to the sounds of your choice, you can tune in to the electromagnetic waves of your choice by employing appropriate tuners.

CHAPTER 16

GAPS

An introduction to this kind of topic is best done by our familiar Inner Brat. Here he goes.

"Do you know how big the universe is?" he asks. "Even if you do not know it in terms of light-years, bla, bla, just close your eyes and begin to imagine its immensity. Especially try to guess the number of nebulae, galaxies, stars, and planets it contains."

Let us cut him short, for once you give him an inch, he will grab an ell. The number of the discrete entities he has mentioned is impossible to imagine visually; it will run into trillions and quadrillions. Brat has a devious sense of humor. What he wanted to tell you was to imagine something far more bizarre and difficult. Imagine the whole universe–we mean, the whole of it–as being made of one lump! The brat is asking us to repeat that, so we do it. The whole goddamn universe as one solid lump, *one continuous solid lump without a break or border!* At first glance it may sound outrageous, ridiculous, dotty, but The Brat has a point there. (Please do not bring in the Big Bang and all that jazz. For one thing, the discussion will diverge vastly. Besides, the world now is as it is, so let us get on with it, he persuades us, tongue in cheek.)

Okay, if everything is one goddamn super lump, there won't be any story to write. There will not be any you or I to tell and hear anything, let alone galaxies or stars or planets. Leaving aside Big Bang and big science, let us be romantic for a moment and conclude that Nature decided to have not one lump, but innumerable lumps. With the creation of innumerable lumps, it was natural to have lumps with innumerable characteristics as well. (That makes sense, as the charming Yankee phrase puts it.) Next comes the main point. When Nature intended to make separate lumps, it wanted to keep them apart by introducing gaps in between them. Nature wanted the gaps to be as explicit as possible. Wondering what The Brat means by that? How about the gaps being a million miles wide? Or 10 million? In outer space, those distances (of gap) are quite common. Distances (read gaps) between galaxies, between stars and stars, even stars and planets, are quite enormous by comparison with the puny distances which we earthlings are accustomed to deal with on our little planet. Nature wanted gaps, and it does not do anything in half measures. You get gaps with a vengeance!

Then comes the next joke of Nature, humorous and subtle at the same time. The overall size of the cosmos is almost infinite and therefore we may feel it okay, when there are such large gaps in space. (If you are given a small spoonful of grains and asked to spread it around a football field, it is natural that between grains there will be enormous gaps. Thus.) Zooming in on the small objects and solid matter, we may feel fairly confident that such solid matter (say, a ball of iron) must be fairly tightly packed (dense, as you feel). After all, if you punch it with your bare hands, you break your fingers and wrist. (Isn't that solid enough?) Even a middle grade science student knows the answer to that. The iron ball is, in scientific terms, a conglomeration of *atoms* of iron held tightly together. The bottom line is that all matter, solid or liquid or gas, is made up of particular kinds of atoms. An inspection of the atom will straightaway push you down into the abyss of our familiar world of gaps! The atom is a mini-micro version of the solar system. The atom consists of a nucleus around which electrons revolve–their numbers depending on the particular atom of a particular element. There are neutrons and protons inside the nucleus–their numbers too, depending upon the particular element being considered. Our main concern here is the relative distances–gaps, as we said–between the nucleus and the outer fringe of the atom. Even though the atom is too small to imagine, the funny thing is that much of the atom is hollow. The gaps inside the atom can be compared to that between the earth and the moon, or more! There is so much hollow space inside. To give a sci-fi kind of illustration regarding these gaps, imagine a human body to have been blown up to the size of the universe. If you peer inside that body, you will see uncountable numbers of atoms and their electrons and neutrons and protons. (That is all that your vaunted flesh and blood and bones are made of.) Then, the gaps between these atomic particles will be comparable to those between galaxies in the universe. The human body is so hollow (including the body of Mister Universe)! We just have to reiterate what we said about Nature and gape in wonder at the gaps–gaps that exist at the macroscopic level of the cosmos and the microscopic level of the atoms. Mystics and poets go into trances and raptures over the contemplation of such phenomena.

The parallels do not end there. They are, as incessantly repeated in these pages, being reflected in many spheres. Ah, take a person's thinking activity; even that of a most busy, active 'thinker.' There will be plenty of gaps in that stream of thought–psychological studies have shown that. Ancient esoteric texts too claim that in between thoughts there are gaps, wherein the mind will be in a state of Original Bliss for the briefest of time. Most human beings, they (the teachings) claim, are not aware of that etc, etc.

*Conversation is thoughts being exteriorized and exchanged. Most of the times, in a normal (relaxed) conversation, you will see that a brief lull in the flow surfaces up spontaneously–hiatus, as it is so beautifully called.

*It seems that almost nothing can exist, or manifest without being properly (!), or appropriately if you will, interspersed with gaps. Go on scanning Nature in action and you will certainly find gaps in one form or another. All right, call our Brat again. What he orates can be epitomized thus: "I said there that Nature did not like one super-macro-macro-mammoth lump covering the whole of universe. Without gaps, it does not make sense. You were about to laugh at that (I know, I know, you can't hide it from me). Well, my dearest reader, consider the sentences that you have been reading here (and elsewhere, or anywhere for that matter). (Sorry from us; once The Brat starts going, there is no stopping him.) *Without the proper and appropriate gaps between the individual words, you can neither read the sentences, nor make sense out of them!* Duh. Poetry, songs, music all need suitable gaps in between narrations.

*Breathing involves acts of inhaling and exhaling air. But between inhaling and exhaling, there is a small gap of time during which the inhaled air just stays in the lungs. (In yoga, this is called *kumbhaka*.) And yes, a similar thing happens with the eyes when we are looking at objects. The muscles of the eyes regularly take a break (nap, gap) by blinking.

*Even physical activities of almost all living creatures (especially humans) need breaks; they cannot continue uninterrupted endlessly. The nap is the gap that refreshes you at your workplace–please do not demur. (Even if you are the one who refuses to take a short break during the day, you cannot help hitting the sack after the end of a hectic day.) Apart from the daily break, you (almost all humans, or most) get a weekly gap, which goes by the name of Sunday.

*This creation of gaps between objects is sensible in many ways. As far as living beings are concerned, there is no question about it at all. "Living beings need to move, for god's sake," cries our Brat. The simple, ordinary act of looking at a person or object itself needs a certain amount of distance (gap, gap, gap) between the looker-on and the looked-at. Inanimate objects also need a gap between them—even if there are noticeable borders around them. Otherwise, they will start reacting to one another, and something else–other than the original objects–are apt to be created. Hydrogen is one object, oxygen is another object. When they come together, water—something else altogether—is formed.

Contumacious argument. Mon, your house is one thing and my house is another thing. The two cannot join together. There has got to be a gap: that compound, that common wall in a condominium, for example. Even if you call that wall a border, the wall has gotta have a certain amount of thickness. If it is not a gap, what else is it? ("Eh, even borders between countries have neutral gaps called no-man's land," Brat interlopes again.)

LOL, there is (must be) a gap in your working hours, else will you go mad. Sundays and Saturdays constitute the gap.

Which directly reminds us of the gap Nature created for our sanity's sake. That most welcome and beneficial gap in our waking hours is made of sleep.

*Research says that even during our states of continuous alertness as in daytime, our brains go into a state of what is called microsleep: a very brief period of sleep.

LOL, or a bon mot, as you prefer. One cannot know everything about every thing. There are inevitable *gaps* in our knowledge. Probably, you may argue that these days Google knows everything (we have coined the neologism googlescient, which fights with omniscient for the first spot). Folks, allow us to remind you that Google is not a person. Even if you take it in a metaphorical sense, then it is a conglomeration of many—plenty of—persons. If you still think Google knows everything, just ask it in its famous search box if there is anything it does not know. (Please answer either you know or you do not know, as the lawyer insisted.) If it answers it knows, we have won. If it is a "do not know," you have lost!

CHAPTER 17

THE THREE ACTS

Drama: This time, you are inside a theater to see the latest play by your favorite playwright. For the present, let alone the various acts and scenes and consider the whole play in an abstracted, distilled form. Under such a condition, we can enumerate the most common occurrences as follows. There is the stage. The actors enter and do their act. They exit.

This metaphor should be applied in all fairness, to the original, primordial act of creation. Empty space–or emptiness–is the grand stage. Nature creates objects on that stage. Soon the objects disappear. That 'soon' is only as brief as some billions of years, that is all.

As a parallel, the same drama occurs continuously in the world, all the time. People come into your life. They do their act. They depart. Your mind is the stage there. Only, the period is not in terms of those billions of years, thank god.

If you start counting each example, it is impossible to enumerate all. The metaphor is very basic to creation. We will be stumbling against examples at every turn of the page here, as is inevitable. The readers will automatically recognize them. This brief chapter has served its purpose as a harbinger.

This is so, since as even kids know these days that nothing is permanent.

CHAPTER 18

ILLUSIONS PLETHORA

Unfortunately (that is, if you dislike philosophy), one cannot utter the word 'illusion' without associating it with philosophy; there are systems of philosophy which emphatically declare (not only that, but they assure us too) that the world is an illusion—on the grandest imaginable scale. As we have said often, let us leave the grand scales and deep depths to the serious thinker-geeks. Joy, we said, and with joy we will contemplate illusion—whatever it is—with poetic delight. In our humble opinion, that is a more sensible approach, especially when we are discussing a lot of topics and sharing many ideas.

*The first instance worthy of mentioning is the way distance plays with our senses. Like the good old Greek thinkers, we declare that our 'seeing/perception' of the objects in the world depend on the way our five instruments of sensing work: sight, sound, touch, taste, smell. Distance plays its own game with all the five of them. The image of a person or object seen from a distance is quite different from that as seen from near. A bird seen from very far in the sky appears like a speck. The same bird, when seen from near, presents you with magnificent colors and exquisite details...

CHAPTER 19

NATURE'S NUMEROPHILIA

It has been pointed out again and again at various places in these pages about Nature's propinquity for joy in its acts of creation. That joy has many kinds of outlets, colors, and vibrations. And even plain whims. For, it seems that Nature likes numbers (just as we humans do)! Begin compiling lists of various kinds of items, and you cannot avoid noticing and appreciating Nature's love for numbers. Wondering what we mean? Just play the short game of Lists we have prepared, in earnestness for a few minutes, and wonder at the obvious:

*One: There is the popular phrase "one of its kind." But it is a bit difficult to pinpoint direct examples. It may be so because probably Nature wants to proliferate immensely. However, we can circumvent the difficulty and prove our point in other, oblique ways! (We said this is a game, after all!) Imitating the spirit of the clever old Greek philosophers, we can declare that–just because of the difficulty in finding direct examples–Nature itself is a grand example of our statement. It is one of its kind. You cannot deny it. Note: We did not use the word universe because many serious science buffs can easily argue that there are multiple universes. Our word 'Nature' encompasses all those 'verses and much more. By now, you may even be thinking of the word god. But it is saner and safer to stick to words like Nature, Creation, Manifestation, etc., given the present state of our world

122

(even though the scientists themselves talk of some mysterious thing called God Particle!).

Ah, by cogitating a bit, you can point out another example for an act that is one of its kind, a grand act, in fact. (In this context, a phrase, "hapaxlegomenon" is reverberating inside our skull. With bashful apologies we ask the dear reader to Google search it.) In fact, that act has a respectable scientific name too. Just teasing you a bit. It is the Big Bang, which, as nobody is tired of repeating, occurred some 14 billion years ago. In our humble opinion, that act is still continuing, and so you have to agree that it is the original one-of-a-kind-phenomenon.

You cogitate a bit more and you get another beautiful example. It is also an example for the saying that one oft overlooks the obvious. What are we talking about? It is our earth, dear earth! In the process we obtained one more example—we, the human beings. Forget all about the aliens roaming in the fifth dimension and all that jazz. As far as plain-thinking folks like you and we are concerned, there is only one *Gaia* and only one set of human beings. (Even if they are going to create cyborgs in the foreseeable future.)

*Science: Under this heading, the gravitational force may be said to be unique, one of its kind, fit enough to represent the number one. You see, there are other forces like electrical, magnetic, and even the mechanical (as in machines, hand or power operated) which are dual in nature like pushing/pulling, attracting/repulsing. But the gravitational force is always attractive. One of the greatest wonders of Nature. Of course, seeing from a practical level, if things do not get attracted, nothing can stay put together and *then there won't be anything bigger than an atom in this universe, and nothing else can exist, let alone humans to contemplate such a situation and burst into rapturous rhapsodies over it!* We must really thank the two Ns—Nature and Newton—for that. (Even though we occasionally stumble and fall down from horses and stairs and bruise ourselves!)

We judiciously leave it to the intelligent reader to add more items to this list.

Tailpiece: If the number can be interpreted in the sense of 'uniqueness' (why not? It is a valid assumption), then we can obtain a lot more examples, all the while appreciating again, Nature's clever scheme of combining the unique with the multiple. Take for example, the human fingerprints. The fingerprint of every individual human is unique. At the same time, there are more than seven billion of them! The same goes for irises and voice-prints. That leads us to the subject of the DNA. The DNA print of every human is unique. Repeat—at the same time there are more than seven billion of them. A similar statement applies to the DNA of all the other millions of life-forms: static, moving, unicellular, multicellular, and so on.

*Two: All types of opposites can be easily grouped under this heading. Male-female, positive-negative, and so on are good candidates for this category. (As usual, you can here divert to the chapter on opposites and come back—if you are not diverted there to some other place! Remember please, that we are enjoying a leisurely stroll in a vast garden, that one road offers as good a view as the other, that there is no fixed, rigid route to cover the place.) We will, for the sake of formality, mention the most noticeable category-duo; the inert and the living.

*Speaking from the platform of philosophy, we have to first mention the two primordial categories of matter and spirit (or awareness, if you prefer a different word).

*Attractive and repulsive forces are the obvious choices for categorization in this bracket.

*The duo set need not necessarily be of opposite nature. Speaking lightly, a carriage can be drawn by two horses. (Tongue in cheek—both male.) Two things can complement each other and can support expansion. Take a ladder with two legs. It can support many rungs and be of use in a vertical expansion. Ah, that qualifying phrase was deliberately introduced here to bring an image from biology to your mind. In the present age, that image of a ladder immediately induces most readers to think of the DNA structure! See the beautiful analogy of Nature. The DNA structure is made of *two* strands intertwining around each other. That picture of intertwining strands must surely make you all think of a creeper, for one thing; a creeper which depicts the image of life on the move. If DNA is not life, what else is? (Nature is the supreme poet and artist combined, not to mention the engineering marvel!) For another, the spiraling strands also represent the allegory of the male and female in close embrace—thereby paving way for a new generation of growth. Parallels galore in Nature.

*Another example can be seen in shapes of objects—straight lines and curves. All the shapes of all objects can be derived from a combination of these two basic shapes. There is a small irony here. It seems Nature vastly prefers the curve, though men (and women), especially the mathematical folks and engineers, deal, create and employ innumerable quantities of the straight-lined shapes. It must be due to the fact that *there are all types of forces acting* at every conceivable space-spot of Nature.

*Three: The word that comes to mind is Trinity! That, of course, belongs primarily to the study of theosophy. But we can think of a few items in the physical world too. You see, when Nature created the category of the opposites, it being cleverer than us, forestalled our anticipation and created a category that is at the same time neither of the opposites and a composite of both the opposites! (You gotta hand it to Nature.) It is the famous neuter gender!

The Internet offers you plenty of sites that can reel off endless lists of interesting things and trivia. (Listly and Listverse are two of the well-known sites.) Such lists are huge indeed. But what are relevant to us here are only those items which are direct adjuncts, or which qualify the workings of Nature. Seen from that perspective, we can offer here one of the most conspicuous (and enchanting) aspects of Nature. Nature delights in exhibiting everything in three states or stages. [That must be why mystics and theosophists say that the number two denotes the act of creation and the number three represents expansion of creation.]

Take the three stages. The Eastern philosophical systems have with extraordinary, deep all-encompassing insight described the whole of creation in just three simple words: Birth, Existence, Dissolution! Simply grand, if you really meditate on those three words. (That is why we have capitalized the words—nothing less will do justice to that majestic vision.) These three words apply unerringly not only to our universe taken as a whole, but also to every single object that exists in that universe. First, there was nothing to see or talk about. Then occurred the Big Bang; that is the birth. After that, the universe has been in existence for 14 billion years, and is likely to continue to exist for as many years. Then, the scientists postulate about the inevitable death of the universe as we know it. Some mysterious thing called entropy (in science it is greater than God) ensures that inescapable end. The involved time span is so unimaginably vast compared to our paltry 100 years of a human lifespan that it is difficult to conceive that the universe is going to end. But rest assured it is going to: both science and theosophy guarantee the result.

On the other hand, the destruction (death, dissolution) of many individual constituents of the universe is either easy to believe, or plainly visible. Since we, as humans, are witnessing and theorizing about the world around us, let us take the case of humans as a first example. The following observation is so obvious as to be beyond dispute. First, an individual human being is born. *Birth*. He/she lives for a 100 (supposed) years (hopefully). *Existence*. Then he/she dies (surely). *Death/dissolution*. The same goes for all living beings—birds, animals, reptiles, amphibians, etc., including plant life. The three stages of birth, existence, and dissolution are invariable. The only difference occurs in the middle stage, that of existence. Some live for but a brief period and some live for a considerably longer time. One may be tempted to think that this kind of impermanence applies only to life, and not to inert matter. Not so if you look deeper (and for longer). Only the time scale of existence (in a particular form) is comparatively big; that is all. Hills and mountains get eroded. Rivers dry up and vanish. Even seas do. The vast Sahara Desert was a sea millions of years ago, the geologists say. The crust of the earth itself heaves and moves–the tectonic plates shift. Continents merge or drift apart...Everything changes its form, sooner or later. Even the most fundamental level of matter, the atoms and their subatomic contents, are no exception. All of them have limited life spans! (A list showing the breathtaking range of the life spans of such particles has already been given somewhere else in these pages dealing with ranges. You can go back to those pages, relish the data, come back and appreciate the power of the immutability of the Law of the Three States!)

Tailpiece: Note the word 'state' in the preceding paragraph. It is just a slight nuance on stage. But it is interesting to briefly look at a small list of 'states' of some things. We repeat, this book is about parallel phenomena; so let us examine the mind and its 'states' too. We will observe a surprising similarity here also. The most famous and well-known three states of the mind are those mentioned (and discoursed) in the Upanishads of Indian philosophy: dreaming, wakefulness, and deep sleep (dreamlessness). The dreamless deep-sleep state can be compared to the 'death' or dissolution of the mind/ego. It is born in wakefulness and is maintained during both wakeful and dream states. If you can appreciate poetic imagery, you can say that this diurnal cycle of states is a micro-reflection (yeah, say, a holographic piece) of the longer-lasting phenomenon of a human being's birth, life, and death! For further joy in this matter, take a leisurely jaunt along the road marked 'holography' and come back here–if you escape the abounding lures thronging that road.

*Sound: Take another phenomenon which is entwined with almost every moment in our daily lives–that of sound. There are so many innumerable kinds of sounds as to be almost impossible to enumerate: sounds made by human beings, animals, birds, lifeless material things (even immaterial things like wind, water, and fire) and so on. But, at the base of it there is a common factor, which is not immediately observable. Just ask about the *shape* of sound, and you will immediately get the clue! Sounds are waves in the air and waves have defined shapes. Look at a waveform (a graph). You will see that invariably the wave rises at a certain point on the graph's baseline. *Birth*. The wave then usually rises up following a particular style of curve (depending on the nature of the original sound), descends after reaching a max, and comes down. *Existence*! Then it touches the baseline. In mathematical parlance that point represents zero. *Death, dissolution*! We are back, gazing at the familiar scene of The Three Stages!

*While we are at it, we would like you to recall that declaration in your old textbook on physics. It said that there are *three states* of matter, namely: solid, liquid, and gaseous.

*And why not add your day to the list! Yes, the sun rises–birth of the day. Sun continues to stay in the sky–existence/duration. The sun sets–night, end of the day, dissolution.

*Another item for the list of threes. Take movement. An object can be static, unmoving. Then it can move at what is defined as a uniform velocity–second state. Ah, here comes the whim of Nature. (Just reminding you; that velocity there is typified by qualifiers like 30 miles per second, 300 mph, and so on. Excuse us for what may appear as unwanted clarification. That phrase 300 mph means that at any moment along the journey of our object, *its speed will be the same*.) Under most circumstances, the speed of the object itself can keep on increasing–or decreasing. This mode of movement is called acceleration. If you measure the speed of such an object, it will be, say x mph at one instant and in another instant it will be more than x (or less). The speed keeps on changing every moment! If you look at it with the naïve eyes of a kid (sans the goggles of science), it will appear to be a most astounding, fascinating phenomenon. A most familiar example for this is that of an object falling from a height onto the surface of the earth. As the height (from which the object falls) increases, the object will gain more and more speed (all the time) and its impact on the surface of the earth will be proportionately greater. This is due to the effect of the power of the gravitational pull of the Earth on the object. As we said elsewhere, the enthusiastic reader (you, who else?) can find umpteen examples that can be appended to this list of triads.

*Troikas: If you focus just on the number three in terms of groups, you can go on compiling a long list of three. Take time to play the game here for a very brief spurt. Right ho, here you go.

*At the most basic level, the world consists of three kinds of people. Yeah, that is right. Perplexed? Easy—I, you, and s/he (naturally, that includes the plurals also) make up the whole population of the world!

*Language-wise, you have the comparative degree. You can obtain a huge list of threes from all the adjectives in the dictionary. Big, bigger, biggest. Good, better, best. High, higher, highest. Lastly, beautiful, more beautiful, most beautiful (you, you, and all of you).

*Position-wise: Left, center, right. Back, center, front. Down/bottom, center, up/top. Time-wise: Yesterday, today, tomorrow (past, present, future). Maths: Minus/division, zero, plus/multiplication. Gender: Masculine, feminine, neuter. Measurement: Line, area, volume. (Forget the Theory of Relativity; our whole physical world can be said to have been made out of these three units.). Oh, you can go on inventing a lot of them.

*Science, physics: The famous RYB (or RGB where G stands for green), red, yellow, blue colors, designated as the three basic or fundamental colors. All the millions of other colors which we are able to distinguish are in fact the result of innumerable permutations and combinations among these three basic colors.

*An area is created when a minimum of three lines (sides) are linked, as in a triangle. When three such triangles are stacked together to form an apex, a three-dimensional space can be created.

*Assorted tidbits: Have you not heard of the famous love-triangle? Perhaps the *ménage à trois?*

*Four: We have the four major directions–east, west, north, south. They are, of course, synonymous and interconnected with our way of perceiving, mainly with the eyes, as reflected in the words front, back, left, and right. Since we are deeply bound by the gravitational power of the earth, we use two additional directions–up and down.

There are four fundamental forces in the universe.

*Recall the DNA and the two strands back there. Well, speaking of the number four, we immediately see that the DNA is made of four base molecules, A, C, T and G. (Adenine, cytosine, thiamine, and guanine). All DNAs are the outcome of intricate combinations of these four base molecules. Mindboggling, if you think of all the enormous forms of life on this planet. *The scope for the combinations and permutations of the DNA strands is so huge that there is a separate DNA print (like the human fingerprint) for every individual on earth!* Similarly, even the counterpart, the RNA, too has four bases, A, C and G being common, the fourth one being U (Uracil).

Tidbits: There are four branches of mystic knowledge (Vedas) as per Indian philosophy. There are four states of consciousness/awareness according to the same Eastern system–sleep, wakefulness, dreamless deep sleep, and a state above and beyond in which all these three exist, called the *tureeya,* the fourth. Ah, usually most moving animals (and furniture too!) have four legs. Man too has four limbs. Our hearts have four chambers.

*Five: As soon as this number is mentioned you immediately connect it with the five senses and the corresponding sensory organs: sight, hearing, touch, smell, taste, eyes, ears, skin, nose, tongue. These are the most fundamental faculties which constitute the rich fabric of our human lives. (And of almost all well-evolved forms of life.) And come to think of it, isn't it a fantastic coincidence that we humans have five fingers in each hand and foot? May be it is not a coincidence, but a deliberate, well-planned construction of Nature, with a deep purpose behind it. Then have a look at this; the Indian system of philosophy asserts that all that the universe contains is made out of five fundamental elements, or principles, namely, earth, water, fire, air, and space. The wording may sound simplistic to the modern ears, but if you look at the abstract principle behind the classification, it makes a lot of sense.

*Six: The most famous phrase here that come to mind immediately is "Six degrees of separation," popularized by Frigyes Karinthy. (Microsoft is supposed to have even proved that theory experimentally!) There is the more famous hexagram, the Star of David. As per Indian yoga, there are supposed to be six chakras, energy centers in the human body.

*Seven: Seven is a splendid number. Looks like Nature is fond of this number. Mystically, it seems that this number symbolizes perfection or completion of creation. A few examples will suffice to underline the delightful manifestations of this number in different realms.

*Start from the most mundane level of our drudgery-infested daily lives. What is (or are) it that relentlessly fills our days in an unending, repetitive cycle? It is the week (very strong) *tightly packed with seven days!* Should we repeat, Sunday, Monday…sorry there, we got carried away by the delightful discovery. That takes us immediately to the related parallel phenomenon of astronomy—the good old seven celestial bodies…

*Then we have the seven seas, the seven continents, the seven wonders of the world, seven worlds (*lokas*) of Indian mythology, seven deadly sins, seven virtues, the seven chakras in the human body (in Indian yoga system), the seven stars in the sky (as per Indian reckoning; the Ursa Major), the seven Great Sages (Indian mythology), the Sun god with a chariot drawn by seven horses, and so on, just to mention a few. (Incidentally, that metaphor of the Sun god riding seven horses must be more than a strange coincidence if you remember that the sunlight shows seven colors when passed through a prism—or the clouds. In Indian marriage ceremonies, there is the ancient system of '*saptapadi*'—the revered ritual of the bride and bridegroom going around the sacred fire seven times. There must surely be many rituals and mythological stories connected with the number seven in different countries all around the world. (In Japanese mythology, there are seven lucky gods and there is a seven-edged sword). And, ah, not to be outdone, even the spy-thrillers like the number seven–who has not heard of the great and the one and only 007? How about the seven-year itch?

*As a parallel, we have the seven musical notes in the field of sound (seven *swaras* in Indian music). As regards light, we have the famous seven colors, VIBGYOR (recall the rainbow!). Curiously, even in the field of scientific units of measurements, there are seven base units, out of which all other units can be derived: second, kilogram, meter, ampere, mole, kelvin, candela. The seven seas was a famous phrase during yesteryears.

The lists of numbers can go on and on; but it will deflect us from our main topic. Let us close it with a most familiar number. How about 365? Fair enough, we think.

CHAPTER 20

HOLOGRAPHY AND MINI-METAPHORS

"To see a universe in a grain of sand," – the great poet said. That is a beautiful line, worthy of the highest rank of inspiring poems. You can also say it is a highly romantic idea. After your poetic fervor and inspirational zeal have cooled down, you may ruefully look around the mundane world, and think that the poet was probably being highly fanciful. Think so? If so, *cool down again* and think again!

When the poet wrote that line, astronomy and the sciences of astrophysics and nuclear physics had not grown to the mammoth size that they have attained now. In the light of the latest body of knowledge, we can detect many wonderful parallels for those famous words.

Take that grain of sand. It is one grain among the countless grains on the beach. Can you count them? As a parallel, the same simile holds good if you replace the beach with the cosmic space and the grains with the stars. Before the modern super telescopes were invented, people (even highly educated) thought that there were probably a few hundred thousand stars in the sky. Many thought that that number was on the higher side. Now we smile condescendingly at that. At present, even school students know a good deal about astronomy. Nevertheless, two sentences here will not be redundant. Now we know that even a single, small-sized galaxy contains more stars than what our forefathers daringly imagined. The further joke is that the number of such galaxies itself exceeds many, many billions! Many millions more are waiting to be discovered. Think of this and go back to those grains of sand on the beach. You will then appreciate the superb parallel between those grains and the galaxies in the universe. Stretching the imagery further, we observe that the grains exist along the side of the sea and in a way come out of it. All ancient poets have compared the vastness of the sea to that of the sky. You have to admit that is a beautiful simile.

CHAPTER 21

NATURAL LAWS

Birth and Death: Even though the title of the chapter reads 'Physical laws,' in our opinion, Nature's first and greatest law is the law of Birth and Death. It concisely states the whole business of our world, our universe. The first rung in this ladder of parallels starts from the creation of the physical world that we see and live in. That is birth for you. The scientists (apart from many religions and philosophies) assure us that this our universe is going to end—even if it takes a few more billion years. Creation and dissolution—that is one heck of a long process. So, Nature, being kind to curious and impatient guys like human beings, enacts the same drama in various levels (as usual). The topic is big and only professional philosophers and thinkers can do full justice to it. There must be countless musty tomes on this subject filling the racks in the libraries of all countries. Let us simply enumerate a couple of examples and that will be enough to act as pointers indicating the vastness of the route.

*Human life: Nature reflects in our lives what takes billions of years for the Universe. Creation and Dissolution are reflected in the birth and death of human beings—in a brief span of 100 years. Death is not the privilege solely of human beings. All living beings die sooner or later. (Tongue in cheek: Hope nobody challenges that statement.) What is born must die, that is all. Elsewhere we have shown that Nature enjoys displaying huge ranges. That is so in the field of life span also. Some species of trees have been recorded to have lived for more than a couple of thousand years. On the lower end of the scale, there are some subatomic particles that live for less than a millionth of a second! (Here, there is a diverting signpost which reads Ranges. If you want you can go along the route and come back after the enchanting stroll.)

*Everything else too: In both an esoteric and scientific (damn practical) way (Nature's), a theme song of birth and death is essential for creation!! Wondering how? Repeat, it is damn simple and *damn practical*. Look all around you and scrutinize Nature's phenomena everywhere. Without birth and death, nothing can be created. The words birth and death are only metaphors. Instead, use descriptions like being and not being, existence and nonexistence, display and deletion, rise and fall, and so on. Now, each of those phrases will provide you with a refreshingly new outlook at the grand game that Nature is playing. Take "rise and fall" for instance…

Rise-and-fall is the process of creation, as we said above of birth and death! Yes, take for example the simple act of singing (talking, communicating). We use words (finely chiseled, elaborately constructed, decorative, etc.). Okay? Then, just look one stage behind (or deeper), and you will see that all words–of all languages–are nothing but sounds manipulated in particular ways. Then again, what are sounds? Sounds are the vibrations of air, waves; the rate of vibration (cycle, as they say) and the volume (strength, pressure) change from source to source. This is the base stage, where our idea of rise and fall is much relevant. Usually, the wave is represented as a graph in physics. One look at the picture of a sound wave graph will show you the meaning of 'rise and fall.'

*Intimately connected, and running parallel with the birth and death of humans, is the activities of Man on earth. Civilizations perfectly reflect the activities and aspirations of mankind. The grand theme of birth and death is beautifully painted across the pages of history in the form of civilizations. How many civilizations were born, thrived, and declined on the vast stage of this earth! Even cultures, beliefs, religious beliefs, cults are born, thrive, and subside down. Birth and death, existence and dissolution, are the grand themes of Nature's esoteric dance across the pages of Time.

*In the earlier paragraphs we said that birth and death are essential for creation (two sides of the same coin). Note the use of the word 'practical' there. Puzzled about the word? The word is apt, we insist; explanation will soon follow. First, take the general, common sense approach. The surface area of the earth on which we exist and upon which we depend for our lives is constant, that is fixed forever. The earth is not going to become bigger and bigger by either tomorrow or the next year. (Forget about all those meteors and asteroids slamming into the earth. Their contribution toward the increase in the size of the earth is negligible.) On the contrary, consider the rate at which life grows. Try to count the number of the new lives (of all the living creatures—of all types) that are being born every instant. To borrow the time-honored cliché, it is mindboggling. That is nothing. Just attempt to add up the numbers of all the living creatures that were ever born on earth from the very beginning of the creation of life! It is impossible to estimate such a humongous number. Here lies the practical nature of Nature. If all those creatures did not die at all, and if they go on multiplying at a tremendous rate, then there would be no space to stand on over the surface of the earth! *Let alone solving the problem of food.* There won't be any left. As said, Nature is eminently practical.

*Steam: Put some water in an open vessel and start heating. Gradually the water gets hotter and hotter, and after it reaches a certain temperature (normally 100 degrees centigrade) it begins to boil. Under this condition, all the water will be converted into steam, given enough time. Before such a thing happens, place a lid above the vessel. The process of escaping of the steam will stop. But you and I (including Archimedes and George Stevenson) know that it is so only for a short time. As the steam inside the vessel gets hotter, its pressure begins to build up (since there is no way out for it to escape) and at a certain point it pushes the lid up and escapes with a low hiss, so that the extra built-up pressure comes down. Again—if the heating of the vessel is continuous—the pressure builds up and the steam escapes by pushing the lid up. By keeping a heavier lid over the vessel, you can build up more pressure, and so on. Every kindergarten kid knows that this pressure of steam is (rather was) utilized to run the steam railway-train, and the steam turbines in a thermal power plant... Let it be. What is of interest to the topic we are following is that there is a certain limit (small or big), above which the steam invariably comes out. If there is no way for the steam to come out, the vessel holding the steam bursts into pieces under the built-up enormous pressure. By dropping the scientific wording and suitably rephrasing the above phenomenon, we can see similar parallels in other areas. *That which has been forcibly contained tends to find an outlet, or damages that which is containing it if there is no outlet.* As you have correctly guessed, we are talking of the mind and its emotions. You will even recall the familiar idiom "letting off the steam" coined after the phenomenon. In fact, the word 'boiling' too is aptly used to describe the emotions held under constraint.

*A parallel of this principle is best reflected in the human mind when (whenever) its inclination for natural, automatic responses or emotions are held under constraints (either external or self-imposed). Neurosis and repression are the favorite terms of the psychoanalysts. Under this same imagery, we can see a different and beautiful, poetic simile. When the water is boiling and steam rises, *and if there are no constraints*, the outrushing steam gushes out in all directions, reaching out to greater and greater areas in space. This is a physical phenomenon, but the same description with suitable alteration of the words can be beautifully applied to the mind too. *When the mind is 'heated up' by inspiration, it expands and begins to explore new realms.* How wonderful an analogy! We can even go further and dare to propose that just as the nature of water in the heated vessel changes—what was in a liquid state turns into a gaseous state—so too, the nature of the mind changes. What was dull and inert becomes supple and quick. This is not entirely a 'poetic' description: there is scientific support too. Nowadays, it is common knowledge that the brain produces different kinds of electrical waves in certain areas corresponding to different types of mental states like sleep, wakefulness, alertness, concentrated thinking, joy, sorrow, meditation, and so on. The effects of such corresponding brain frequencies have been copiously recorded. And alternately, such frequencies can even be fed to the brain by different methods to induce appropriate responses in the human mind, as through the ear, via appropriate sound waves. The technique consists of feeding two sound frequencies differing by a designed low margin into the right and left ears simultaneously. The low difference in the two frequencies is called a beat frequency. The human ear by itself cannot 'hear' such low frequencies if fed from an external source, but the brain is able to respond to those small (beat) frequencies by somehow detecting the difference between two frequencies fed separately through the two ears. Without our conscious knowledge, the 'brain' is able to do addition and subtraction—not of arithmetical numbers as such (which are abstract symbols), but of the physically sensed stimulations themselves! Ah, the brain does many more extraordinary things, such as extracting different wave forms when all of them are 'mixed' and fed to the ears. As an example, look at the simply marvelous (but most essential too) ability of the brain to independently filter out individual conversations in a crowded room wherein the air is actually a fantastic, macaronic mixture of innumerable sounds. It is indeed a most marvelous gift of Nature if you ponder it properly, for which we should be highly thankful to Mother Nature; otherwise, you simply cannot even walk along in the streets without getting your bones broken (or life squeezed out by a speeding vehicle!). We have discussed this phenomenon in another chapter, and if you are tempted to jump there, please go there and come back at your leisure, provided you are not tempted to branch out to someplace else *there!* Amen.

*Chain reactions

This is the most familiar phrase to all the readers. Who has not heard of nuclear bombs? Most probably none. The nuclear bomb explodes because of the chain reaction. Without going too technical on the topic, chain reaction may be explained briefly as follows. When an energetic 'ray' enters the nucleus of a fissile atom (an atom that can be split; only a few heavy atoms can be split), the atom breaks into two parts, releasing a small amount of energy. The energy so released is extremely small and will be of no practical use to us–industrially or otherwise. What happens when the atom splits is that apart from the energy released, one or more 'rays' (particles, as they say in scientific parlance) are released. This is the important thing. These rays enter the nucleus of another neighboring atom and split it, which action again releases further small amounts of energy and the 'rays.' These rays again split another atom…and so on. Thus, this kind of phenomenon is called a chain reaction. The total number of the atoms is numerically very large even in a small amount of matter. (Like, say a six-inch diameter of uranium.) Hence, even the minute amounts of energy released at the single atomic level add up to produce an enormous amount of energy. That energy is hundreds and thousands of times greater than that which can be produced by conventional methods like burning, dynamiting, etc. Actually, the word 'chain reaction' is a kind of misnomer; it does not invoke in the mind the superfast lightning speed at which the *millions and millions of atoms split*, all done in a fraction of a second! It is this staggering speed of the reaction which is responsible for the nuclear explosion. The technologists have developed a method to contain the speed and quantity of the ray emissions by employing what is called a moderator, thereby facilitating the way to harness the enormous nuclear power for industrial and other uses. Nowadays, it is a routine scene where the thus harnessed (imagine a super-super Godzilla held under leash) nuclear power is employed to produce electricity, to run ships and submarines, and so on. (Imagine too what rampage the above Godzilla could perpetrate if it breaks the leash. If a nuclear power in a power reactor breaks its leash too–accidentally–then it could cause far more damage than your Godzilla. Recall the recent disaster at the Japanese nuclear plant, Fukushima, and the terrifying Chernobyl disaster in Russia some years back. They have coined a famous word, 'meltdown,' which describes a scenario where the nuclear reaction goes out of control. The heat produced will be so intense that the nuclear fuel will go on melting whatever it encounters on earth, digging deeper and deeper till it reaches the center of the earth. There was a joke circulating some decades back that such a burning mass would bore a hole straight through the earth and come up on the other side at Peking!)

Leaving aside all such information glut, let us focus once again on the topic we are pursuing–chain reaction *per se*, which we saw, is a long concatenation of actions and reactions. If we zoom out from the nuclear interiors and zoom in on the words themselves, namely, chain and reaction, then we can perceive many analogies offering us that imagery in other spheres.

The first and most obvious thought (distant pun intended) we get is that of thought itself! First, you start thinking about some object, topic, etc. That is enough for the incredible wheel of the mind to set about spinning at incredible speeds. (The speed, of course, depends on the topic and its urgency, intensity, appeal, and so on.) One thought will immediately stimulate another thought–or group of thoughts–and that thought will automatically give birth to other series of thoughts and so on. Comparing this phenomenon with that of a nuclear chain reaction is indeed justified, because the speed of thoughts, though not comparable with that of nuclear particles, is nothing to be scoffed at. We may stretch the analogy a bit further, justifying ourselves with poetic license. Often, the outcome of a great inspired thought-chain will end in the production of scintillating insights or brilliant works of art, literature, etc. (There is a flip side too, of course, as with everything in Nature. The mind may also get terribly neurotic, or psychotic, depending on the nature and uncontrollability of the induced thought-chains.)

*Speaking humorously, we can point our fingers at the phrase "pecking order," which exists both in the human and animal kingdom! The big boss pecks his subordinate who, at the earliest opportunity, takes the peck out of his system by pecking his sub, who…and so on down the line. Another humorous example is the game with cards we used to play as kids. Arrange a number of cards standing on their edges, each card being supported by another card next to it, etc. down the line. Topple the first card with a flick of the finger and it will lean heavily on the next one, making it lose balance and create a similar effect on its neighbor. All the cards will fall on their face one by one.

*There is an amusing analogy of this among us humans too—that of rumors! You, no doubt, have heard of the saying that a rumor travels with a speed faster than that of truth. (Wags claim that it is faster than the speed of light.) An analogy inside an analogy: (air) waves propagate in a medium. Right? Rumors too propagate more effectively through not medium, but the media! Right? Further, if the spreading and proliferation of a rumor is likened to that of a chain reaction, the effect of it, the damage done by it can be equally devastating.

*In the phrase chain reaction, the root cause is represented by 'reaction.' Reaction is, naturally, the response to the original first 'action.' Reaction in turn may act as an action to beget a next response, and so on. The affair may be short-lived or a long-drawn one (as in your chain reaction). If we look around, we may find plenty of analogous chains of this sort in all spheres of mundane living.

Chain reactions (slow): The most famous parallel is the one so expressively indicated in Eastern philosophy by the word Karma, which is as large as Life itself! It is a beautiful parallel for the physical domain of actions and reactions; which does not need lengthy explanations. Here too, the phenomenon occurs at two levels. The most obvious ones are plainly visible at personal levels—those that occur face-to-face. You smile and speak kind words to a person, and most often you get back reactions in the same kind and level. You get angry and behave rudely. It is obvious what you are going to get back. These kinds of reactions may seem to be short-lived on the surface of it. Ask any psychiatrist, and he will smile indulgently at you.

In an intercourse between two persons, A and B, the immediate reactions are between the two, naturally. But later on, what has transpired between them sinks in, and creates unique impressions on the psyches of both, lying dormant. The outcome is that later on, the dormant impressions will affect how B will behave when he meets and interacts with another person C. Person A will induce a similar effect on another person D...and so on, the chain reaction extends, though not as fast as the physical one. These things described above occur on the surface level. But Karma–essentially similar in nature–works in a more subtle way. Actions and their potential effects are reflected back on the original actor and stored in what might be termed as the karmic fields (of both the doer and the done-upon). To adduce another parallel, this may be compared to the way seeds lie in the soil, patiently waiting for the appropriate environment to sprout–and bear fruit. (The proverb 'as you sow, so you reap' comes to our mind, does it not?)

*World Population: This is one of the very exquisite examples of Nature's slow, long-drawn-out dance sequences. The phrase 'world population' seems to unconsciously suggest the image of humans, so 'earth population' would look more appropriate. But 'world' has been retained because earth population, when taken in its entirety, includes all the countless forms of living beings; the example of one typical form like that of human beings will suffice to illustrate what we are going to inspect now.

A simple observation first. Look at the time scale involved and compare it with that of the superfast nuclear chain reaction discussed earlier. That, once again, points its fingers toward the wondrous phenomenon of range. (There we go again; you are free to go back to the chapter on range and return hither!)

*Chain reaction, game of words: This is an old, famous saying among lexicologists and linguists and philosophers and, last but not least, logicians. You can take this seriously or humorously, as you like, but this is really serious for them. The wonder starts like this. You cannot define (definition being the simplest and shortest way of an explanation) *anything by itself;* you can only define (also, one way of understanding) a thing in relation to other things to which it is related. One illustration will suffice here:

Start with the word 'talk.' (One word.) Talk is a meaningful sound employed by humans to communicate their thoughts and feelings. (That is eight words, excluding prepositions and pronouns. Total of nine words at this stage.) If you are unswervingly faithful to logic, you will see that now you have to explain (okay define) those seven *new* words. Begin the Sisyphus-like labor again with any new word, say, humans. Humans are erect, tailless mammals which talk, dress, and shave among other things. (At least five new words. Total is now 9+5=14 words.) Oh god, we have to define those five words if we are faithful to logic and our oath. You have to tell your audience what a tail is, what mammals are, what dress means, what a shave is, and so on. Probably, you could be using an average of four to five new words again. Go on adding up the words, remembering all the while that you have not completed tackling even the second word (humans) at all! If you are patient, persevering, and productive, you can manage to use all the words in the dictionary! This is a type of chain reaction indeed, but one that goes on at a leisurely and (safe, thank god) pace.

*Other derivative parallels to words: Words should remind us of the spoken kind automatically. The spoken kind branches off into oration, conversation, debate, quarrel, social gossip, drama, songs, and so on. Among them, the most amenable to chain reactions are debate, quarrel (unfailingly), and gossip; one sentence from one participant will ignite one or more from the other, and the chain usually grows long. In the case of gossip and quarrel, the chain, even if broken once (or temporarily), tends to pick up at a later suitable occasion. The spoken kind should in turn make you think of the written kind (of words). The written kind may not be as fast and furious as the spoken type, but it certainly is quite a longer chain. Words suggesting and supporting, evoking more and more, automatically arranging themselves into paragraphs and chapters and a complete book, are beautiful examples of the slow process of chain reactions.

As you have found out by now, every idea, concept is interlinked with another one (this, in itself is a grand chain reaction) and so often we go back and touch a point again, or return to a solid concept repeatedly. ("Life is like that," jests the great Digest.) Accordingly, we have to go back to the Big Bang and Creation again and again. The beautiful syllogism can be traced along the theosophical or scientific paths of reasoning as follows. Karma is now an international word and almost everyone is aware of it. Action of any kind (physical, mental) is karma, and we are assured that it always begets more karma (good or bad). This kind of karma, according to Eastern philosophy, goes on building up not only over a person's lifetime, but is carried over to that person's next life. (And countless life cycles, we are assured!) Seen from this angle, this karmic chain must be the longest imaginable! If you think that is all hypothetical speculation or indulgence in fantasy, okay then, let us step back into the mundane world of objects: the objects of Newtonian physics. Begin with a single object to which energy is imparted. The object begins to move, initiating a chain reaction. The object, let us say, meets another object. The second object now moves, receiving energy from the first one, and keeps on moving until it meets a third object. It can go on and on indefinitely, since physics assures us that energy cannot be lost. Also, a moving object keeps on moving unless it meets resistance of some kind–air, water, gravitational, magnetic, electric, etc. This is an ideal scenario. In the practical world, the object may meet an immovable/fixed object (adjectives refer to objects on our earth; they have no meaning in outer space.) What happens then? No worries. The rigid object will be shattered if it is brittle, and its fragments will carry on the merry dance previously described. If the object is not brittle, it will absorb the energy and begin to vibrate. These vibrations will impart energy to the air surrounding the object, and to the 'base' to which the object is attached, and the base too will transmit energy to another object (plenty of them, for sure) touching or lying on it. The dance continues. See, this is really grand karma on the mechanical level!

Tailpiece: Quiz–What is the longest chain reaction, then? Simple. It is the Big Bang, the act of Creation itself! (Oh, we are again touching that revered topic. Seems unavoidable. And natural, in a funny logical way. After all, we are all immersed in the universe, and a part of Creation.) The cosmos is still expanding, for one, and all its trillions and trillions of parts are constantly interacting. *The chain reaction of the birth of the universe is still continuing; both metaphysically and physically.* Amen.

*Brownian movement

The phrase is coined in honor of the scientist who discovered this phenomenon. If you pour water (or any liquid) into a glass tumbler and watch it normally, you may not see much, except the clear, undisturbed, calm content of water. Think a bit below the appearance and you will remember that water is made up of molecules. (Just like the way most solid objects are.) In a solid object, its constituent molecules are tightly bound, whereas in a liquid, the molecules are not so rigidly held together–that is why liquids flow. Air and gasses are different; their molecules are not rigidly bound to one another, and they tend to flow out of a container unless you seal the container. Well, it was discovered that the molecules in a liquid also are under constant random movement. This is the famous Brownian movement.

Now, to the topic of our concern, that of parallels. When you look around, you will find plenty of parallel phenomena, activities, etc., for movement is a ubiquitous phenomenon. (There is a beautiful word in Sanskrit for the world, which connotes that which is always moving. True indeed.) We will quickly enumerate a couple examples here and move on.

The first and foremost example of this constant movement is that of, what else but thoughts! From birth to death, the minds of human beings are under constant motion. (It does not stop even in sleep; we all dream.) There is a two-tier parallel here. One is that of an individual person. Compare his mind to that of the water tumbler above; his thoughts are under constant sand random motion. The second level is from the view of all of us on earth taken together. The earth is the glass tumbler and the seven odd billions of human brains are the water molecules. (Allow us to hark back, "What happens here is reflected there.") Please jump to the Haiku section for further poetic thoughts on Brownian type movements.)

*Gravitation: Gravity is omnipresent–ah, like God. So, naturally, it crops up in every topic under the sun. So, we will obediently take it up once again for a brief mention (venerable force, without which there is no universe, nor earth, nor you nor me!) Physical force, as you can easily observe all around you, can be of two kinds–push (repulsive) or pull (attractive). In technical parlance, they are called positive or negative. There are equivalent kinds in science as in the electric and magnetic fields, which exhibit both attractive and repulsive forces. Bodies with like charges (positive and positive pair, or negative and negative pair) repel each other, and those with opposite charges attract each other and so on. This is a universal law. But look at gravity again. It only attracts, it does not repel! That is, two objects (any two) always attract each other gravitation-wise. Gravitational force is unique. It is the only force among the known forces in science that acts in one way only!

There is a reason why we elaborated on this unique property of gravity. To point out a wonderful parallel in another sphere–that of the mind. (We are not ashamed to admit that we prefer to use the word heart in this context.) Now you got it. We are thinking of love! Love, the ideal, pure kind of love on which philosophers and mystics go into raptures, is like gravity, a force which attracts. (The Great Bard – "The whole world loves a lover.") Recall again that the word magnetism is usually employed to denote the attractive quality of love. We venture to speculate that Nature is expressing the same thing through the phenomenon of gravity among inanimate objects what it enjoys doing among human beings, nay, all living forms. Embrace everything within your reach with love. We can go a little further on this road of metaphor. When love becomes too strong, it does not let go of the object (of its love) from its grip. Agreed? It is a common enough scenery all over the world, not only among humans but also among animals. *That, dear friends, is what a black hole does! We even venture to say that were the Great Bard alive now, he would have written a befitting sonnet on Black Holes and Love; amen. (Free tip. Ask a pop song writer to write of the crushing power of the heart that is more powerful than the black hole.)*

*Further sauntering along the by-lanes on this road. As gravity grabs more and more mass, its power increases and the mass increases. See how beautifully a similarity manifests ubiquitously in many other fields. Do we have to remind you of the famous saying, "much becomes more?" Initially, an enterprising person earns a respectable amount of money. There is a certain stage after which the process of accumulation seems to increase automatically. Finally, the person becomes a millionaire, then a billionaire, then tops the list on Forbes. This is quite a familiar process… Oh, you can go on and on. Remember the old adage of your school days about little drops. Little drops of rain fall on the ground. Eagerly they search for conducive opportunities to gather together following the lay of the land. Soon puddles begin to form. Pools, small streams develop at suitable places. Streams eagerly run hither and thither seeking kindred companions. Soon they all join the nearest river! (Much becomes more.) There are rivulets, rivers, and mighty rivers hundreds of miles long all over the face of the earth. Things come together, grow and grow, attracting more and more of the same—we said, look at the way gravity works ending in super-massive black holes. The points of no return. Thus again, it happens here too on the surface, on a different level. The rivers end at the sea, continuously discharging everything they have into it. (The point of no return!) To quote from a poet (plebeian, budding, aspiring), "The sea loves water, the way a black hole loves matter." "The embrace of love is akin to that of gravity." "Black hole devours matter; the sea devours water." And other sonnets of that ilk.

*Yes, one can go on and on in this vein; Nature and Life are bounteous in similar acts and actions and activities. Bodies, gravity, attraction, love;

so, the song runs, doesn't it? So, let it be. For, when you physicists talk of bodies and gravitation, we mere meager mortals are reminded of biological bodies and your gravitational attraction becomes in our sphere, the attraction indeed of love! Taking cue from much becoming more, we can justifiably extend the phenomenon of accretion in one more way. Begin with one person. Like gravity, he has enough mass (read love power) to attract people coming into contact with him. Here too, we use the words "personal magnetism," magnetism as in science. See, see the parallel! Gradually, that person's activities begin to attract more and more people. See the parallel with gravity again. The force of gravity extends far and wide, we noticed above. In like fashion, the person's influence extends far, especially in these days of instant infinite communication. He has attracted innumerable persons–he has become a star. See again: star, powerful gravitational attractive power. Our hero star too wields immense power.

*It works in a different way too, somewhat the other way. The example in the above paragraph was individual oriented–one person attracting many toward him. Look at a big mass held together by gravity on the other hand. If you inspect it keenly, you will see that it is a congregation of a lot of individual particles. Each particle is endowed with gravity and the combined effect of that gravity is holding all the individual particles in the shape of a single object. Now swap the words gravity with love, and particles with individual persons. Just as the particles coalesce and are held together by gravity, a number of individuals can come together (love, a common interest, etc.) and work as a single unit. That unit is a club or a society dedicated to a common goal! Oh, let us rant further, for other metaphors beckon and propel us to elaborate along. You see, the objects formed by gravitational attraction vary in their sizes and composition. The sky is studded with countless objects of all sizes, right? Well, bring down the metaphor down-to-earth (so to say!) and you will find a striking similarity in terms of both sizes and contents. There are small societies, big ones (recall Society for Prevention of Cruelty to Animals, for one), clubs of all imaginable sorts (fan clubs, for one) and sizes, small and big organizations, and so on. People getting bound together by ideas and ideals. Then humans stay bound together in a different way too. Love, we said (gravity). Patriotism, love of one's land, is the most common (almost essential) force that binds humans together—the geographical boundaries too are there, of course, but are secondary. Coincidentally, most of the time language (another powerful, gravitational-like force) too plays a strong part in holding humans together. Just like stellar objects, these earthly objects (entities) exist in various sizes and shapes. Many countries have their own national languages; just look at the countries of Europe (and try to enumerate all their languages!) Yes, shapes too; that is the funny and remarkable thing. Simply look at all those funny contours of the borders of all the countries of the world. Then, apart from languages, ideas too hold people together. And their binding power can be more powerful. Remember how vast the idea of communism had spread many decades ago. We have kept the most powerful and long-lasting ideas (ideals) for the final mention. Religion, of course! Nobody can deny the vast spread of the major religions of the world. And how ancient some of them have been!

A small, humorous (but relevant, nevertheless) diversion here. We started this topic by saying that ideas hold people together. They are very powerful too. Then some cynic or heckler in the crowd is sure to shout thus, "If they are so powerful, if love binds all together, then the whole of this earth should have become one single nation long back! More than 4000 years of recorded history shows that such an event has not happened." That is really an astute and accurate observation. One has to appreciate it. Having said that, we ask our dear (beloved) cynical-heckler friend to look above at the sky. This is not a comedy—we mean what we said and we said what we meant, as the dialog in a mediocre film runs. Did our dear heckler get confused? If so, here is the un-heckling for his benefit. Gravity and love are equivalent as metaphors, we have established. The billions of objects in space vary in sizes tremendously, and in shapes too. *If gravity were to gobble up everything, binding it all together, then our universe too should have become one immense lump long back!!* You and I would not have been here indulging in these stimulating speculations. Obviously, it has not been so. It means that Nature wants variety and range. (The signpost reads Range. If you want you can go to that chapter, browse, and retrace your steps. (Serious students and geeks have to excuse us here. This is not a textbook on science. Romantic thinking–not entirely devoid of reasoning–is more accentuated here.) So, just as there are objects of various sizes in space, here on earth too, there are units (countries) of different sizes and shapes. Nature has seen to it–that is what we mean. (All things are interconnected; ranges again. Life is like that, as the good old Reader's Digest used to assure us.)

*The above thread is not finished yet. Our heckler is correct in a way unsuspected by him. He seriously asked why the whole of earth has not become a single, unbroken Nation. Great emperors in the past have tried to bring the whole of earth under their control. Alexander, Chengis Khan, Kublai Khan, Napoleon, Hitler, even communism, and so on are a few examples on that score. Heckler the interloper will immediately shout that none of those quoted above succeeded. Patience. The answer again is in the skies. But, "You yourself already accepted that the sky contains only differentiated blobs of matter. Blab bla?" We were again teasing the impatient heckler. The answer, to adopt the manner of the Grecian Oracles, lies in the final solution! Do not shudder at the phrase. We are referring to the Dissolution in fact. It is not the Dissolution of our earth, which religious texts prophecy. It is the dissolution of the whole universe as we know it–well, kind of. Scientists, the kind called cosmologists, predict that as opposed to the Big Bang, there must be a Big Crunch. That means that on some future date (measured in terms not less than billions of years) the universe gets bored expanding (which it has been doing for the past 14 billion years. Poor thing, it is justified in getting bored) and starts contracting. In the end, all of this immeasurable universe will condense into an unimaginably small, *single, undifferentiated tight mass.* The science geeks cannot be wrong, we assure you. Mr. Heckler, read the words in italics and you have the answer. Still frowning? We will resolve your doubt. Your first query is answered–the universe turning into a single mass under the power of gravity-love. Well, *in that same year your earth also is going to be united as one single nation! It is guaranteed, but you have to wait patiently.* QED [comment: Nature is kind to us, see?]

*There is one more by-lane crossing the main road of gravity-love, worth a bit of trekking. A bit of nitpicking only. A few more parallels. A single small object possesses minute, almost negligible gravity, as already explained. But when a number of such objects come together, their gravitational pull adds up. And more to the point, the combined mass acts gravitationally as a single mass. In general, when things come together, their power increases. Likewise, in the working of the atomic bomb or nuclear power generation. The energy released by the fission of a single atomic nucleus is ridiculously small as to be negligible. But when such atoms combine together into a mass of six or eight-inch diameter, the total energy is devastating enough to wipe out a large city. If a single molecule of air, even if traveling at 100 miles per hour, hits you, you won't feel it at all. When millions of such molecules join hands and assail you, they can blow you off your feet! The examples are countless. That said, we will enumerate a couple of examples in the human sphere and leave you to go an adding to the list–as an exciting game.

*The obvious similarity is that of us, human beings. A single human being's capacity of output, even if it be considerable, is limited. It is always enhanced by the addition of more persons of like interest. That is obvious and needs no further embellishments. Just look at the countless fields of endeavor in which persons work together. (In fact, no civilization can survive without the cooperative effort of human beings. No organization or government can too. All quite basic and obvious…) Even the best athlete in the world can never build the pyramid–even if he labors for his whole life. The same argument applies to the construction of the Panama Canal. In fact, it is true of any big undertaking.

*A single soldier, even if he is the best in the world, cannot charge forth and conquer a fort. The same thing can be accomplished when many such soldiers group together and act as a unit. (Yes, little drops of rain…)

*A single strand of cotton yarn (almost any thin strand for that matter) can be simply broken with a snap of the fingers of one hand. Join a number of such strands, twisting them around. You get a rope of surprising strength, capable of hauling up objects of immense weight; for example, the lifts in multi-storied buildings etc. Even bridges can be hung using them. The list for material objects like this is almost endless.

*For variety, here is a parallel in the mental (psychic) sphere. Some readers may feel this is farfetched, but we would like to include it here. We are alluding to the intention-oriented mental (psychic and spiritual) efforts coordinated together by a group like prayer, healing sessions, etc. The belief is that when a group of people engage in a mental act in synchronization, there will be a palpable effect of that action across the human consciousness of the world. Almost all religions believe in the efficacy of this kind of group effort. The idea may cross the realm of pure faith and extend into the tangible/measurable world of actual living. A lot of serious research is being carried out in many scientific labs on this subject. Most of the readers have heard of the famous Maharshi Effect. It is said that even the government of USA has introduced some training courses based on that. The Maharshi Effect states that in a city, *when a certain ratio of the population practice the exercises of meditation and peace, the crime rate in the city decreases!* Recently, the book "The Intention Experiment" by Lynne McTaggart is also well-known among reading circles. There is a phenomenon along similar lines. About 30 years back, the book "Hundredth Monkey" was very popular. The theme of the book was quite interesting. It was discovered by scientists that when monkeys in an island were taught a new skill, other and more monkeys learned that knowledge through direct observation and imitation.

That is nothing spectacular. But here comes the kicker. When a particular number of monkeys learned the skill–say 100–monkeys in an altogether new and isolated area learned the same new skill *without direct contact with the original monkeys of the first island!* Somehow, knowledge had jumped across the intervening space, as if there was an unknown mental connection between monkeys all over the world! If this is true, then it bolsters what we have been saying again and again in these pages, writing as if Nature is superconscious: as if it has a will, an intention, a design in the ways of its unfolding. Many ancient rituals conform to this belief. The Indian system especially had the *yaga* and *yagna* sacred rituals designed for the purpose of invoking general welfare of the populace.

*Black holes!! It is impossible to imagine even a man-in-the-street who has not heard of the black holes, let alone high-school students. To the uninitiated, a black hole can be summed up quickly as follows. All matter is endowed with gravitational power. (The earth we live on never lets us forget it.) The pulling power of gravity depends on the mass of the object. For example, the sun has more mass than the earth and therefore its total gravitational pull is many times that of the earth. The sun is a star. There are plenty of stars in space that are far more massive than our sun. Consequently, they are endowed with far greater gravitational forces. The next bit to remember is that all objects have what the scientists call 'center of gravity.' The phrase means that the total gravitational pull of the object behaves as if its pull is acting from that center of gravity. That is to say that *the gravity of the object is pulling every bit of matter (of which the object is constituted) inwards, toward the center of that object.* (It is a good thing for us and the living beings populating the surface of the earth. Otherwise we–and everything making up the earth–would have dispersed and floated away into space long back!) In effect, the gravity of an object is always trying to 'shrink' the object.

*Tidbitty small talk: Things entering a black hole and not returning have many diluted (thin) parallels in many fields, though not as awesome and spectacular. Even a deep well in your village is a kind of black hole! You let things drop in and they are gone. Forget about deep divers and all that jazz, for that aspect is irrelevant to our postulate. Well, you want something deeper and bigger? Yes, Nature can accommodate you. Think of the deep sea! Things go in and settle comfortably at its bottom forever. Thus, this too is a kind of black hole. (Again, don't mention the scuba divers. Think of the mammoth amount of ships and other kinds of objects–yeah, meteors–that have fallen into the seas all around the world for thousands of years.) Thus, the sea is a mini mock black hole of sorts.

*Stretching the similarities (and humor) further, we can focus on one aspect of black holes. That is, that things enter its maw and do not return. Rephrasing the idea, you can say that things move only in one direction under the influence of a black hole. If you vaguely suspect that we are speaking of one-way streets, we assure you that indeed was our object. A black hole is a one-way street. Imagine that the one-way street is infinitely long and our simile is perfectly tenable. Stretch the fun a bit more. Can we find any more similar phenomenon (in a different field) where things move one way? Yes. In electricity, there are special materials called diodes. A diode allows electricity to flow in one direction only, along a wire. Usually, the electricity that we use in our residences flows in both directions; it is called AC, alternating current… So, a diode too is a distantly distant cousin of a black hole. (Don't scowl, for god's sake. We are not discussing pure geeky science here. Scowls, frowns, and seriously knit brows are prohibited in these pages.)

*Ah, when it comes to gobbling up completely, relentlessly, we have the greatest of all epithets. It is called death! Death is a black hole for life; you simply have to agree there! It is a beautiful and grand metaphor that Nature itself has created for its pleasure. Infinite numbers of lives of all kind have been swallowed by this special black hole from time immemorial, never to come up above…

*While we are still in a humorous mood, we can as well jocularly think of things that travel one way and never return. There is an old Sanskrit saying which assures us that three things when placed into the hands of others will never come back: woman, money, and books! It holds true even today. That is an example of a micro-black hole for you. Money; can you think of another instance when the money travels only one way and does not return to you? No, not "down the drain" kind. It is the tax you pay, whether you like it or not!

*The big billionaires of the world too are a kind of metaphor for black holes! When money, land, power (anything along those lines), reaches their zones of attraction they are sucked in in toto. À la black holes, their (the billionaires') mass (read money, wealth) grows: and then *that* helps attract more money inwards. Much becomes more, again. See the statistics in the US; 90%of the total wealth of the country is owned by 3% of the population! The same modus applies to power also.

*Relativity: While discussing natural laws, we cannot ignore the venerable Theory of Relativity. One important branch of this theory describes the behavior of time for a moving object. If the object moves at a very fast rate, time slows down for it. Many sci-fi books have been written on this theme. This phenomenon is on the physical level, and it has been experimentally verified. Well, there is a parallel in the mental world (but in a slightly humorous way, of course). When you are extremely busy and engaged continuously in intense action, the day seems to have passed faster than usual. The reverse is also true. If you are totally idle, alone and bored, the day never seems to end. Everyone knows the famous joke about time (attributed to Einstein). If you are listening to the tirade of your boss, the passage of one minute seems like one hour. If you are chatting with your lover, one hour seems to have passed in one minute.

*Viewpoints. As mentioned elsewhere, the same object, when viewed from different angles, presents different images. Thus, the image of the object is relative. A parallel analogy exists in the area of mental perceptions and judgments. An incident (even if recorded as a non-judgmental video) is seen and commented on by different people in as many different ways. Nature wants us to appreciate that relativity need not necessarily be shrouded in mysterious formulas and scientific jargon!

*Inertia

Inertia, as in science, is a bit different from the inertia we know in general usage. But the abstract concept behind the words tally. And we can find a lot of parallels for the concept in fields other than science. In our daily parlance, inertia implies a kind of laziness, sloth, sluggishness, etc.–a persisting resistance against movement or action. In science also, inertia is defined as that quality of an object, under the influence of which the object, if at rest (not moving) will be at rest only unless an external force is applied on it. That is understandable, and jells with our common sense too. The other definition is a bit startling. It needed the genius of Newton to expound it. *If the object is moving, it keeps on moving forever!* (Unless and until an external, opposing force is applied on it.) Usually we expect that the moving object stops, sooner or later. That is so with all objects we see on earth, which is surrounded by air, and which possesses gravitational pull. In outer space, away from the pull of earth's gravity, a moving object keeps on moving. All our rockets and space vehicles take advantage of this property; otherwise we will never be able to reach other planets, let alone the moon. Enough. Now to the parallels of this quality of inertia, in a few interesting fields.

The very first instance...doesn't begin. Yeah, that is correct. The scenario is like this. You have got a great idea for a blockbuster novel. You wrote the idea in your notebook three years back. Today you are holding your pen (uncapped) ready in hand, paper spread on the table. You are knitting your brows intensely, and staring into deep space furiously, ready to burn paper the moment inspiration flows. Inspiration has not flown yet; not even trickles are in distant sight. After a while you put down the pen, deciding to watch your favorite series on TV, hoping that after the show you may get the mood. You have been doing this act for the past six months. Or, in the other scenario, you are the macho who prefers to peck fast and furiously on the digital keyboard of the laptop you specifically purchased with the fond hope of writing a bestseller. You want to check up your email before opening that blessed MS Word document (new, blank, untitled). Force of habit makes you click on a link. A new page opens. You browse, see another link to an alluring video, click it, and so on. Before you say goddamnit, you have wasted three hours—you have not yet opened the blessed MS Word document. Time up. You have been doing that for the past six months. Then, you realize that there is a word for what you are experiencing—writer's block. You also realize now with surprising clarity the meaning of inertia. You thought it occurred in physics, but now you see that it has been sitting heavily inside your head all these days.

There are umpteen other types. People spend years of their lives wanting to change their way of life. Usually only a lucky few succeed. In physical inertia, a minor force also is enough to show its effect on an object. Alas, in mental inertia, most often, even the strongest efforts are often ineffectual.

*Inertia, second type: that which moves keeps on moving. As said earlier, a profound insight into one of Nature's physical laws. As before, Nature paints parallel scenes in other fields. The most striking and familiar one is in the realm of the mind. A single word 'habit' says it all. The propelling force of habit is truly greater than that of a juggernaut. Once the mind develops a familiar track along which it can move (pleasurably or otherwise), it will keep on moving along the same track for an astonishing length of time, often spanning a lifetime. (You surely remember the wise-crack your teacher made in high school illustrating the power of habit. Remove h from habit and yet 'a bit' of it remains. Remove a again and yet 'bit' of it remains. Remove b also from it and still 'it' remains!)

Habits can be good or bad. But there is something more persistent and far more deadly than habits. It is drug addiction! The very hearing of that word sends a chill down one's spine. Something which moves keeps on moving, and in this case, in contrast to the physics law, nothing can stop it. Terrible. One gets suspicious that Nature has somehow overdone what it intended.

Resistance in general: It seems Nature does not like its contents to move (grow, rise, whatever) easily. There is, in almost all cases, a resistance to movement unless, of course, the object is moving in pure vacuum, as in outer space. Especially on our earth, since it is covered in a layer of air, there is always resistance to movement of objects.

*Arrow in air

The arrow moves in the air, the air offers resistance to the arrow, the arrow overcomes it and moves on. If the air-resistance is less, the movement of the arrow is not much affected. If the resistance is considerable and unpredictable, then the arrow's journey in air is erratic. The arrow may not even hit the target.

Similarly, there is usually a resistance to movement in human enterprise of all sorts; movement in the sense, especially of progress. This has been the case since time immemorial.

Except the daily routines, almost all achievements are encountered by challenges and obstacles. "Excuse me, please." The great Newton himself showed that action and reaction are equal and opposite. A most profound theorem, if ever there was one. From that profound fount of wisdom (*and* science) flows much insights and parallel observations, haikus, mini-haikus, and macro-haikus (and pardonable rave rantings too).

*The leader of the great party, X, proposes a legislation purported to wipe the tears of the citizens. The leader (and all members) of the opposition party vociferously object. Many hot words are exchanged and much hot air flows. Sometimes, fisticuffs too ensue. (Normal, as you all know, in those high places, ostentatiously governing a country.) Ask any of those leaders and they will condescendingly inform you that that is how progress is made. If our arrow-making progress against the wind had the gift to understand those words, it would nod its head appreciatively.

*Likewise, mention the above lines to a psychotherapist. He will wholeheartedly agree with the idea of resistance. ("There is always plenty of resistance to therapy. It is unbelievable.") The patients who come and lie down on his couch week after week, month after month, for years often, bear eloquent testimony to that (that the headshrinker benefits financially is a different matter). The hidden wit in you is entitled to coin the epigram, "The mind can be more stubborn than a hard-boiled mule."

*The yogis and most spiritual leaders have also observed a parallel phenomenon in the course of the moral, spiritual advancement of the acolytes. It is common to see that most spiritual seekers struggle for years and years to achieve progress. Here, recall the saying, "Many are called, few are chosen."

*It is so even in the fields of science, technology, and arts. Who does not know about the monumental effort and patience of Edison? To find the perfect material for his world-changing invention, the electric bulb, he had to test and reject about *one thousand materials!* That was in the old days–so to say. Now, any task in science and technology requires a group effort–especially in technology. Science brings us to the subject of medicine. In the field of medicine also, there are umpteen numbers of diseases that offer resistance at every step. Indeed, there are some fatal diseases that cannot be cured once they get hold of a foot inside the human body. Cancer, rabies, tetanus, fatal doses of radiation, fatal doses of poison, AIDS, and so on. (That was a small list. Ask your family doctor and he will give you names of many more strange, deadly diseases.)

*Thus it is with arts too. A painter, sculptor, or a dancer will struggle long and arduously to achieve a perfect expression through the chosen medium. Thus it is with music. The history of the struggles undergone by classical singers for achieving mastery in some forms of Indian music is legendary. (Gift of a golden voice is purely secondary.) Lastly, I (we, you) need not point out that the path of love between two lovers is not straight, nor is it strewn with roses. Far better writers and poets than you and I have penned the most eloquent words on this subject.

PS to above: Even animals share a similar experience. Nothing comes easy. That reminds you of the famous dictum of Darwin, struggle for existence. *Struggle*, see? A deer may seem like an easy prey to a tiger. But no deer will go and stand before the tiger asking to be consumed. To mimic the popular phrase, the deer will give the tiger a good run for its life.

*Nothing comes easy, yes. Ask those guys who mine for gold how many tons of earth are to be excavated and processed before the earth yields a few grams of gold. Uranium gives you unimaginable amounts of energy which can be utilized in many ways. Again, ask those guys how much of physical labor and man hours and machinery equipment are needed to extract small amounts of uranium from the bowels of the earth.

Ask those rare guys who manage to climb to the summit of Mount Everest.

Ask the guy who wins the grueling marathon at the Olympics.

Ask the guys who manage to swim across the English Channel.

Ask the masters of Shaolin.

Ask all the guys who moved from rags to riches.

Or the daredevil who walks on a rope stretched across the tops of two skyscrapers.

Such examples are aplenty.

Humorously, but seriously: In the beginning of this topic we talked of resistance to movement. A striking parallel exists in politics. Just try to enter and move freely in a country other than yours and see what happens! There would be some totalitarian countries where even its own citizens cannot move freely inside their own land. Even in liberal, dedicated democratic countries also, there are many sensitive areas, which ordinary citizens cannot enter. (LOL take: There are some places, which, once you enter do not let go of you easily. Once a guy enters the cooler, the guy cannot walk out as and when he likes.)

*Facets: Suppose there is a beautiful piece of art—say, a marble statue—located in the center of the hall. Visitors marvel at it and go around it gazing in admiration. Each visitor takes a photo of the statue from a different angle…

As is obvious, *each photo is visually different from another*, though the object, the subject (*excusez moi*) of their interest is the same. This phenomenon is universal, without doubt, since we live in a three-dimensional world. Every object can be viewed from an infinite number of points. What did we say, viewpoints, eh? That should immediately remind you of a parallel—striking, you should admit. Yes, that is my point of view (!). Points of view are also relevant in the field of thinking, ideas, conversations, etc. Somebody writes a piece of essay on a topic. What he expresses is his point of view. Most naturally, many of his readers and critics have their own points of view. The similarity between the acts of physically viewing an object and mentally viewing a concept is striking. Notice that we even use the same phrase to describe both acts.

*Facets II: We said every object displays a different facet to different viewers placed at different points. This aspect has another related parallel. (Again, Nature is wonderful, we must admit.) Start from the human side first. Humans not only give rise—and breed different opinions (points of view), they also react in different ways while dealing with other human beings. To put it in an alternate way, a single person will react differently with all those around him/her under varying circumstances. The funny thing is that the same person in turn presents a multitude of faces to all others viewing him—and we are not saying this in the physical sense, though that too is true. This kind of behavior is quite common, and in a way natural, given the enormous varieties of persons, objects, and circumstances that a person encounters while living in this world.

Nature exhibits the very same phenomenon in its inanimate creations. (Nature loves metaphors!)

*Viewpoints: Apart from human beings, the content of the previous paragraphs can be applied to the behavior of inanimate objects and other phenomena. An occurrence or reaction can be seen and interpreted as a study in the various disciplines of science. Observe the case of a person suffering from a disease. A doctor will study him from the angle of biology and physiology. If the person is to be diagnosed, the person's body and organs will be examined as complexes of chemical reactions. The same goes for prescription of drugs to combat the disease. Even psychology is not ruled out. Many patients with physical symptoms are given psychological therapy. In the extreme view, (seriously, this is also a valid view point) everything that happens in the patient's body can be seen as a long, complex activity reflecting the laws of physics, because all matter, under sub-microscopic levels, is just play and interactions of *unchanging* particles like electrons and protons and neutrons!

CHAPTER 22

RANDOMNESS

Randomness: If you thought I picked up this topic at random, you are right! But I must confess that this topic used to haunt me often in the good ole college days when I came across it first while studying atomic decay. In that sense, the act of my picking the topic was not random! In keeping with the spirit of this book, we will scrutinize all these things mixed with a slew of emotions—wonder, poetry, purely prosaic, philosophy, tentative exploration, curiosity, awe, joy, etc. We do not mind including even rashness in the list!

Most probably there is no educated adult around here who has not heard of the word 'radioactivity' or the name of Marie Curie. Stripped of the technical jargon, the phenomenon of radioactivity can be described as follows. All atoms have a nucleus at the core. The atoms of various elements contain different numbers of nuclear particles inside the nucleus, the number being unique to each element. Generally, heavier and heavier atoms contain more and more of these particles inside their nuclei. (*The particles, like neutrons and protons, are the same in every atom but their numbers are different.* That is another fantastic wonder of Nature, which needs a whole lifetime of admiration and deeply erudite books of explanation). And it also follows that the heavier nuclei of the elements contain more energy. Now, it is seen that many of these elements give out or "spew out" energy from their nuclei in the form of radiation. This action is constant and continuous–occurring all the time. Such elements are called–you guessed it–radioactive elements. There are many such elements and so on. But what is relevant to our topic is just the process of radioactive decay as it is termed. Take a certain amount of the radioactive material. There are millions and millions of atoms in it. The atoms go on leaking out radiation energy (decaying), and after some time the original quantity gets reduced by half. It is termed as the 'half-life' of that particular element. (The 'half-lives' of various elements vary by an enormous range; vide the table we have furnished elsewhere in the chapter covering ranges. You again have a chance to wonder at the mindboggling expanse of Nature's ranges in every field of manifestation.)

Having said all that, we will zoom in on the heading of this topic, randomness, and see how Nature reflects it in many other fields as well. Now, the decay ('half-life') of a given amount of material can be very accurately calculated. There is what we can call a measurable certainty in the process–fairly understandable. But Nature is quite fond of playing with our judgments and convictions. You see, the point is like this. In a certain given mass of the radioactive element, there exist, as you all know, millions and millions of individual atoms. When we talk of the half-life of the element, we essentially mean that half of its constituent atoms 'decay.' That is, if you have 10 million atoms to begin with, you can be sure that 5 million of them will decay after the 'half-life' period. Now, 10 million atoms make a huge number, and *you are not sure which among them are going to decay and which are going to survive*. To repeat the idea in a different way, you simply cannot pinpoint to a certain single atom among those 10 million, and predict that that particular atom is going to decay next. This applies to every atom! We simply do not know which atom is going to decay when–but on the whole you can bet your shirt that half of them are surely going "out." Randomness is the technical jargon for this phenomenon. There is a famous branch of mathematics called statistics, which has a special flair for making astonishingly accurate calculations about such seemingly 'uncertain' phenomena. This is because of the strange vagary of Nature. You can even dub it as an irony. You see, in a large group, the behavior of individual participants (particles, molecules, objects, etc.) cannot be predicted accurately, but the behavior of the group as a whole can be formulated fairly accurately. A lot of physical laws and formulas have been derived in science employing the powerful equations of statistics.

*This act of randomness is reflected in quite another field—among us and other living creatures. You know what we are hinting at? It is death! The astonishing parallel here with radioactivity can be seen thus. It was pointed out above that in a given lump of radioactive material consisting of millions of atoms, we cannot pick a particular atom and predict when exactly it is going to decay. Now consider the population of a big country. The deaths of its citizens occur at random. You cannot pick a particular person and predict when exactly that person dies (forget astrology and other fancy-mancy things).

*While we are at it, we cannot help introducing dame luck here! The whims of that dame are functions of pure randomness. (You cannot say whom she chooses and when.) On the other hand, it is safe to say that probably there is no country in the world where people do not gamble. Go and ask the guys who run all those casinos. Their fortunes are built on the firm foundation of randomness. Luck. That same luck smiles on the guy who has won the jackpot, on the one whose horse has won the race in the Derby, even on the one who found a 100-rupee note on the road.

*Randomness and Luck. Yes, Nature plays (eternally) this humorous game on us in the field of politics too! Take a long look at the results of the innumerable elections that are held in all democratic countries. The contestants' winning in the elections is a matter of unpredictability.

*Mutation: The division of living cells follows a standard routine. Suppose a particular cell has defined biological characteristics, say a, b, c. As you know, cells multiply by division. A cell manages to divide itself into two parts, each part being a copy of the original. This is the process by which living bodies manage to grow in size, repair the damages done on them and so on. The main point of our concern here is that each new replicated cell is an exact copy of the original one. This kind of process keeps on occurring as a standardized mechanism all the time. (That is how a growing mouse keeps on growing as a mouse and a growing human baby keeps on growing, preserving its human form.) All the time? Well, almost. Nature loves to play the game of randomness too (among its plethora of games). Mutation is the name of the special game in this context. You see, the above-mentioned splitting cells take a fancy once in a while and instead of acquiring characteristics a, b, c, they will acquire something else, deviating from the original cell, say x, y, z. This kind of deviation happens at random. Thank god, otherwise nothing will be stable in the world of the living creatures. (When the normal cell division and the cells' death rate change inside the human body, cancer raises its ugly head: an example.) We need not go deeper into the subject, enquiring why mutation happens at all. Mutation need not be of the adverse kind. For, mutation is seen to help the process of evolution. The focus here is on the randomness of the act; as for other issues, Nature knows best!

*Dents: When you hit on the surface of metallic (and other) objects, a dent is naturally formed on the surface. Most objects behave in this way. Some may be fragile and shatter, but that is okay for our topic here. Replace the word dent with impression–you will immediately get links of similarity in other fields. That word resonates with our idea of mental functions. Impression, depression, dent: all connote the same thing. A mark is formed on the mind, which stays that way. This is the essence of memory! (If you feel that the idea is crude, recall that memory is stored in the human brain as changes in the neurons. A fine parallel.)

*A dent on the material, apart from being the result of interaction of two objects, can also be interpreted as memory. Dent, impression, mark, all are synonymous with memory, which is also an indication of a change of state. Memory can also be defined as a record. The word record was used with the intent of reminding you of the famous gramophone records of yore. (For the benefit of the young generation of today who may not have seen or heard of it. That great genius of thousand patents, Edison, invented the method of creating impressions of our sounds, talk, on a hard disk which was hard yet pliant. The impressions were permanent and could be played back to recreate the original sound. A la parallelism of our topic, the dent quoted above need not necessarily be on a solid object. Drop a pebble in a pool of water. Dents/impressions are created; but they are called waves, which can travel. One more. Waves and traveling remind us again of the audio waves, which are also dents or impressions created on air particles.

*Yes, go ahead and stretch the idea a bit more. Dents and impressions need not be hard, but be soft and static. We use them all the time. Perhaps we would not exist without them. Nor would civilization and culture have progressed without them. Wondering what we are talking about? Yeah, it is the invention of writing! (Add printing too.)

*Another trivia. Dent is formed by the contact—soft or forceful—between objects. We saw that an impression is created. The impression can be temporary or permanent. The waves in the earlier example above are temporary. But there are impressions which can be both temporary and permanent! Now, don't blow your lid. We meant what we said. Come this way and see for yourself what that lad and lass are doing in yonder secluded patch under the trees in that park. Oh, what they are doing right now can be defined as a kiss. That kiss, dear friends, is a temporary superficial impression on their skins, so far as the physical aspect is concerned. But far deeper and permanent impressions are produced in their hearts. Was that a poetic explanation, even if true? Easy; the permanent impressions of one more kind (real, actual) are created in their brains as memories! Nature, see?

CHAPTER 23

EXCHANGE

The nucleus of every atom contains protons and neutrons. The protons are positively charged particles. The neutrons are neutral, charge-wise. That is to say, they do not carry any charge, either positive or negative. Pardon the repetition—both of the above particles reside inside the nucleus. The nucleus is like a strong-walled fort holding them inside, taking much care to see that its 'prisoners' do not break out. This is how most of the matter that we see in our daily life is stable. (Salt remains as salt and sugar remains as sugar, our breathing oxygen remains as oxygen, and so on and so forth.) The reason for the repetition was that we wanted to draw your attention to a strange phenomenon occurring inside the nucleus. We said that protons are positively charged. Well, recall your basic science lessons and note that opposite charges attract each other and like charges repel one another. That means the protons inside the nucleus are always repelling one another. So by all means the protons should move away from the nucleus—they have no business to stay inside! The neutrons have neutral charge and there is nothing to hold them tightly inside the nucleus as they are free to move away! Yet, the wonder is that both of these particles stay inside the nucleus, and it is very difficult to dislodge them under ordinary circumstances. To explain this strange activity, the scientists first put forth a theoretical hypothesis that a sort of constant, continuous *exchange* of new particles between the protons and protons was taking place such that the repelling force due to their being of same charge was kept at bay all the time. The idea was both ingenious and, ah, kind of desperate! But it worked—and was vindicated soon in the experiments carried out in many laboratories. The newly named mesons were discovered, in many varieties.

The operative word that is of interest to us here is 'exchange,' apart from the other technical intricacies. *'Exchange' between entities has been conducive to the stability of the environment containing them.* It is that occurrence from which we wish to draw a parallel in a different field. See below!

*Man and woman (or lad and lass): Since this is a very obvious parallel we will not elaborate much. Imagine a man and a woman who happen to be physically together at some place. (Leave aside all other environmental descriptions to the novelists.) Be assured that Nature will not allow them to sit silent for long! Soon, there will be an interaction between them. It can take many shapes, usually starting with a conversation.

Stop there for a while. What is a conversation but an exchange of words? *Exchange*, you see, we have come back to that word—which we came upon in the context of internal nuclear reactions. The exchange there promoted stability of the nucleus, by way of a mutual bond among the participants. Similarly, here too, in the context of two persons, the exchange—of words—promotes a mutual bond between the participants! A poetic parallel, indeed; and Nature seems to be fond of it. For, soon apart from the *exchange* of words, there will be an exchange of ideas, and most of the times it goes further, culminating in the exchange of hearts! Is there a cynic out there who does not like people loving each other? Perhaps, also he may want to bring in the idea of dislike or hatred between two persons. Our positive thinking idealist poet is ready to welcome that aspect too. Dislike too, he points out, is an *exchange*! (The physicist standing by his side may chuckle and then add that it is a particular illustration of like poles repelling one another. You can stare back and say that anyhow an exchange is an exchange; be assured that we will support you. We will even help you by throwing the venerable proverb at him from behind your shoulder – "Birds of a feather flock together.") There is a lighter side to this, which nevertheless illustrates the wonderful power of exchange. If A dislikes B dislikes C dislikes…etc, one may wonder if there is any chance of their coming together at all. Not to worry. Suppose there is some topic (or person) those ABC (and more) guys all hate equally, then they will form a club where they can exchange their hate! There is another addictive form of exchange that is most powerful and irresistible. You guessed it; it is gossip, whose addictive grip is impossible to underestimate.

This generic idea applies to the positive aspect too. If, instead of hate or dislike, you choose like and love, there is no problem at all. Immediately–and as quickly as possible–umpteen numbers of fan clubs will mushroom up in all conducive environments. Note that here too, exchange is the operative word.

*Exchange (back again to): While we are at it, we can as well pan around and scout for further associations and metaphors on this wonderful, but one of the most basic activities ever invented by Nature. If we are permitted to wax in poetic sentiment, we will say that Exchange (yes, it deserves a capital E) is the vast and variegated foundation on which Nature builds its immeasurable empire in all its realms of manifestation.

The subtle link to the appreciation of that idea runs briefly along this line of reasoning. Any kind of expansion, proliferation, at the fundamental-most level needs *two* things, since then only does there arise the basic perception of duality, a differentiation from which all further acts of creation can bountifully proceed. Two things (let alone entities) need to establish their separateness first. Nature facilitates this by creating one or more differences (however minute, however subtle) between them. *That*, by itself, is enough for Nature to force them into a game of exchange. That is the wonder and beauty of Nature. The exchange will create stability and a mutual bond between them, while at the same time helping them to maintain their individual separateness!

*Exchange, barter, money: Many of the activities in the world (and of, too) involve exchanges of one kind or another. The most common one was barter before coins came to be accepted as the primary form of payment. Payment is nothing but a symbolic *exchange of value* in a universally accepted form. The whole of international economics is a huge complex web of exchanges only.

*Exchange involves giving and taking. Considered from that angle, a very interesting perception arises when we look at life itself. We mean all forms of life. In an abstract form, life is a unit with a boundary existing in (and subsisting on) the environment separate from it. *The awe-inspiring beauty is that the life-form needs the environment to get its supply of energy (read food) in order to survive.* This is a universal truth applicable to all forms of life, whether it is a simple single-celled unit or a complexly organized one like that of humans. (You have to get food for your body from outside; yes or yes?) No doubt, a scientist will explain this in terms of energy gradients, entropy, and so on. But what is of interest to us in terms of non-technical language is that Nature has designed life such that there is an exchange between the external environment and the walled-in unit of life; Nature itself is feeding and maintaining what it has created.

*The word energy prods us to think of temporary/artificial living forms created by man. Puzzled? Just teasing. We are talking of machines here! Machines too, like living organisms, require external energy to be fed into them. You must have heard of the impossibility of constructing perpetually moving machines. (For example, you may remember those toy ducks displayed in many store windows, eternally seeming to dip down and drink water from the bowls beneath their beaks, without seemingly requiring an external source of power. The toy does take energy from the bowl of water in which the beak of the duck dips. A seemingly innocent and charming action. The material in which the beak is made is such that it absorbs water. When the beak comes out of the water in the bowl, the water slowly evaporates. This creates an imbalance in the weights of the two portions of the toy, which is finely balanced on a delicate fulcrum. Due to this, the duck dips again, takes in water once more–and the cycle of the duck's dipping and rising continues forever. That 'forever' has a modifier attached to it. Forever means, as long as there is water available in the bowl within reach of the duck's innocent beak. A fantastic game of parallels played by Nature.

*Exchange occurs even among the lifeless. Seemingly volition-less objects. Take the case of 'inert' matter, classified as chemicals. Many chemicals react quite vigorously when brought into contact with one another. (Some reactions could be dangerous too. Ask any chemist, he will confirm it and caution you.) What is relevant to our topic is the action of mutual exchange. There is what are called chemical compounds which are made of multiple elements held together. For example, calcium carbonate is a compound consisting of the elements calcium, carbon, and oxygen. In some cases of chemical reaction, a damn decent (yes, they behave so decently, read on and see) kind of *'exchange'* takes place, reminding us of the barter-trading! "Hey, trader, what have you got there? Can you give it to me?" – "Sure, gimme what you have stowed there in your basket and I will gladly give thee what you asked for.") The upshot will be thus. Chemical One is (A+B) being made of A and B. Chemical Two is of (C+D). When they are brought together, a chemical reaction occurs, the kind of barter indicated in the previous dialog takes place and the result will be two new compounds made of (A+D) and (C+B)! That is why we used the qualifier decent in the beginning of this paragraph. This kind of chemical reaction is called double displacement. (Here is an actual textbook example. When barium chloride and sodium sulfate are mixed, the chemical reaction will result with the end products barium sulfate and sodium chloride.)

*Exchange, even entropy: Entropy is one of a few gods of modern science. (Brat says, "Just as it is impossible to understand God, it is impossible to understand entropy too. If you doubt it, go to Wikipedia, read the pages and come back here!") In a general sense, entropy means that in a given field if there are areas of dissimilar concentrations, sooner or later everything will tend to get into a state of uniform distribution. (Brat again, "It is a kind of voluntary communism. The rich will gladly give away what they have to the poor.) That is, there is a kind of exchange between the areas of dissimilar potentials.

CHAPTER 24

BRAMHAPUCHHA

In one sacred text of ancient India, there is a (seemingly) peculiar statement. It says that the Creation, as we observe it, is only the tail of the Brahman. (Brahman is The Creator.)

Many ancient books are fond of metaphors and indirect statements. (Remember the famous metaphor of the pointing finger? The finger is pointing at something beyond. But the unsuspecting neophyte is busy staring at the finger!) The commentary for the puzzling tail runs thus. To begin with, it says we *see only the tail* of the Creator, not His whole entirety. The thing to note here is that the tail is only a tiny part of the body. Secondly—and in a more subtle way—the main body is more important than the tail; is it not so? If you are religiously inclined (or otherwise), you will appreciate and agree with that.

Let us focus on the other, physical aspect—that of size and proportion. The tail is only a small portion of the rest of the body. After that, the rest is easy to guess.

What the commentary explains is that the unseen is vaster, far than the seen. *Creation manifests only a part of itself.* The invisible empire is bigger than the visible. So beautiful! This then further leads us to innumerable similes, parallels.

The hidden is more than the openly seen. The very first image one gets on reading this line is that of the tip of the iceberg–who has not heard of this all-familiar phrase. Familiar, but nevertheless absolutely true! The submerged portion of the iceberg outweighs the open tip by a factor of nine! (90 percent of the iceberg lies under water). This parallel may seem to be a bit of poetic to some, but it is a physical, verifiable fact also.

We were only teasing you employing the 'indirect way' mentioned above–though the simile stands right on its own weight (pardon the 'indirect' pun). Well, just a bit more teasing. Consider the sea in which the iceberg floats. The same old texts are fond of comparing the sea to something else–which is in fact exceedingly immense than the former. It is the sky, which is another word for space! What follows next is most probably quite obvious to most of the readers.

We are talking of dark matter and dark energy! A few words for those who may be unfamiliar with the subject. (Very unlikely these days.) Scientists have been able to estimate the amount of matter contained in our universe. Elsewhere in these pages, the size of the universe as we are aware of at present has been indicated, quite mindboggling by itself. Estimating the amount of matter contained in that vast expanse of space is a highly specialized task; but it has been done. This is how the puzzlement and the heartache and the adventure and the excitement, all arise in science. Usually, any achievement or breakthrough, sooner or later, brings in its wake other unforeseen problems and puzzles! This is what happened when the scientists calculated the amount of matter in the universe. (As a spoiler, we will add the qualifier, "visible" to that word matter. You are about to appreciate it very soon.) Let us leave out abstruse technical details like universal background radiation, cosmological constant, the rate of expansion of the universe, and so on. After cross-checking with such forces and parameters, the scientists were shocked. According to these calculations, the universe should contain quite a lot more of matter than what we see! That means that space contains some other kind of matter which we have been unable to observe or detect so far. Such a kind of hidden matter has been dubbed as 'dark matter.' The astrophysicists performed, again, another kind of audit on energy (apart from matter)–again still remaining undetected so far. Such a kind of energy is called dark energy. As per the equations of the scientists, *the combined amount of dark matter and dark energy exceeds that of the "visible" matter observable energies in the universe.* Nothing can be more ironic than this!!

Wonder how, in what way? Just look at the numbers. The percentage of dark energy is 68% and the percentage of dark matter is 27%. Normal universe–that which we are allowed to see (!) or detect makes up only 5%! *Truly, at the grandest level, more is hidden in Nature than is being shown!* (No, we do not have a fetish or OCD about exclamation marks. They are being forced down our humble, trembling hands automatically by the sheer grandeur of Nature.)

Now you can appreciate why the ancient texts talked of the tail and the body.

*Earth and life: À propos the above topic of the invisible being (overwhelmingly) vaster than the visible, our earth itself illustrates the theme beautifully, in a slightly altered angle of view. We have been living on the surface of the earth from time immemorial. Note the word surface. Though by now we have studied almost every square meter of the earth and the earth is being watched every second by countless satellites, we have not been able to see inside the vast depths of the earth–leave aside the indirect images and ideas assembled by scientific instruments. The unseen portion of the earth is immensely bigger than the seen, in terms of sheer physical size.

The above was for starters; there is another beautiful parallel, which we are going to put before you in a new angle designed to surprise you.

Ponder the phenomenon of Life on Earth. That Life is meant to represent life in all of its forms. We are going to use peculiar arguments here, but yet there is logic behind it. Begin it thus. Right now, in the present tense, try your best to estimate the *total number of all living creatures on earth*. The number will be very large indeed. Then imagine the total surface area of earth. Obviously, the area (surface, please bear in mind) is far greater than the area occupied by the living creatures. This may seem obvious and not of much consequence. Now think again in a different way. The number of the living creatures that we asked you to compute was only for the present time, right now. Living creatures die, you die (sorry there), I die, we all die. Everybody dies. From the very beginning of creation, everything that is born has been dying. Now just imagine, hypothetically, *that there was no death on planet earth*–from the very genesis. You simply cannot compute the total number of living beings that would have populated the surface of earth: (and still be living) man, animals, birds, insects, and all.

In that case, there would not be enough standing space for all of us. Let alone the secondary problem of finding enough food for all the creatures. Hence, we can safely guess that Mother Nature found a way to solve the problems of both Mother Nature and all living creatures by introducing the inevitable and beautiful controlling device called death! (In fact, in the ancient Indian scriptures, the God of death is called Yama, which literally means "control.") Not only does death directly control the limit of Life, but clever Nature, endowed with a supreme sense of humor, has managed the affair such that life itself eats up life in countless ways–look at all those carnivores! If some of you are tempted to think that you are pure vegans, think again. Trees, plants, and herbs too are living beings. (See comment below this paragraph.) That is one aspect of creation of life. The other one, as pointed above, is that the total presence of inert matter far outweighs that of all life-forms combined. Another beautiful parallel to that quaint word tail, introduced at the beginning of this topic. The 'tail' (life) is only a small part of the huge body of the earth. Since life, even that which feeds on inert matter, needs something else apart from itself to survive and grow and propagate, Nature seems to have created a major portion as 'inert' and a suitably minor portion as life. The deduction is very tempting.

*Humorous aside: That ratio of the seen versus the unseen seems to be universal. Nature is indulging in the famous game of 'hiding in plain sight.'

It seems so funny yet obvious. In nature, wherever you cast your glance you see only the tail (partly revealed portion) and not the body (the hidden portion). Tarry, please. Yeah, look at the human body itself in all its naked glory. No sinister allusions intended. When you look at the body, you see only the skin. Everything else, flesh, bones, and blood is hidden from plain sight. Words like biological necessity, survival techniques, functionality are irrelevant from the angle that we are looking. *Mass-wise, that which is seen is a fraction of that which is hidden*; that is all we want to point out. This is true of other living creatures also.

This further inspires you to gush in awe at even inert matter! Look at a hillock. You see only its contour. Compare it to the mass of what lies inside; the ratio of the seen versus the hidden is immense. (The URL here links back to those lines on dark matter and dark energy referred earlier. Another URL takes you directly to the enchanting litany–what happens there happens here too.) You cannot simply stop there. You are compelled to look at the deepest level of matter and discover the atom, the fundamental unit. Did you look at it properly? Boy, the ratio again stares back at you sternly like the Sphinx. The inner mass (hidden, that is, inside the nucleus) of the atom is enormously more than that of its outer ('seen') constituents like electrons! (Tail and body, you got to accept it, what say?)

*Further down in these chapters, the interesting case of the division of cells in a living body is discussed. (Please see Anomalies.) The cells in a living body go on dividing and multiplying–parallel again, with the way life-forms multiply and grow on (and in) the body of the earth. Nature has put a splendid control over the growth of such cells, since if left unchecked, the proliferating cells will destroy the mother body in which they grow. On another scale, *on the bigger stage of the earth, the same play is being enacted!* This strongly points to the existence of a Great Supreme Intelligence. (But most atheists and professionals will balk at the idea.)

That which manifests, manifests only a part of itself–as if it does not want to reveal everything about itself!

*Even in this side of our regularly enfolding universe, we can observe a similar process being mirrored in intergalactic space. Consider the black holes, the most famous objects in the universe. A very brief explanation here though, as before, it is highly improbable that the readers may be unaware of what black holes are. Avoiding scientific jargon and using the common man's language serves a good purpose in this context.

Gravitational force is the star actor (pun intended) in this almost fiction-like drama of the formation of black holes. Begin with observing with what we think is a highly dense state of matter. Usually a material having high density appears to be very compact to us. (Steel, gold, platinum, and so on.) All kinds of matter (materials), it is needless to point out, are composed of molecules of various kinds. That is to say, the molecules are tightly packed together to present a solid appearance to our eyes. Intermolecular forces are responsible for such tight packing. (Try to pulverize or compress a piece of steel by squeezing it in your fist and you will know what we mean.) To put it in a different way, that steel ball appears to be very compact because we cannot reduce its size. This holds true in the case of almost all kinds of conceivable forces we may employ to act on the surface of that steel ball.

Now, turn your attention on gravity. And matter itself. All matter is endowed with gravitational power. The gravitational force is one of the four fundamental forces in nature, as discovered so far. Secondly, the effect of gravity begins to add up as the amount of matter in a given place adds up. That is, *as an object becomes more and more massive, its gravitational power/pull too grows proportionately*. Thus, the planet Jupiter, being more massive than Earth, has more gravitational power. The Sun, being more massive (containing more mass), has greater gravitational force than Jupiter, and so on. Most of the objects we see are almost fixed in size. But it was not so during the formative period of the universe; especially as regards things like stars. Stars began to get formed out of the primordial gas in the universe. Once the gas condenses into a particular shape at a particular spot, the effect of gravity becomes marked. The mass attracts more and more gas all around it, increasing in size and mass–the process becomes cumulative. When the object acquires a particular size (mass), the gravitational power would have become so enormous in the interior of the object that nuclear fusion will take place (given the availability of suitable atoms (like as in our Sun), and the object attains the status of a star. There are many kinds of stars. It is not necessary to go into all that here.

The next stage in our story was scripted initially as a pure fancy. Scientists fancied some intriguing situation. (That is their business.) They began to wonder what would happen if the star went on gobbling up more and more mass unto itself–thereby acquiring unimaginable gravitational power. What could be predicted?

Two funny things. One: as the gravity of the star increases, it begins to crush itself in its hypothetical (poetic) gravitational fist. Under such power, the object/star begins to shrink! Try this as an exercise in imagination. Go back to the steel ball we mentioned a few paragraphs above. Imagine it being compressed by a hydraulic machine. The steel ball does shrink– which, though invisible to the naked eye, can be measured by instruments. That is nothing. Next, imagine the fate of that ball if you put the Empire State Building on it. It requires special vocabulary to describe it. Ah, that is nothing. Now put the weight of the entire earth on that poor steel ball and imagine the hellish (and beyond) crushing power acting on it! Words fail to do justice here. Ah, again for the last time. Take a star (baby, mass-wise, compared to a black hole.) Imagine the sun standing on the top of the poor, poor, poor ball and that weight crushing the ball!

That is the kind of force scientists imagined acting inside a super-massive star and they calculated the result. The star, under such crushing power, would shrink to an unbelievable size. The original diameter which usually runs into a hundred thousand miles will be crunched into, probably around a few kilometers! Can you imagine it? If so, be ready for the shocker, for black holes come in a wide range of sizes and mass. In fact, they have calculated a limit, mathematically, to the size of a star, when it begins to shrink, etc.–called the Chandrashekhar Limit. This bizarre object was named a black hole. Why black, why hole, you may wonder. The peculiar name is justified, when you read what follows next.

It has been pointed out above several times that the gravitational power of the star goes on increasing. That gravity, apart from compressing the stellar object, does something else extraordinary. Its power finally becomes so immense that no object, once it enters the influential circle of the black hole, can escape from its clutches, whatever be the size or speed of the object! Wait; what is the object which can travel at the limit of the highest speed in the universe? It is light, as you all know. Well, the black hole is ready to grapple with light also. *If light comes near the influential field of the black hole's gravity, it (the hole) simply gobbles up light!*

What does it mean in practical terms? Since an object is 'visible' if and only if light bounces off from its surface (like the moon), or if the object itself emits light (like a candle, the sun), we will not be able to see the black hole! Even any and all other forms of waves will not be able to escape the gravity of the black hole. How then, can we know about the presence of a black hole? Scientists are clever guys. They infer the presence of a black hole by the way its gravity acts on other (naturally, very distant) objects… Let us leave further and other technical details. Just remember that the existence of black holes was theoretically deduced; later they were detected. They have found plenty of them since they know how and where to look.

The main point of interest for our purpose is that the black hole has far greater mass than an ordinary visible star and is hidden from our direct view. That is it. *What is hidden is more immense than the visible!*

*Small tidbit: Back there we said that black holes come in a wide variety of sizes and masses and asked you to brace up for the shocker. Take mass. Just as we take a meter as a measuring unit, we take the mass of the sun as a measuring unit when dealing with black holes! The sun, as shown earlier, is millions of times more massive than our Earth. Such a huge mass is, so to say, taken as one unit in order to measure the mass of a black hole and is referred to as one solar mass. Now, a super massive black hole can be 10^5 to 10^{10} times the solar mass! More than a billion times. Even the intermediate ones among these giants can be a thousand times more massive than the sun. We talked of the range. There is a variety called the micro hole, as massive as the Moon. Let us round this up with the sizes. Black holes can be a 1000 kilometers wide, 30 kilometers wide. The micro ones–hold your breath–can be as small as 0.1 millimeter wide! (Don't blame us. We got this info from the pages of venerable Google itself.)

Tailpiece: Somewhere in these pages you would have noticed the witty adage of yore, that Life and Nature are so vast and variegated that for any kind of broad remark that you make (or find) you may rest assured that Life (and Nature) will throw up an example contradicting it! It is true, apart from being witty. Being nudged by those lines, we can find exceptions for the main theme of this chapter. The chapter proceeded (breezily, we hope) exploring at length the great propinquity Nature has of hiding more than what it reveals. Since people are much fond of arguing any point put forward ("That is the way of progress and innovation," they justify themselves), we will satisfy their appetite with an example. (They are sure to dig out more instances. No worries; be merry. That is the intention of Nature, really.)

Well, take the example of the tree–one with lots of branches and plenty of foliage. That is, look at all that is visible above the ground. And look at its roots below the ground, hidden from view. In this case, that which is visible is more than that which is hidden.

In a lighter mood, you can even put forward the case of manmade structures like buildings, castles, towers, skyscrapers, etc. As in the case of trees, a portion of the object is hidden from view. Maybe, Nature's laws take delight in hiding things partially from view; who knows!

Another parallel is the sense of touch. It does not need much explanation. In most of the normal cases, you can touch (feel) only the surface of an object–not its interior. (Again, leave aside your modern instruments of probing.) And again too, Nature must have had some purpose in designing our world that way.

A variation: The main theme, that of the hidden immensely outweighing the visible portion, is truly awesome. There must be some reason behind it, apart from philosophical, mystical speculations. Science will soon (we hope) discover some deeply fundamental and satisfying law behind that phenomenon. Meanwhile, as we found earlier, Nature enjoys displaying ranges in everything it creates. Here too, we can enjoy observing it in action. Various things are hidden in various proportions.

*Take 50-50, as an example! Normally, if you look at a person (no mirrors in the rear, please!) you normally see only the front portion of his body; the back is hidden. Hope you all agree without grumbling or quibbling about it. Of course, this is true of all objects that we see. Maybe Nature had some intention there, when it created the instruments of visual perception. "Is the intention hidden too?" we hear some wag quipping.

*The final word on that. We have to seriously believe that Nature hides things *in all spheres*. Intrigued why we are repeating? Well, the final word, dear readers, refers to knowledge! If we believe what we discussed in the above paragraphs, it looks like that knowledge too is hidden. The statement may sound glum or pessimistic, but then if you look back and survey all the vast and continuous efforts that man is making toward obtaining a final knowledge of the universe and realize that there is still plenty of unsolved, unresolved riddles, then most probably you may (sadly) accept that there will always be some quantum of hidden knowledge lurking deep in the womb of Nature.

*Nature mirrors this concept in a different, subtle way. The metaphor is being exhibited—executed is a better word—everywhere in all that we see and experience the universe around us; in toto and mercilessly, if you please. If you are puzzled, then we recommend you to jump to the chapter Morsels and come back—sobered!

CHAPTER 25

POTENTIAL ENERGY

In physics, there is a term called potential energy. It can be explained in simple terms as follows. Everyone is familiar with the mundane phenomenon related to height. An object falling down to earth has greater and greater impact if it falls from a greater and greater height than before. To generalize, an object placed at a high level has more energy. That is it. That is what we wish to draw a parallel from. Simply focus on the words high level and replace energy with power. You have the perfect analogy of man!

A man placed in a high position certainly wields high power. You simply cannot argue against that statement. Just like our above object, the higher and higher a person is placed, the greater power doth he wield. Your local boss of a small business establishment, the head of a firm, senators, governors, ministers of the state, and finally the head of the state itself... the progression of the level of position and consequent power keeps on increasing.

Another funny analogy too holds good. The object at the highest holds the highest amount of energy, no doubt, but remember too that if it comes crashing down it will be smashed. The same result is true of a human being who falls down from the position of high power! History is replete with innumerable instances illustrating it.

CHAPTER 26

THRESHOLD (THUS FAR AND NO FURTHER)

Nature likes creating enchanting mysteries. After a bit of understanding or laying bare, the mystery becomes then more enchanting and more meaningful. For many activities, phenomena, Nature has put up beautiful barricades. The activity comes to our cognition or is 'ignited' only after the involved parameters cross the threshold. If you go on searching, you can find oodles and oodles of examples. A few sample parallels will suffice for our purpose.

*You can begin this series with one of the essential faculties of the human senses–that of hearing. The ear receives sound waves from external sources and sends appropriate signals to the brain; we hear. There is a certain threshold of sound intensity below which the human ear ignores the sound waves; that is, we will not hear the sound even though the sound waves enter our ears. (You see two persons engaged in conversation at a certain distance across the street. You see their lips moving, accompanied by vigorous movements of their hands, heads, legs, and chest, etc. But their words are inaudible to you because of the distance. The distance makes the arriving sound waves too weak to be interpreted by the brain.) That is the lower threshold. The upper threshold can be said to exist, but its function is different. The brain interprets such sounds as being either too unpleasant or dangerous. The music from a loudspeaker may be good, but if the volume is too high it becomes unpleasant. The sound of an explosion is obviously not only unbearable but also dangerous–your eardrums may be damaged. There is another kind of threshold also with regard to sound. (Nature enjoys variety, we have said and said, and we say it again.) The sound waves are characterized by vibrations. Vibration can be slow or fast, indicated and measured by the *frequency* of the sound waves. Puzzlingly, Nature has put up two thresholds in this event. If the frequency of the sound waves is too low, below the lower threshold, we humans cannot hear the sound even though the sound exists and is reaching our ears! Similarly, in the upper level, there is what is called ultrasonic sound vibrating at a very high level. Human ears cannot hear such sounds too. But dogs and other animals can. (Does it seem like Nature is partial to them?)

The eyes come next. They too have threshold limits, though they operate in a far wider range. Naturally, Nature has designed them so, since eyes are the most prominent sense organs of the human body and of all other living creatures. (Except, probably bats! Another example of an anomaly. Jump to that chapter and come back if you want.) The human eyes cannot see objects smaller than a certain size. If you doubt it, try to read printed letters smaller than diamond size. In a different way, we also cannot see objects bigger than a certain size. If you doubt it, go stand at the trunk of a giant sequoia tree and try to see the *whole* of it at one go! (Diversion as usual: this should remind you of the way we–or all creatures–eat. We humans need a certain quantity of food to sustain life, say. But we do not gobble up the whole of it at one go, right? (Brat's diversion to a diversion: Nature has a sense of humor too. We do not swallow all the food we need at one go, obviously because there is a big difference between the sizes of our mouths and stomachs! Either Nature could have designed our bodies such that our mouth could have been the same size as that of the stomach. I espy wrinkles of distaste on the noses of some dear readers. Okay, or, Nature could have designed our stomach having the same size as that of the mouth. Then gourmet chefs all around the world would have vehemently protested, right? Exit Brat.) The signpost reads Morsels. If you are tempted, you can saunter along that route.) Along similar lines, the eyes cannot clearly see objects which are too near or too far. Yup, again try reading the same newspaper from a distance of 20 feet. Parallel to the audible strengths of sound, there exists the light's strength in the case of the eyes. If an object is in the dark or is dimly lit, we cannot see it. Also, in parallel with the frequency range of sound waves, there are frequency thresholds for our sensitivity to light. You are all familiar with the famous seven letters VIBGYOR, indicating the seven colors of the rainbow. V stands for the violet color of light, which has the highest frequency among light waves. At the bottom, we have R for red colored light, which has the lowest frequency. Frequencies below red are called infrared and we cannot see them (though they exist and are used in many gadgets). Rays with frequencies above that of the violet are called ultraviolet rays.

*Thresholds seem to exist naturally for the body's other senses also. Skin is sensitive to touch. If the touch is soft and tender, the body (brain) interprets it as likable or pleasurable. If the touch is harsh or abrasive or invasive, the brain immediately classifies it as being unpleasant or even dangerous. The skin responds along similar lines to heat and cold, since both of them can be either conducive to health, dangerous, or downright fatal. (If you touch a red-hot iron rod, the arm jerks back automatically.) The tongue is not far behind, equipped with the ability to distinguish an astonishing array of tastes. Along the threshold lines, there are some tastes which could trigger a sense of danger too. But this is more prominent (and finely tuned) among the animal kingdoms. (Human sense of taste is not that finely tuned. Remember the widespread anecdote of the bitter almonds taste? The chemist who discovered the substance possessing that taste, put it on his tongue and noted down the taste of bitter almonds in his diary. Later, he was found dead, because the substance was one of the deadliest poisons known to mankind-cyanide! The story is so popular that most early whodunit novels would simply mention the smell of bitter almonds in the air, confident that the reader would know that the instrument of death was cyanide.) Lastly, there is the sense of smell which acts almost along the similar lines of taste. The difference is that in the case of taste, there is a direct contact with the scanned object, while in the case of smell, the object being sensed can be near or quite far. Elephants are legendary in this capacity for smelling. It is said that they can smell a human even from a distance of one kilometer! There is a certain kind of moth which also possesses a similar sensitivity. It is said that that moth can sense as minute a quantity as a couple of molecules of a particular fragrance emanating from another moth of the opposite sex!

Emotions. The above lines were about human senses. Equally important are the emotions of humans. Here too, Nature has equipped human beings with discernible thresholds. The most notable capacity for us is that of patience, tolerance–especially for unpleasant situations. Every person puts up with a very unpleasant situation up to a certain limit, and then blows up. (He lets off steam, he blows his fuse; picturesque parallels.)

Apart from the living creatures, there are thresholds in other fields of Nature too. The ice that is created and accumulated on the slope of a mountain's shoulder will keep quiet till the quantity of ice reaches a certain limit (depending on the angle of the slope, the atmospheric pressure, temperature, wind, vibrations, etc.). Then an awesome avalanche is set in motion, and woe to whoever stands in its way.

Water rises up from the sea (and rivers and lakes, etc.) and forms clouds up in the sky. The clouds stay as clouds until the appropriate environmental parameters like atmospheric pressure, relative humidity, temperature, wind force, etc. are conducive. Then there will be rain–gentle, severe, storm, thunder showers, cloudburst, cyclone, and so on.

Manmade limits. Man, being the creation of Nature, has inherited many genes (so to say, but true, really!) from her. Like Nature, he enthusiastically creates thresholds and limits on everything he can *create* (gene, see?), or take control of. Manmade thresholds have technical names like valves, fuses, controls, walls (weirs), dams (!), and so on.

*A fuse. As long as the machine is using up a predetermined amount of electric power, the fuse installed in it keeps mum. If there is an excess of current flowing through the wires/machine, the fuse blows, protecting the machine from damage.

*A weir, put up by an engineer, acts like a threshold; it stops the body of water behind it from flowing out until the water level crosses the height of the weir. A dam too acts similarly, but chooses to let out the water behind it at a controlled rate.

*The safety valve in a steam engine or a pressure cooker lets off steam when the built-up pressure exceeds a certain limit; it holds back the steam inside the container *until then*. (Again, go back and tally this kind of action with bodily functions designed by Nature. Consider the function of the urinary bladder. It collects and holds the urine till it gets filled to a certain amount. Then, when that threshold is reached, it sends signals to the brain to evacuate. Working in tandem with that mechanism is that of the disposal of waste matter from the bowels. Both are wonderful mechanisms which the most inventive engineer has to acknowledge and admire. Just imagine the horror of human beings if the above two kinds of waste matter keep on discharging as they rise, without being stored for long times inside the body. There would not have been a human *civilization* in the first place. And, most probably all human beings on the planet, with unvarying consensus, would commit one mammoth mass suicide, while all other creatures would watch down in condescending sympathy. Nature knows all this, whether we believe it or not. Because, you see, *the other kinds of waste matter like sweat and impure air from the lungs are being continuously expelled from the body without being stocked inside. Nature knows!*)

*LOL. Man, (and lady, thou too, with respect) while you are earning money merrily, the eyes of the government–and equivalents of the IRS of other countries–are silently watching you (seeing-seeing thee, we: CCTV). The moment your income exceeds the predetermined *threshold limit, you gotta pay your tax.* No arguing, no mercy.

Life abounds with a zillion things like this.

*Blood pressure is necessary for the blood in the body to circulate properly in all the arteries and veins and capillaries. However, there is a certain limit to that pressure beyond which the blood vessels are apt to burst; that is the end for the body. The threshold exists for the lower range also. If the blood pressure is too low, the brain will go into a funk first, since it demands a hefty percentage of blood to perform efficiently. (Better not write down the values here, since the very mention of those crucial figures will induce anxiety and phobia in sensitive persons! We want our readers to be calm, peace-filled, and healthy.)

Closely related to the above is the pulse rate of the heart. The moment a person is seized with strong emotions (especially fear), the heartbeat increases. Fever too raises the pulse rate.

While we are at it, we can as well mention the name of sugar. (Once more, *absit omen!*) Sugar is most essential for the body to function and survive. It is the source of energy for the body. The funny (no, sorry, tragic) part is that if there is excess sugar in the blood (god forbid, we do not want even to name that nasty disease), a host of maladies invade the body and will refuse to go away. Doctors solemnly declare that there is a certain type of this disease which cannot be cured, but only controlled...bla bla. Enough of that.

CHAPTER 27

LAYERS

We must add to our litany on Nature's likes that it is also fond of producing things in layers. When that word layer is uttered, the immediate image we think up is that of the onion! You go on peeling layer after layer of the onion and yet one more layer remains–while a few drops of tears trickle down from your eyes. Laying layer on layer is Nature's habit. Remember the old school-days' quip about the word habit, how stubbornly it clings to us?

Okay. A bit more refined approach then. What is the most conspicuous thing in our world? It is light; the light of the sun. Forget technology for the present and ignore all those billions of artificial, manmade, android lights. This white light, as we see it, has seven layers–go back to your school days and recall the acronym VIBGYOR, which stands for the seven colors (V for violet, I for indigo, B for blue … R for red). The layers here refer to the varying frequencies–depth–of vibration of the light waves. All the seven layers when added up, compose the natural white light. And vice versa, white light when broken up separates into those seven colors. Remember the rainbows. Recall the experiment in school where a beam of light was passed through a glass prism and the above-mentioned seven colors came out on the other face of the prism.

There are plenty of examples of things arranged in layers abounding in Nature. We are giving below just a couple of items. (Once the idea catches on, you will be surprised to observe an example at every turn you take.)

*Earth's six layers (culled from Google pages)

Inner core, made out of iron and nickel

Outer core, made out of liquid iron and nickel

Mantle, made out of hot rock, silicon, oxygen, iron, and magnesium

Asthenosphere, soft, flexible made out of the outermost part of the mantle and the crust

Lithosphere

Hottest layer

Earth's atmosphere

Earth's atmosphere is divided into five main layers: the exosphere, the thermosphere, the mesosphere, the stratosphere, and the troposphere.

*Ocean's layer

Below is a summary of the ocean's five layers.

Hadalpelagic Zone (The Trenches): The Hadalpelagic zone is also called the Trenches and is found from the ocean basin and below

Abyssopelagic Zone (Abyss)

Bathypelagic Zone (Midnight Zone)

Mesopelagic Zone (Twilight Zone)

Epipelagic Zone (Sunlight Zone)

*Brain–layers:

In between the skull and the brain are three layers of tissue called meninges. They protect the brain. The strong, outermost layer is named the dura mater. The middle layer, the arachnoid mater, is a thin membrane made of blood vessels and elastic tissue.

*Skin has three layers:

The epidermis, the outermost layer of skin, provides a waterproof barrier and creates our skin tone.

The dermis, beneath the epidermis, contains tough connective tissue, hair follicles, and sweat glands.

The deeper subcutaneous tissue (hypodermis) is made of fat and connective tissue.

*Sun! (yes, even the Sun)

From the center out, the layers of the Sun are as follows:

The solar interior composed of the core (which occupies the innermost quarter or so of the Sun's radius)

The radiative zone

The convective zone

Then there is the visible surface known as:

The photosphere

The chromosphere

Addendum:

'*UpamaKalidasasya*' is a well-known saying in the Sanskrit language. Kalidasa was the most famous poet in Sanskrit literature, endowed with a flair for composing exquisite similes. *Upama* is a figure of speech synonymous with the word simile in English.

This naturally resonates with the main topic of our discussions throughout this book, namely parallelism. To state the obvious, the simile describes succinctly all that a parallel phenomenon can say about itself. Hence, we find it appropriate to include a few similes in this section—the way a good chef adds a few chosen ingredients to the main dish he is preparing to enhance its taste. (There, you have an instance of a simile!) Here we go:

*Like a reflection in the mirror

You see the image of an object reflected in the mirror. In physics, this kind of image is called a virtual image. What is meant by that is that the image is not captured on a screen, a specific surface, etc.–unlike the way an image is projected on a screen by a projector.

Apart from that there is the old traditional, philosophical interpretation on the image reflected in a mirror. The image, to repeat a farcical joke, is unreal; it is not the object. Apart from the shape of the object, the image does not possess any other properties of the real object in the real world like smell, touch, and a host of other things–quite obviously.

Starting from this simplistic interpretation, philosophy goes to the next step and declares that the so-called object (and more, the world in which it exists) itself is unreal! All the "real" perceived properties of the object: the way it reacts with other objects, its physical and chemical reactions, everything is dubbed as unreal. The whole universe is equivalent to scenery observed in a mirror, the mystical texts declare unequivocally, though such a statement sounds very puzzling to the average "normal" people like us. Then, where or what is the mirror? You may begin to wonder. Simple, the old texts declare. Consciousness is the mirror in which the world is being reflected. The C in that word is a capital C according to them. And so on, it gets subtler and subtler, and tougher and tougher to grasp... Even what we see and assume as solid matter becomes immaterial and ends up being just an effect of reflection in consciousness. How about that as an act of subtlety in ratiocination? Let us leave those more abstract ideas to the professional philosophers.

And take one more similar and simple parallel. Mirage! The mirage is also an image, but of a different type–not of the reflection but more of the refraction kind. That is, light passes through a medium, gets displaced/distorted, and creates an image of a distant object. The victim (the poor seer, usually being in the desert) feels that the object (of his dire need, usually water) is very near. In fact, there is no water either there or anywhere near.

This kind of mirage effect is not limited to the desert only. Nature exhibits parallels, we are not tired of repeating. Yes, you can find a similar phenomenon out there in the vast depths of space too. The modified form of a mirage happens there due to the effect of gravity. Some interstellar objects have so much mass that their gravitational power can bend light passing near them. Remember what you studied about lens in your school days? A lens bends light rays (in different ways depending on its configuration), thereby creating altered images of objects whose light passes through it. Since the gravity of the stellar objects bends light, it can also create an 'image' of distant galaxies etc on the other side, whose light passes through the powerful gravitational field. Such an effect is called a gravitational lens effect. Astrophysicists have observed many such instances…

Once more, we can see a diluted analogy of reflection. Apart from the physical reflection of light, there is a reflection of immaterial things—like thoughts! Indeed, the word 'reflect' is used regularly to denote the activity of thinking. Here, the mind's ability of consciousness is akin to a mirror in which thoughts are being reflected.

Stretching the word further, we can observe reflections of diverse other sorts too. How about an echo? That is a good example; sound waves get reflected off a surface, creating an echo. (A whisper in your ear. Why stop there? Even material objects get reflected/deflected when they strike suitable kinds of surfaces. If you are in a lighter mood, you can also bring in emotional activities and the responses—reflections, what else?—that they beget. Anger and hatred are immediately reflected back at the sources.)

Back to the mirage. In a nutshell, a mirage is an illusion. That is what philosophers never tire of telling us about this world we live in.

The parallel can still be further stretched and interpreted in a different angle, even taking in the latest theories in physics. It goes like this. Initially, we all (including scientists) thought that the world we live in is made up of three dimensions: length, breadth, and height. It looked obvious until one genius added time to it and proved it by many ingenious (and irrefutable) mathematical expressions. After his Theory of Relativity, four dimensions came to be accepted as the norm! Ordinary persons like you and me were already beginning to feel uncomfortable. That continued for almost a half century. What has popped up in recent times will make us dizzy. Candidates for the latest theories on the origin of the universe are called String Theories. These theories propose that our world is a consequence of interactions in…5, 6, 7 dimensions? No, brace yourself, it is *10* dimensions! Wait. There is a 'king' among those theories called M theory. It proposes 11 dimensions!

You and I know and are familiar with three dimensions. What are those extra seven dimensions? Where exactly–by god–are they located? By god! Do not swear and sweat. It is easier to accept the contention of old-time philosophers that the world is unreal, an illusion, than to break your head trying to imagine seven more unseen, unseeable dimensions. The subtle joke is that if what the String Theory says is proved to be true (through testable experimentation), then after all, reality–the world in which we all live and die–is founded on something unseen. That is as good as saying something unreal, imaginary. Then you can as well admit unabashedly that our world is an illusion!

*Reflection, another angle

When you read about reflection, you cannot help quipping, "How about the reflection of a reflection?" in jest. Jest or no jest, you are justified in your quest. (No, this is not a line taken from the scratch book of a wannabe song-writer.) Remember the famous phrase 'house of mirrors?' (Yes, you are right; that straightaway makes us remember the famous last fighting scene of Bruce Lee in the film Enter the Dragon.)

In fact, we wanted to introduce the fascinating childhood toy of our 'good old gone those days,' the kaleidoscope. In its simple form, it consists of three or more mirror strips bound together to form a kind of triangular tube, with one end of it closed by a transparent sheet. You drop small colorful beads into the tube and view down from the open top. Since there are multiple mirrors, each colored bead will be reflected off each of those mirrors. Again, the reflections of the original will be re-reflected from the other mirrors. As a result you will see a fascinating geometric pattern being obtained from all those multiple reflections. Gently tap the tube and the beads in the base will be rearranged. Now you will see an altogether different pattern. With each tap and shake of the beads, different sets of reflection-patterns will be obtained. As a kid, you must have spent countless joyful hours playing with the toy kaleidoscope.

Now, move to the parallel in a different field. I see you—physically, with my eyes. Okay? You think it is a simple and banal statement? Wait till you hear the funny game one of our olden classmates used to indulge in and exasperate us with. During a conversation in our group, if some unsuspecting guy uttered, "I see," then off he would go unrelentingly, like a dachshund waiting for the signal. (We will leave out the inverted commas.)You see? Oh, I too see. I see you. I also see you seeing me. Naturally, then, you see me seeing you; don't you? But then, we cannot leave out him (tapping his other pal on the chest) from the scenery. You see, he also sees you—and of course me. Therefore, he sees me seeing you seeing him (not to mention me). Do you see? Did you see him seeing me seeing you?... We will stop this, being merciful; our man would go on concatenating at least 50 seeings seeing him-me-you seeings. This is called the Kaleidoscope Effect. We hope we have successfully demonstrated it.

Humor apart, the above paragraph is valid on wider circles and many planes. The unquestionable fact is that humans are social animals. With the advance in communication technology, the old phrase 'global village' has never been more true. Every minute we are all engaged in the acts of observing, being observed, sharing our observations, advertising our observations, observing our observations being observed (selfies, CCTVs, surveillance cameras, stage cameras, media cameras, spy cams); oh, the staggering loops within loops grow intricately complicated.

In fact, this phenomenon exists on a vast scale and encompasses the whole surface of our globe. You see, even without the intrusion of all those horrible gadgets, the situation can be described in two simple sentences. I see the world. In turn the world sees me. All the time, all our lives. Thus: I see you. I see him, and all of them. I see myself–in a mirror or the mind. In turn, you see me; I am reflected in you. He sees me; I am reflected in him, and all of them that see me. Ah, do not smile. You are also reflected in him, because, he sees you also. (Him and all of them.) If this is not a super Kaleidoscopic Effect, what else is? Next, we observe that this act is inevitable. Nature itself has designed it! The seer and the seen–everything can be compressed into those two words. That, as a matter of fact, is the supreme insight of a few Eastern (especially ancient Indian) philosophical systems. This insight is not limited to philosophy alone; it spreads into the realm of modern science also.

The beauty of the insight is irresistible too. If you care to concentrate and think about it, the almost hidden core idea runs like this. To begin with, let us say the world out there exists. That, you may (or some may?) assert is a stark fact. As a response to this, the mystic smiles and points his wagging finger at you. Mystified yet? You see, the subtle irony here is that you are the person asserting the fact. (Asserting, acknowledging, avowing, the terminology does not matter.) That is of equal importance as that of the existence of the fact. To put it more strongly, *the existence of something is invalid unless and until it is acknowledged by an entity apart from it.* If you are still unsatisfied or wavering, we only have to remind you of the good old conundrum touted about by all philosophers and scientists–if a tree crashes down deep inside a distant forest, and if nobody sees it or hears it, then has the tree really fallen down? It has to be witnessed; we must repeat it. Scientists too are not far behind. Scientists, especially particle physicists, proponents of Quantum Physics gleefully sanction the above proposition. You must have heard of the famous (darned?) Schrödinger's cat. It is somewhat similar to the falling tree told above. Like the tree, a cat is enclosed in a container/sealed box and some special method is chosen to kill the cat such that you cannot guess or calculate its death in advance. After all that complicated jazz, you are left in an uncertain state of knowledge about the cat's death versus life position. And more jazz. The final upshot is that you gotta open the lid of the box to know if the cat is dead or alive. And so on and so on. (Please Google again for precise technical details.) The upshot is that the act of observation is the deciding factor. Quantum physics goes further and proclaims that everything is in a state of flux hovering around (mysterious) infinite probabilities until the precise act of observation happens! Please do not ask us to explain more than this; far greater intellects shiver when treading the land of Quantum Physics!

Philosophically, the observer and the observed are intimately bound together—one cannot exist without the other. Ancient Indian philosophy adds one more important act entwined around the previous other two to make a compact and comprehensive trinity. It is awareness, or consciousness: crucial to the very act of observation.

*The bottom line for the above: There is an ancient philosophical apothegm that says that all wise (and true) groups of statements wisely meld together to produce the simplest of dictums (being the distilled essence of wisdom). All the above mega-scaled activities of seeing in all of its variations of passive and active forms, distil down to a profound intuition contained in three words—the observer, the observed, and the act of observation. The whole bloody shebang of Creation is compressed in those three words. Mystics will go into raptures over it! We dare not fly into those rarefied heights, lest we get our wings scorched like Icarus.

*Let us step down a rung on the ladder of seriousness and have a quick '*dekho*' at other parallels á propos reflection. Reflection can also be of things other than light, of course. Refer back to the observer and observed etc. It is curious to see that, even thinking too is often described as reflection! ("A little reflection will convince us..." and so on) Intuitively, we feel that while in deep thought, our thoughts are being reflected in the mirror of the mind, specifically that faculty of mind which is awareness. You have to agree that it is a beautiful imagery. The same burden of Nature's song–action and a witness to that action.

*Apart from light and thought, more solid things too are prone to reflect and get reflected. Take air; you get echoes when sound waves are reflected off surfaces. Echoes can also be echoed back under certain conditions like in rooms, halls with closed hard walls, or long tunnels, etc. Metaphorically speaking, sounds can be reflected off human beings too. As when a well-intentioned advice is being administered to an unwilling dour youth. Or when the Theory of Relativity is being explained, complete with mathematics to a blooming moron. In a slight variation of this sound waves and echo, we can include the ubiquitous and addictive phenomenon of rumormongering. Rumor-spreading can be described as a special or distorted form of propagation of echoes. (Remember the funny game of Chinese Whispers? You whisper a statement into the ears of your neighbor, who will transmit it to another person by the same method of whispering. The process keeps on going. After a certain stage, when the last whisper is checked, it will be seen that the original message would have been totally distorted beyond recognition. That is rumors for you. In a local language of India, there is a funny saying illustrating this effect. Roughly translated, it runs thus – "Eagle flew…ends up as, the buffalo flew.")

*Though it is obvious, we will mention the reflection of other objects since we are enumerating lists parallels. Things a bit more solid than air, like water waves too get reflected when they strike certain boundaries or surfaces, producing charming patterns. (In physics, they are called interference patterns.) And then, almost all solid, hard objects are reflected or deflected when they hit comparable solid surfaces. (Go, watch a game of billiards.)

*A similar action is assured of in the (ancient again) Eastern theory of karma. What you give out (throw at) to the world, comes back to you (sometimes multiplied). Karma is very wide and works in mysterious ways in innumerable spheres.

*Dark as night

A nice imagery and a good parallel here. You can see things clearly in daytime. But when darkness descends the same things become invisible. For god's sake, do not mention electric lights, floodlights, torchlights, and so on. We are thinking of the pristine darkness of the olden days.

*The main analogy here is that we know that things are there, but we cannot see them in darkness. The immediate similarity we are reminded of are the black holes! (We have already talked of them at length earlier.) They are there; we do not see them. How apt the imagery of darkness is!

*Psychology: We need not even prompt you on this topic nor mention the name of Sigmund Freud. The subconscious of psychology needs no introduction. The subconscious of traditional psychology is a huge repository of repressed emotions, thoughts, and memories. All those things are hidden from the normal waking consciousness of our lives. The subject and study of the subconscious has been around for more than 70 years; innumerable books have been written on this. Leaving aside all the intricacies and subtleties, we need to just focus on the feature that is of interest for us. That is the analogy of the hidden/the submerged. The mind too has a hidden part. Creation (Nature) as we are not tired of repeating, enjoys playing similar tunes across different fields of its expression.

*To speak in a lighter mood, take the case of even hills and buildings (apart from trees we mentioned earlier). Seems as if everything needs to be partly hidden at least to have a firm foundation, so to speak! Except, of course, those that move. (Naturally. Otherwise—excuse us for the tongue-in-cheek—the earth will be continuously plowed forever!) We were joking when we said we are talking in a lighter mood. We can seriously contend about moving objects too having their foundation hidden. The persuasive, speculative argument runs thus. Remember that all things in the world, moving or fixed, are made of molecules, atoms, fundamental particles, in that order. These particles are always in constant motion.

For the next step in our argument, we need to remind you of that weird String Theory with its weirder 11 dimensions mentioned earlier. Now calmly think of the sane, normal world we see every day. (In fact, we human beings have been seeing it as it is for thousands of years–irrespective of our various languages, geological differences, etc.) We are seeing the world in three dimensions, which means what? It means that all those particles, matter, et al are showing us only three tenths of their whole being! You guessed it. The rest seven tenths is hidden in all those seven dimensions of the String Theorists. It must be so, we feel instinctively. (We are actually giving away a great idea for the would-be Einsteins of theoretical physics. The icebergs were silently, but frantically signaling to the scientists for these 2000 and odd years. Oh, ye scientists of the world, are you listening? Busy yourself on this new, profound concept that nine tenth of everything at all levels is hidden and only one tenth is being manifested up here. You will soon be touching your toes. No, the toe is not a yoga posture. It is TOE– Theory of Everything, to construct which every scientist has been striving.) Hide-and-seek, that is the game Nature likes to play with zest and zing.

*There are other kinds of parallels, some profound as above, some not so profound, but noteworthy nevertheless. Let us take the lighter topic. In the previous paragraph, it was said that Nature likes to play the game of hide-and-seek. We, human beings, are not far behind! Not surprising because, after all, we are the offspring of Nature. Apart from the subconscious (of psychology), we human beings invariably hide personal information in our transactions all our lives. We are not making moral judgments here, but stating what can be observed universally. In fact, it is a natural and universal phenomenon, and part of life itself.

That is one aspect, reflecting the lives as individual entities. The other facet is that of humans as grouped into societies–the wider, organized ones called governments. The administrative functioning of the government–

any government irrespective of its category, like democratic, socialistic, communistic, whatever–invariably involves hiding things. Defense and espionage are some of the areas which compulsorily involve secrecy. Otherwise, the government cannot run. Nay, it will collapse. Not only the state, but even big corporations and organizations are no exceptions to this rule. Hide, hide, hide. It looks as if things cannot exist without being partly hidden! To point to the poetic simile again, the largest tree cannot exist without its roots (the very foundation) being hidden beneath the earth.

*Not really so farfetched. See our daily lives. Half the day we spend being awake: things seen, being brightly aware, keen physical activity, and so on and so on. All that can be classified as being above the surface–cueing in to the iceberg metaphor. Then the other half: we spend being submerged in sleep and the subconscious, beneath the surface, like our dear old iceberg. Again, we harp on our old theme of Nature's variations. Remember the phenomenon called hibernation of animals. That is just a sort of variation on the night/sleep/semiconscious theme. Search and you will surely find plenty more allusions and images on this theme. We are limiting examples to save on the bulkiness of the text. Readers are invited to do their own personal exhilarating, joy-filling exploration henceforth.

Action at a Distance

Begin with the simple cases of how force is applied in the physical world. One day, two guys, A and B had a heated argument in the street. The heat rose to an uncontrollable pitch. Unfortunately for A, B was the local boxing champion. B delivered a beautiful punch (from the point of view of boxing buffs) to the jaws of A. The gnathion of A was dislocated, embellished on its way by another beautiful crack. The incident is quoted here to illustrate the case of force being applied directly. Depending on the strength of the applied force, the consequences can be mild or devastating.

Place a red hot iron piece on the anvil. You can beat it down to any shape you require. A hydraulic press generates enormous pressure; you can crush almost any object (including metal pieces) beneath it. And so on.

These are all cases of direct physical action being applied on an object. There are limitless such examples–the whole physical world runs using them all the time.

Relentlessly back to our bee in the bonnet; Nature's propinquity to play a game on different levels, different dimensions. The force seen above need not be of the physical kind when it comes to the perspective of life–especially human beings. The force can be indirect also, apart from being direct.

The most blatant force can be that of a parent dealing moral pressure on his son. Almost all families abound in unlimited moral pressures. (Both positive and negative.)

On the social level, it can be and is indirect most of the times. The irony is that the indirect, distant force will be having a far greater power and wide range, undoubtedly. Think of a small scenario. Look at a tough guy in the area. He is tough in physical confrontation and adamant in arguments etc. He is kinda immovable… Kinda only, if you think of it. Usually (again) in the local area, there will always be a person who has more push, either politically or financially, or in other ways. If you want our man to be controlled, you only have to approach one of those. Your job will be done. The irony is that the distant force is more powerful than the direct one. Think you may find somebody more powerful and stubborn? Think again. Now all you have to do is to go farther than your local heavyweight–jump from the small area of a town and move to a wider circle, say of the state. Say, a senator. And so on, the wider the circle of influence, the greater will be the power wielded by the person controlling that circle. The farthest point in this kind of progression is of course, the position of the president (or the head of the state). The power and influence emanating from that position is supreme. An interesting observation can be made in this context. More than men and living things, the power rests supreme in inanimate things. Intrigued? Ah, try to remember that there are things called constitutions! Sacred religious texts do not lag far behind. (We have intentionally left out the leverage employed by the illegal and criminal groups like blackmailers, the mafia, and institutions of similar nature.)

*As a natural extension of the previous paragraph, we can see that the instance of indirect force acting across large distances has a beautiful parallel in the way a country runs. (Ideologies and time do not make any difference.) All the citizens obey/follow the constitution if the country is democratic, or the dictator's diktat, or the king's firman.

*While we are at it, we cannot help extending the metaphor of the indirect and point out that our very existence on earth is under the control of a very distant object. Yes, it is the sun! That the earth's wellbeing and fate is firmly under the control of the regular, unerring activity of the sun is beyond contention. From there, we are tempted to move even farther, almost invisible, but the most powerful presence. You guessed it; it is God we are talking about. (Or the Creator of the Universe if you are a bit of an atheist.)

*Lest you forget, we would like to remind you of the famous declaration of Archimedes. "Give me a lever of sufficient length and a place to stand (outside) and I will move the earth." This statement of the great Greek was meant to show the power of a lever. If you look at the working of the lever with innocent, wondering eyes, you should admit that it is a magical tool, though being the oldest. Look at it again please with your childhood eyes. You can dislodge *heavier and heavier objects as you operate the lever farther and farther away from them!* Not for nothing is the word 'leverage' so popular (and expressive too). This is one of the best examples for what we discussed in the above paragraphs.

There is another aspect also to this force and distance. When a very distant object has the capacity to influence even from such a position, it means that its intrinsic power/force must be immense. This has reference to the physical sciences. Take gravity for instance. The sun is millions of miles distant from the earth. Yet, our earth is held under its gravitational pull. Just try to imagine the might of the original power that has the capacity to act even from a distance of millions of miles! (Do not spoil your sense of wonderment by thinking in terms of laws of physics and mathematics.)

*Side-note: There is a flip side to this scenario, just as Nature generally brings up an opposite to almost every manifestation it parades. (Back to our old signposts. There is a signpost with 'opposites' written on it, at this juncture. If you feel like it, you can follow it and land into the chapter on opposites, browse through it and come back, or stroll from there to yet one more diversion.) The gravitational power, as we saw in the case of the sun, extends over enormous distances.

Above, you saw the breathtaking power of gravity; the tentacles of gravitational force stretch millions of miles across space. But hold your breath again. Scientists (wonderful but factful irony here) classify your gravitational force as a weak force! Inside the atom and deeper still inside the nucleus, there are what are called strong forces, keeping strange nuclear particles in check. And, pardon us again—for you are being asked to hold your breath one more time—another irony is in the offing here. In fact, it is a super-irony kind of thing. You see, if gravity which acts across unimaginably vast distances is dubbed a weak force, then, can you begin to guess how far this strong force can spread? Poof! Hold there. The strong force acts only across less than a millionth of a millimeter of distance! Normal day-to-day logic cannot comprehend this. That is why we said that Nature enjoys playing exquisite games. (If it swings to an extreme end on this side it can as well swing to the extreme on the other side too. Even so, this particular irony discussed above is incomprehensible.)

Quantum entanglement: We can justifiably include quantum entanglement in this list. Some action occurring at a specified spot has an effect on another object—not physically connected—far away. To describe it very briefly, two particles are said to exist in a state of quantum entanglement under certain circumstances. Particle A and B, say, are separated from each other by a long distance; could be even a thousand miles. If you alter the state of particle A here, particle B somehow senses it and its state changes accordingly! At the risk of repetition, it is stressed that there is no physical connection between the two. Roughly a century back this was looked upon as a quaint proposition. Now, many laboratory tests have been conducted, confirming that such an action actually takes place. (As is the case with technology, very soon quantum computers are going to enter the market! Brat – "That will be the day when the Devil will flee from the earth. He would have had enough of humans and especially the Quantum.")

Acupressure! We have been discussing action at a distance. Parallels, you said. Yes, acupressure deserves an inclusion, we propose. You have to agree. See the funny analogy here. The practitioner of acupressure pricks on a tiny spot on a certain area of the patient's body, and that action has a healing effect on an organ located at a distant part of the body. "The greater the distance, the better," the proponents of this therapy claim.

CHAPTER 28

BUILDING BLOCKS

Part 1: Adding A to A can result in things far more interesting than just a collection of As. The result can be very profound and vast and enriching. It is impossible in these pages to pay full tribute to Nature's endless intelligent schemes. Allow us to tease you with innocuous (and seemingly insipid) instances. Take a grain of rice and go on adding more grains to it. What do you get? You get rice only. Maybe the volume increases; you get more and more rice, that is all. Similarly, if you go on adding grains of sand you will get more and more sand, a sand dune, a fine beach, even a desert. Lastly, take one drop of water and go on adding drops. You get a puddle, a stream, a river, or even the ocean. By adding more and more of the same thing, you get the same thing, but in greater and greater volumes. Right?

Right and not completely right!

Please do not think we are raving. We were just teasing you in a friendly way! Let us become sober now and pick up the thread, but with a twist. Take the extreme case of something inanimate, like a straight line. Now remember that we were adding things to similar things. Add another straight line to the existing one.

Ah, at this stage you will notice (obviously) that there are different ways of adding one line to another; not in the simple way of adding grains

209

of sand or drops of water. (This itself is a wonderful phenomenon in its own right.) You can use the second line to *cut* the first one. If you add (cut) at right angles, you will get a plus sign—which is brim-full with meanings, mathematical and otherwise. If you cut the line at an angle, you will get the mathematical sign of multiplication.

Reminding you of what was said earlier. Put a single dot on a paper. It is a dot, is a dot, is a dot. Yes? Dots are dots. Bring them together and something marvelous happens. Three dots placed in a triangular formation will represent the 'therefore' symbol of mathematics. If that is inverted it means 'hence;' yet they are the original three dots only! Bringing sufficient number of dots and arranging them properly, you can depict any picture on earth; *yet each of them is a dot, and even by count, they are all dots only!*

These kinds of things shown above are the building blocks—the simplest kind, and yet out of which, the most amazingly complex structures can be formed. At the risk of repetition (please remember that all things are either interconnected or interrelated), one would like to remind the reader that electrons, protons, and neutrons are the simplest kind of building blocks, and yet Nature has constructed the whole of our universe out of them. Hats off to Nature for the umpteenth time!

If you have got the time (and the inclination, as Pisa said to Big Ben) you can go on preparing quite a long list of these building blocks. No limit. You have got the whole of the universe to play with.

Part 2: We human beings may think we are smart. But then Nature will be laughing in its sleeves. It is far smarter and has plenty of common sense than we realize.

Consider the simple act of building or constructing things that are large and small. A staff or a walking stick can be taken as one sample for small-sized things. You can go on manufacturing them in different lengths (there is a natural practical limit, of course). There won't be any problem or inconvenience. There are umpteen number of articles of this type in our day-to-day lives. Cups, saucers, plates, spoons, books, food stuff like biscuits, cakes, and so on.

Go to something bigger like a wall. Walls can vary a lot more in terms of size and length. (Think of the Great Wall of China). Here comes the ticklish part. Yes, it tickles you when you think of it with the mind of a wondering child. (You may giggle and laugh–there is nobody watching over you.) Let us say, a mason is asked to build walls of 4-feet length, 10-feet length, 100-feet length, etc. He no doubt builds them, but not as single, whole (uninterrupted) units/blocks. Tarry, tarry, we are going to clarify before you burst out in indignant remonstration. Please look at all those walls in raw state–before they are plastered. All the walls have been built up using required *numbers of small units*; bricks or stones. This is so even with other kinds of big structures like all kinds of buildings. It is so; technical, engineering analysis dictates it. Besides, it is eminently sensible and practical. (Apart from industrial and commercial considerations.) Generalizing, we can say that all large constructions are *built up using small uniformly similar blocks*. Fabrication of machines too follows a similar principle; instead of similar parts, they are an assembly of many different parts working toward a common purpose. All this involves plenty of engineering and mathematical analyses. Whole libraries are filled with technical books dealing with this aspect. So we, humans, are a brainy species. Okay?

A funny angle to it then. The twisted reasoning (sic, really?) runs like this. For one thing, the we humans referred to above are a part of Nature. Accept it, no point in arguing it. Therefore, Nature too is brainy. Accept this too. Nature has been doing what we think we discovered or invented. Indeed, they are hackneyed statements to say that we invented flying by watching birds, that we invented submarines by watching fish and whales, that we invented radar by studying bats, and so on and so on. There are plenty more such examples; and all of them sync perfectly with our main theme of parallels and metaphors. Let us just limit ourselves to this one item—of the building blocks. (Nature is marvelous, we are not ashamed to repeat.)

*Life-forms: The number of the diverse kinds of living things on earth is mindboggling: single and multicell organisms, insects, worms, birds, animals, apes, men. We were talking of large things, so consider something large like an elephant. In the previous paragraphs, we mentioned machines assembled out of functioning parts and other objects built up by similar small units. Well, Nature is equally smart (more, no doubt!) The elephant has been equipped with different moving parts, just like the way we design a machine. Just as each part of your machine is designed with a specific function in mind, each part of the elephant is designed by Nature to perform a specific function. This is so obvious that it almost sounds redundant to mention it. It is because everything we see everywhere is built on this (simple and beautiful principle). Like the way we saw the wall is made of convenient and sensible smaller units, Nature builds up all large organisms on the same principle. As a parallel to the wall and bricks, look at the skin of the elephant. As bricks are to the wall, so the skin cells are to the skin of the elephant.

Every topic here is invariably linked to every other topic. Hence, we will desist from adding more examples, since the reader would have already come across them in the earlier pages. Besides, the readers can themselves find plenty more illustrations in their own lives. It is enough if the awareness of this kind of parallelism is alive in them as they go on reading, watching, and thinking.

CHAPTER 29

GREGARIOUSNESS

Back in our college days, every text book in the library on sociology would start with the famous saying, "Man is a social animal." That is true, of course. Everywhere on earth we see human beings living together in groups, mixing and interacting with others. It may be argued that it is impossible for a single human being to live alone–with the exception of rare ones in some religious circles. This is obvious. We cannot lead our lives without the basic needs like food, clothing, and shelter. We depend on others for all the three basic needs. Many people work in factories to produce the cloth we need to cover ourselves with. Even then we cannot put it on unless and until tailors agree to stitch and make clothes out of cloths. An engineer, an architect, and masons and plain manual laborers are required to work in coordination if one has to live in a proper shelter. The barest, minimum food we consume requires the efforts of farmers and laborers, the umpteen number of industries needed to manufacture the cooking vessels, kitchen equipment, and so on and so on. (Quite a lot of things. Then, *those things in turn need quite a lot more things*. And so on.) In short, a human being cannot live in total isolation from his fellow beings. Remember the famous saying, "No man is an island." All of us interact with our fellow beings in various capacities and ways. Fellow beings need not (and usually it is not) be humans only. The phrase includes animals, birds, all kinds of living creatures. The list is long indeed. On the top of that, we interact with our environment too. (And manage to pollute it as much as possible!) All this is obvious. Indeed, what is human history but an elaborate list of human beings' actions and reactions with all around them?

*Now to the parallels on this theme. The key word, interaction, is not limited to humans alone. Nature reflects the theme among its inanimate realms too. A cursory glance at the sciences of physics and chemistry (especially) will provide us umpteen examples. There is no need to elaborate about chemistry. Reactions; almost everyone has heard of the phrase, "chemical reaction." Almost every chemical reacts with every other chemical to participate in a "chemical reaction" and gives rise to numerous compounds etc, not to speak of the production of other items like release of heat, electricity. (All topics discussed in this book are interrelated–naturally. Chemical reaction, mentioned just now, is intimately connected with combinations. You can as well jump to that chapter, browse it and come back. Or if you are not particularly insistent, you can divert from there to another by-lane!)

Bottom line: Nature did not create billions and billions of objects solely to let them float inertly in empty space forever! Every specific object (even one belonging to one of its own kind) reacts with every other object in one way or another. That is all, and that is the purpose of creation. Gregariousness is the key word.

CHAPTER 30

RETURN TO THE SOURCE

Nature gives, Nature takes back. That is the principal meaning of Returning to The Source. (We are not excessively fond of those capitals, but the reverence we feel toward Nature impels us here.) As usual let us leave highfalutin polysyllabic Latin-tinged words to the highbrow geeks–no 'r' there, please note–and proceed with joy in our heart and smiles on our faces. The returning to the source occurs at various levels (high, low, mundane) as we can observe all around us. Let us view a few samples at random and move to other fields…

*"Dust thou art, to dust thou returnest," is a most famous saying. This perfectly sensible and irrefutable adage needs no explanation. Almost all religions assert the same sentiment. The ancient Indian philosophy uses the term *panchabhoota* to denote the five fundamental elements out of which the whole creation as we see arises: earth, water, fire, air, and space. [An aside. Instead of the old terms, use solidity, liquidity, radiation, molecules/atoms, and space and you can see it makes very good sense. Leave aside scholarly commentaries.] Our bodies are made out of those elements. The elements are held and function in a boundary (skin) as long as there is life, and after death the body decomposes, allowing the elements to go back and merge with nature. To dust thou returnest. Perfect, you have to agree. (The fear of death or the partiality toward life is irrelevant from this high perspective.)

215

The same event can be viewed theosophically. Apart from bodies that return to dust, many theosophies around the world insist that the souls too return to the Source–that source from which both the material and immaterial worlds spring up.

Sea: The oldest simile for the source and return is naturally, the sea. Sea is, as humans observed from the very beginning, the great source for water in the form of rains. The water of the sea evaporates and rises into the sky, forming all those beautiful clouds (at various heights and in different formations). Clouds travel over the lands of the earth and given the appropriate conditions, will descend on earth as rains. That water will in turn organize into rivers (under suitable conditions of the surface of land) most of the time. The rivers, ah yes, have no option, but to go back to the sea. ("*Nadeenamsaagarogatihi*," a Sanskrit saying goes–the sea is the final destination of all rivers.) It is as if all that immense quantity of water was eagerly waiting to return to its source!

*Humorous tidbits: That water returning to its source should remind you of one more thing very common in most cities. Got it? Think of the city squares. Yeah, we are talking of all those beautiful water fountains in cities all over the world. The water spouts high in all directions and after its glorious journey falls back, returning to the pond, from where it began its journey up. Back to the source!

*Back to the source? Yeah, you go to the library and borrow a couple of books. After reading them, what do you do? What else but return it to the library. Back to the source. Borrowing reminds us about the other more prevalent kind of borrowing; of money. You take the money from your friend (good guy) and later on you return it to him. (You are a gentleman, see?) Back to the source. The cricket player occupies the crease for a long time, mercilessly hitting gallant boundaries and rakish sixers. He has scored 99. Attempts a massive sixer eager to score that prestigious century. Alas, the patient bowler got him; the center wicket topples, followed by flying bails. What does the batsman do? Well, back to the pavilion as the commentators of yore used to say. Ugh, back from where he arrived. The same scenario occurs in all the sports. And in dramas–the actors do their bits on the stage. And then…well, back to the source. (Remember the Bard's famous quote, "All the world is a stage." That line vibes well with our remarks on birth and death in these paragraphs.)

*Earth: Earth should have come first in this list. There could be of plenty of people who may not have seen the sea with their own eyes, but every human being sees the earth daily. It is the earth on which we all live, it is the earth which sustains our lives. It is the giver of food to all living beings; *Gaia*, Mother Earth as all cultures reverently agree. In consonance with our theme, it is the source. In the end, this source somberly takes us back into its vast body. For in the end, our bodies decompose and mix uniformly into the very earth that sustains us. (Only gifted poets and great visionaries can do justice to this grand theme.) Further, it is not only we humans but all living beings that enter into the folds of Mother Earth. (The poet gushes ecstatically that the Mother loves her children so much that she patiently waits till the end and then grabs and embraces her children, and crushes them so that they will become part of her body. Amen.) While we are at it, we may as well enumerate the power (magic, in the ancient days) of gravity here. As you all know, a stone thrown up comes back to the ground (smile). The higher you throw it up, the greater will be its speed of hitting the ground–as if it was more eager to come back into the bosom of Mother Earth. In the olden days (before Newton's Theory of Gravitation), even eminent 'wisemen' explained this phenomenon by declaring that when objects are thrown up, they come back because all things belong to Mother Earth, and hence have to return to her! "Give unto Caesar what belongs to Caesar." One more example of back to the source.

*Let alone Caesar, even the modern-day governments do it. If you are a government employee, the government pays you your salary. (It pays you pension after your retirement from service.) Besides that, the government provides extensive schemes, utilities, and services to keep all of you healthy, comfortable, and safe. Then the government takes it back (oh, do not worry, not entirely) in the form of taxes.

*Yeah, you borrow money. And then you gotta return it. Brat says – Do not challenge it. The loan shark is smiling sadistically at you behind your back. And all those respectable banks and other agencies have their own somber ways to see that the moolah returns to its source; in an enhanced amount, naturally.

CHAPTER 31

GEOGRAPHY INSIDE THE BODY

This concept is one of the bees in our bonnet. There is a powerful compulsion to declaim in great flowery-flowing utterances (to whom else, but friends, Romans, and countrymen–with due apologies). But modesty and fear force us to murmur inaudible, hesitant soliloquies. In the tug-of-war, OCD wins; we proceed. The inspiration has its roots in the ancient yogic texts. There it says that the body of the yogi who has realized the Supreme State reflects the universe itself. (Since that yogi has perfectly merged himself with the Supreme and the universe is nothing but the manifestation of the Supreme.)

Stepping down many rungs down the ladder, we, from our mundane, mortal eyes, can discern little metaphors which hint at those grand unreachable heights of understanding. Looking at the geography of the earth, we can draw some parallels in the human body. (Whether it is poetic fancy or philosophical cogitation or just plain comparison is a purely subjective stance, depending on an individual's conviction and temperament.

*The five elements (Elemental Principles): As already said in the initial pages, the ancient Eastern systems of thought neatly classified everything manifested in the universe under the five great elemental principles: earth, water, fire, air, space. In spite of the modern scientific classifications, the old one holds good astonishingly well. Let us proceed with due respect to the system.

Earth element (*prithvi* in Sanskrit): All things solid come under this category. In the human body, the parallel constituents can be traced to bones, skin, flesh. To go more graphic, in geological terms, the earth has what they call crust (some miles deep). The striking and obvious parallel is that of the skin of the human body! Ayurveda, the traditional system of medicine, goes further and even specifies certain *organs* of the body where the functioning qualities of the elements are reflected in action.

Water element (*aapah* in Sanskrit): The category *aapah* represents all things in liquid form. When it is pointed out that the human body as we all know contains 60% to 70% water, all remonstrance against a parallel to earth subsides. Because, as even kindergarten *kindren* (sorry for that word; but better accept it!) know, the water element on our earth outweighs the land in area. 70% of the Earth's surface is water-covered. Even the ratio in both the cases (Earth and human body) is almost same. That apart, our bodies contain the most essential liquid, blood, which falls under the same *aapah* category. One beautiful poetic imagery cannot be overlooked in this context. The surface of the earth is populated by thousands of rivers in which water *flows continuously*. Well, the body too is populated with thousands of rivers in which fluid *runs continuously*. The micro-rivers are arteries, veins, capillaries, and ducts in our bodies. The fluid is red and is called blood (smile). The *aapah* element exists in other forms also. Fluids from duct glands, bile, fluids inside the stomach, secretions inside the entrails, and more. Parallelly, water exists on (and inside) earth in many forms: underground streams, wells, stagnant waters, etc.

Fire element (*tejas* in Sanskrit): In a general way, temperature is associated with fire. (Cannot deny it, can we?) Human bodies have temperature (98.4 degrees Fahrenheit). Can't deny it, can we? Ayurveda associates 'fire' with the power of digestion—*jataragni* as it is termed. Hence the functioning location of that element is in the stomach. It also resides in the human eyes. (Very appropriate, is it not?) Take this parallel. Just as fire/heat resides inside the stomach of the human body, fire and heat reside inside the *bowels* of the earth; all volcanoes, extinct or active, bear eloquent witness to that! And all the geysers across the surface of the earth support it in their own way... Extending the idea further into the cosmos, light and all kinds of radiations too can be seen as manifestations of the fire element.

Air element (*vayu* in Sanskrit): You cannot question if there is air inside human bodies, (LOL). Try to hold your breath for a minute and all your doubts will vanish. (LOL again.) There is good air and there is bad air; that in the lungs and that in the guts. Ayurveda calls the air that sustains life as *pranavayu*. There are four more other kinds of 'air' as per that classification, acting in different parts of the body and stimulating corresponding bodily functions. Coming back to the earth, you see that the earth too is surrounded by air. If you want to strengthen the simile, take the earth as a body and you see that air resides inside the bowels of the earth. Natural gas they call it and in many countries, that gas is being utilized as fuel. In Russia, gas pipelines stretch thousands of miles. That will give you a good idea of how much gas the earth contains.

Space element (*akasha* in Sanskrit): Notice that as we progress down the list, the 'elements' are getting more and more refined. Space is the vastest of these. All these elements and the whole universe exist inside space. Nature has created a refined humor out of this refined element; not only does matter exist in space but space too permeates matter's inside. That there are enough 'spaces' inside the human body does not need elaboration: ear, nose, throat, mouth, chest, stomach, intestines, and so on. Earth too is not lacking in similarities. There are innumerable caves everywhere on earth: on the surface, on mountains, and underground. In outer space too, there exist vast empty spaces between galaxies.

*There are other general parallels apart from the above classifications, which are succinctly put in the Haiku section of these pages.

CHAPTER 32

WHO WILL GUARD THE GUARDS THEMSELVES? [PHYSICIAN, HEAL THYSELF]

That is a rhetorical question of the good old (dependable) Greek days. If you go on thinking about it, it sure tickles the brain. A simplistic cogitation on it can run as follows. We are the ordinary citizens, not much skilled in self-protection, etc. Somebody more skilled and capable has to protect us. They are the guards. But then guards are also human beings like us, for one. And the more important factor here is that once you admit of being in need of a guard, a natural question will arise as to who is to guard that guard. Don't like it? Look at another parallel.

Ponder this situation. In a society, it is natural that there will always be some aberrant persons indulging in unlawful activities. Human nature itself is like that. (Go back and look up the chapter on ranges and diversities. Nature is Nature.) Sidestepping the moral and philosophical, philanthropical issues we have to focus on the stability of society as a whole, as a functioning unit. Punishment (as a means of deterrent?) is to be imposed on the guilty ones, after an appropriate process of judgment. The judge does such a job. Okay. Now go back to that Greek thinker's conundrum, apply it here too; who will judge the judge? Another judge? Then who will judge the second judge? The doctor treats the patient. Who will treat the doctor? ("Physician, heal thyself," is another famous Hellenic apothegm.)

Such kinds of statements are called infinite regressions. The thinkers of yore were not indulging in idle fancy or intellectual entertainment when they raised such questions. Many such regressions cannot be solved, but in practical life, the process of referring back has to stop.

CHAPTER 33

SIMILE-MACRO-HAIKUS (PROSE-FUELED, INSPIRATION-PROPELLED)

(The topics under review in this book are too numerous to deal in their entirety. Besides, if you go on collecting all the relevant data, it will be too bulky for a single book. So, in the spirit of extreme haikus, we will write a brief list of single-sentence similes, metaphors reflecting the theme of parallels across multiple fields. A word to the purists. What follow are not strictly haikus in the way they are defined. They are inspired haikus. You think of haiku and write down what comes out of your heart, and dedicate all of that to the Goddess of Haiku. The spirit belongs to Haiku, the body is made of prose. That is that. After all, prose has a rose inside it.)

1. Forceful entry

A neutron penetrates the nucleus of an atom; the atom is smashed.

A bullet penetrates a body; the body is smashed.

A stone thrown with force hits a pot; the pot is smashed. (The pot is wrought out of porcelain, dear reader.)

A terrorist penetrates the hostile country; many buildings and lives are smashed. An army too can make a forceful entry into another country. That is war, and the terrible consequences need no explanation. ("*Bella, horridabella.*")

There is a parallel in the field of the mind too. The technique is called brainwashing, which results in terrible consequences. Another technique for invading a mind is called brain mapping.

2. Groups at work

The bees in the beehive are busy working and coordinating their efforts to produce honey.

A hundred workers in an office are busy working and coordinating their efforts.

A thousand workers in a large factory are busy working and coordinating their efforts.

The ants in their colony outweigh the workers of the factory in terms of activity, solidarity, and discipline.

Millions and millions of citizens in a country are busy working and coordinating their efforts to keep their country prosperous and stable.

Millions of cells in a living body are busy working and coordinating their efforts to keep the living organism alive and functioning healthy.

(Willingly, unwillingly or unknowingly, all the nations on earth too are doing a similar thing. Otherwise we earthlings would have self-destructed ourselves by now!)

3. Brownian movement

The molecules inside a liquid are under constant movement. (That is called Brownian movement.)

Vehicles all over the world are constantly moving in all highways, roads, and by-lanes.

Why vehicles, the owners, men and women, walk, loaf, saunter, trek, jog, and run all over the earth, mimicking the Brownian movement.

Competing with them (and even exceeding them), thoughts inside human brains are constantly moving in all the highways, roads, and by-lanes of the mind.

Not to be outdone, other living creatures, animals, and birds too are constantly moving on the surface of the earth—and above.

Ah, this needs a bit more expansion; thus.

More of Brownian movement (with apologies to physics nerds, for extrapolating)

Molecules in liquid swim like frenzied fish. Millions; what a sight! Dance of Nature's delight.

The megacity streets; see it from sky. Vehicles, vehicles, vehicles. Speeding frenziedly, hither, thither, every whither. Brownian in streets. Another city mimics it. All cities on earth do it. That is Brownian movement on earth for you.

Why vehicles only? Men (sorry, and women) are not far behind. People throng in the streets. Walk, saunter, hurry, run, jog, trample hither, thither, every whither. Not only streets, brother (sorry, and sister), but on hill and dale and water, plains and deserts and poles and forests. Humans move constantly, hither, thither, all over the body of earth. That is Brownian movement in human form for you.

Why Men only? Other creatures are vying with them. Birds fly and glide and swoop in the air. They glide on water and dance on land. Fish and whales and dolphins and terrapins do it in water. Animals trot, jump, race, pounce. Snakes and reptiles slither. And worms crawl. Insects of all types and sizes buzz, and sing and dance, and hover. Bugs do it on all living bodies! In cities, parks, forests, all over the earth. That is a mega Brownian movement of the creatures of earth for you.

Why creatures only? Yeah, look around in the air surrounding earth. Let alone the trillions and quadrillions of air molecules. Just like flotsam and jetsam on sea, myriad kinds of things float and flit and fly in the atmosphere:

birds, metal birds, leaves, pollen, parachutes, balloons, anything that can float on air. All of them are fodder for your earth's Brownian.

Why atmosphere only? Peep into space. Meteors and asteroids merrily travel hither and thither and every whither. They are the Brownian dancers of space. Not only asteroids, but regulars like planets around their stars participate in the dance. Galaxies, pregnant with stars, and stars too, do not keep quiet. They spiral, they expand ever so slowly but steadily, running farther and farther from their neighboring galaxies. That is not all. The whole cosmos is expanding frantically. That is the Cosmic Brownian for you. (And, OMG, that brings us back to the Big Bang for the umpteenth time—we cannot escape from it, for we are trapped in it.)

On a lighter level: Vehicular movement mimics Brownian movement, it was said. Now and then (oh, no, quite often; Brat – no, regularly) vehicles dash against one another. This literally happens with humans too on busy streets everywhere. It also happens, a bit figuratively, as when John runs into Jose unexpectedly in that same street or mall. The further funny parallel is that just as there is an exchange (of energy, velocity) in the case of particles, there is an exchange between two humans (energy in the form of greeting, gossip, information, emotions, gifts, money, good wishes, and so on and so on).

A further exotic stretching. Above, you saw that knowledge (info, if you want a bland word) is transmitted the way energy is transmitted among particles in movement. An enchanting Eastern simile likens this unto the way a candle lightens up another candle and that candle lightens the next candle and so on. [If this reminds you of a chain reaction, no problem. There is that signpost right here, on your left. Saunter along that road and return—if another signpost does not tempt you.]

4. Groups of groups of entities

Asteroids. Bigger than them, the planets are. Then, bigger than them the stars are. Bigger than them the solar systems are. Then, nebulae, galaxies; thus, the denizens of the universe.

Individuals. Larger than them, the family is. Then larger than them, the town is. Then states, then the country, then the world. Thus, the denizens of the earth.

Trees. Bigger than them the gardens are. Then bigger than them the parks are. Then forests. Thus, the static denizens of the earth.

Rocks. Bigger than them the hillocks are. Bigger than them the hills are. Then mountains, then the ranges. Thus, the solid lifeless denizens of the earth.

Drops of water. Bigger than them, the ponds are. Bigger than them, the streams are. Then the river. Then the seas and oceans. Thus, the moving, liquid denizens of the earth.

Cells. Bigger than them, the multicellular organisms are. Bigger than them, the humans are. Bigger and more populous, the animal lives are. Thus, the living denizens of the planet earth.

Thoughts. Groups of thoughts bind into patterns of habits. Patterns of habits bind themselves into complexes. Groups of complexes bind themselves into a personality. Thus, the denizens of the mental world.

Books. Why not? When they accumulate, they become libraries. Ponder the fact that every city (and town worth its name) in the world has libraries (note plural). And there are libraries containing a million books. (There could be someone who would perversely argue that books are inanimate objects, that they, by themselves, are incapable of movement. Oh, brother, go tell this to a bibliophile. He will smile at that someone tolerantly, or possibly scornfully. A book by itself may be incapable of physical movement. If that book is a classic, or the latest bestseller, or even if it is listed somewhere, that is enough for the book to *induce a person to move toward it and grab it and move it from the shelf.* If that is not magic in motion, what else is?

A similar argument can be put forward in the case of all consumer goods that accumulate in all the malls and shopping complexes and consumer stores.

5. Woven

Dots, dots, dots, woven together made a photograph.

Pixels woven together brightened up a digital screen.

Threads, woven together made a cloth.

Pearls, strung together made a necklace.

Little drops of water...

Trees, woven together made a garden, a park, and a forest.

Words, words, words, woven together made a novel.

Thoughts, thoughts, thoughts woven together made a personality.

People, woven together made a family and a town and the country.

6. Rise and fall

At this instant, millions of lives are being born and millions are dying.

Brash, blatant parallel – At this instant, billions of people's (and animals') chests are rising and falling in rhythmic breathing.

At this instant, millions of thoughts are being born and vanishing in all our minds.

At this instant, millions of waves are rising and falling all over the oceans.

At this instant, millions of sound waves are being born and vanishing all over the world.

At this instant, billions of manmade electromagnetic waves are being born and subsiding in the ether all over the earth (and above!).

Outdoing this, interstellar space is filled with radiations of all sorts from stars, galaxies, nebulae, neutron stars, blackholes, and other denizens of space.

7. Float or fly

Objects surrounded by a medium are not satisfied with docilely sinking to the bottom. They defy often, to float or to fly. (Objects inert or alert.)

Dry leaves and pollen and minute particles manage to float in air at varying heights.

Man mimics them and outdoes them with his balloons and zeppelins.

The kite at the end of the string manages to float or glide in air.

The other kite, *avis*, flies masterfully in the same air.

Man outdoes the bird and flies faster and farther in his metallic birds.

Flotsam float in water. Fish and whales do that and swim, besides. And humans too do.

Man now out-floats floating itself. He gleefully floats in outer space, far above the pull of earth.

8. Focus (either this or that)

A prose introduction to a haiku. A professional philosopher would gladly write a whole volume on this topic. The thoughtful scientist too, will not be far behind. Creation of the universe may be a big mystery. But Nature, as we repeat and repeat, takes delight in playing double games. It created an experiencer and more subtly, a thinker. (For all living creatures can be said to have experiences.) *The thinker came to understand that though creation seemed to be vast and endless, he experiences it only as a focused entity on a small area—the smallest possible, in fact!* Take a very mundane act, the obvious fact. Physically, you stand in some place and gaze around. Eh, what was that? Around, see that beautiful word. *The world is all around you, but you have to physically turn around to see it.* That is, our view is limited, constrained along one angle, even though the vista extends around 360 degrees. There is more. The turning around in a circle refers to one plane or dimension. There are two more degrees, up and down. Truly, our vision is severely restricted. Still more. That vision along a straight line does not really offer much. For one, our vision is again restricted by distance. We cannot see an object which is too near or too far. Even in that span, if we have to 'see' something clearly, we have to *focus* on that spot. The greatest imaginable restriction indeed to experience the infinite. *It looks as if Nature intended us to experience the infinite, bit by micro-bit.* That is how (or why?) Nature brought in the second greatest mystery after creation, namely, time! If that idea is accepted, mystic (or even poetic, will do) intuition naturally suggests to you that time is another name for joy. (If you doubt that, then that same intuition is asking you right now, "Well, *mon cheri*, you have been sipping that cup of coffee for the past 20 minutes, drop by tasty drop. You are obviously enjoying it, or else, would you have chugalugged the whole content in one go and thrown away the cup? Eh, you are still holding the empty cup!" If you can get joy out of one small cup of coffee, imagine how much joy Nature would be getting in the act of creation. Our mutual friend, the familiar Inner Brat, adds his comment here, "My contribution to one-line haiku goes thus. *'Nature has been sipping its cup of creation for the past 14 billion years!'*" Brilliant, we agree. And it does not look like it is going to put down that cup for a few billion years more.)

Apropos that mystery of focusing on a restricted field/area, let us go back to theology once more. Most revered systems agree that the Creator (God, The Lord, Brahman) created the universe and pervaded it inside-out. The Lord is one only in troth, but He desired to spread and magnify His joy in His own manner. How did He do (does, is doing) that? He pretended to forget His true nature and acted as if He were a limited single entity separate from the rest of the universe. That is the individual ego, *jeevatman*, as they say in Sanskrit. When the individual is focused and limited, he is not aware of his god-nature. When he attains Realization, he renounces his ego. To sum up, the Infinite itself focuses on an infinitesimal part of itself enacting a drama of as a separate individual entity. That jells well as a parallel in the field of matter also. Like individual minds and egos, particles of matter exist and behave as if being separate from the rest of the universe. Let us not elaborate further. Our interest of finding parallels has been satisfied. There are countless numbers of books in all the libraries of the world if you want to research on the finer details of this topic.

Tailpiece: Even while there is a focus on the individual body, the focus again manages to focus on smaller and smaller areas. (That is Nature for you.) Back there we saw that there is a severe filtering down of focus on the barest essentials as regards the outer world. The same thing happens in the case of events inside the individual body. Just as it happens outside, many internal activities continuously occur inside the body. If there is a focus on all of them, again, the mind goes mad under the sheer load of the impressions. That is why Nature has created a system of autonomous nervous responses to take care of them: heart beating, breathing, digestion, cellular growth, cleaning of blood, and secretion are some of the activities which are being carried out without the necessity of a conscious supervision by the mind.

Before you go further you have to decide if you want to go back to a previous (Sirens-tempting) topic or not. Either that or this. How do you decide? Easy—the time-honored way. You fish out that coin from the depths of your pocket and toss! Toss; that is it. When you toss the coin, it is either heads or tails. One of the most ancient examples illustrating that something can happen either this way or that. (LOL: As usual, anomaly peeps its head here too. There was an old movie. The guys wanted to decide something important. The coin was tossed up to choose a course of action. Gosh, the coin came down all right. (It did not fly away.) But then, the bloody thing stolidly and phlegmatically stood on its edge. If it happens in a movie, it could probably happen in real life also. Why not?)

You may have two eyes, but you can focus (really fix) on one object at a time. The other objects blur.

You focus and see better with more details using a magnifying glass. The rest of the visual field blurs.

As a parallel, that is what you do with your mind when you concentrate on an idea, when you contemplate deeply. The rest of the world vanishes.

As a parallel, that is what you do with your mind when you begin reading a book. You read it page by page. In the page, you read it line by line. In the line, you read it one word at a time. The rest of the world vanishes.

As a parallel on the greatest scale, that is what you do with your life. You live through your lifespan of a hundred years (amen), year by year. You live through that year, day by day. You live the day–oh wonder–moment by moment! And mon, the eyes are set to look *forward*. See the significance? That property is reflecting the way time and our lives move–forward! Sure, you can turn your head around and see back. That is the parallel for what we do mentally when we look back at what happened yesterday or yesteryear. (Salute, salute, to thee, oh wondrous, incomprehensible Nature!)

Party in a hall with 20 people inside. You listen (when 'hear' is focused, it becomes 'listen') to your friend's conversation. All the other voices become noises! (Thank you, angel of Haiku!)

That is what One Great Boffin said. When you level your sights on a moving particle, you can know exactly only either its location or its speed; one of the two variables. Either speed or location, not both. This is christened as the Uncertainty Principle. (Reminds you of the egg and omelet proverb, does it not?)

Philosophy and mysticism creep in, in all studies. Either this or that, you saw in the above lines. Well, the Man of God, the Saint says either you (egotistical delusion!) or God (unalloyed immersion into!)–choose.

*Irreverent small talk: You either swim in the sea or walk on the sand.

*You are either healthy or sick. A piece of information is either true or false. You are either silent or talking. You are either standing or sitting. The air is either hot or cold. (Except in the case of some guys who blow hot and cold in the same breath.) The list is endless…

*And lastly, (sorry folks, this is neither irreverent nor small talk. This is factville) you are either alive or dead…

Anomalous postscript: If in the mood, you may follow the signpost anomaly, and come back inspired. There it was shown that almost every natural occurrence is echoed back with an anomaly. The above mod haikus glorified many either-or situations. But then, Nature also reminds us that things can be both either and or! The quiz is simple. As the famous saying goes, there are many shades of gray between black and white, in which cases you can justifiably argue that the objects are both black and white. (A bit of this and a bit of that. No, a bit of this and more of that. No, more of this and a bit of that. Ok, 50-50, what say? Like a half-filled jar is also half-empty. A half-closed door is half-open…)

That light discussion was intentionally introduced so that you may consider more seemingly egregious, but damn, most advanced scientific thought. But enormously bemusing nevertheless, to ordinary guys like you and us. The situation is best illustrated by a most famous animal which goes by the name of Schrödinger's Cat! In a certain kind of experiment which is proposed to be carried out on the cat and designed to terminate the life of the cat, the final result cannot be predicted off the cuff, but can only be determined by actually observing the cat, which cat is hidden from direct view by being placed in a sealed container, and so on. Leave aside the finer details and sophistry of logic. The bottom line is that the nerdy scientists insist that the poor cat is both dead and alive until the deciding moment when you actually observe the state of the cat. Please recall that in the previous paragraphs we were examining (confidently) those states which can only be one of two opposite states. We even said that something is alive or dead. But in this experiment (it is science, ladies and gentlemen), the cat is as bedeviled as you and we are, not understanding how it is both dead and alive at the same time.

(An aside: The members of the SPCA might object to such a cruel experiment on a cat. The actual experiment has not been carried out physically. About a century back, these kinds of brainy, speculative experiments called thought experiments were much popular. They need a lot of discipline, high level of scientific knowledge and imagination. Albert Einstein was very famous for his thought experiments.)

9. Roll call – attendance register

In the olden days, the teacher in your school used to check up the attendance of the students in the classroom by reading out the name of each student. The students acknowledged their presence as each name was called out.

Each student had a separate name.

Nature gave each student a separate face. Nature was not satisfied. It gave each student a separate voice-print.

Nature enjoys overdoing things. So, it gave each student a separate fingerprint.

It overdid again, as usual, for the sheer pleasure of it. It gave each student a separate iris print.

Nature did it once again. It gave each student a separate DNA print! It is wantonly profligate.

(P.S. Do not worry. Even if you were not a student, you too have all those unique prints to identify you.)

Postscript to postscript. Modern man vies with Nature on this score. He gives you a greater number of identities. You get a social security number, a driving license, an email ID (two, three or more of them), a telephone number, a tax registration number—such an endless number of cards and numbers that you cannot remember all of them! (And keep on losing some of them periodically.)

10. Chain reaction

The nucleus of one atom splits, releasing stimulants which enter the adjacent gossiping atoms, persuading them to split and transmit more stimulants. The chain reaction.

The gossiping atoms are the persons in a raucous party. Words, gossip the stimulant. Gossip spreads and spreads around. Chain reaction.

After the party, rumor takes over from gossip. Chain reaction, vaster now. It goes round and round around the globe. Yeah, TV, news media, and Internet born of www are there to hysterically whip it around. Guy A posts a video clip on Twitter. Guys B, C, and D like it. E, F, and G retweet it. The retweets are R/Teed feeding fodder to others, who in turn R/T them. Chain reaction. Soon the atmosphere of the earth is dense with buzzing retweets and sharings.

Author, mister Bullshit, writes a book full of BS. Two famous newspapers and two famous literary magazines (mysteriously) like BS (the stuff) and write—you guessed the correct phrase again—rave reviews. Review sparks sales, sales spark more reviews. Chain reaction. The BS of author Bullshit becomes a BS (bestseller)! If karma smiles at you, nothing can stop you.

11. Much becomes more.

If you doubt it go and ask Midas. He will smile at you.

Mysteriously, much somehow attracts more.

If you doubt it, go and calculate compound interest on the small amount of money you had borrowed 10 years back. If your mouth opens wide at the amount displayed on your calculator, do not blame me.

The reverse is also true. You go on saving money, and keep on adding to it however little the addition may be. Usually there is a certain triggering amount, beyond which what you accumulate begins to grow at a faster rate. (If you do not know how to manage it and play ducks and drakes with it, do not blame the hidden law.)

You were diffident if you could write. You begin, you write a few lines. Once the word count reaches a certain figure, the much becomes more and lo! Your first book is smiling at you from your desktop. More can become even more. Soon you have a dozen books to your credit. One of your books improves in sales. After it crosses a certain figure, you are surprised to see it straddling the bestseller lists!

Mister Good Guy, your neighbor, was what his name suggested. He did good deeds. He was a gifted talker. (A tremendous asset, especially in politics.) His reputation built up step by step over the years. Once it reached and crossed the crucial threshold, his career shot up like a rocket. Yes, today he is Mister President. (Much became more and more until it became most.)

Absit omen. The human body has amazing capacity to fight infection and invading diseases. At a certain stage (nobody is sure how), the disease gains the upper hand–in spite of the best care and treatment. The threshold (a deadly word) is reached. Again, *absit omen*; let nobody ever fall sick in the whole world. The threshold is crossed. Much became more. But the body can take it no more. The inevitable happens. The organism stops functioning.

One eats. One enjoys eating. He/she begins to eat more, and oftener. Then one gets fat. One eats more and compulsively. Much becomes more– fat, that is. There are cases where the person becomes so obese that the person will not be able to move about in a normal fashion.

*The mention of a body's sickness leads us automatically to another kind of sickness–both physical and mental. Yes, that is addiction we are talking about, where the act of much becoming more is relentless and deadly to boot. Guy smokes one cigarette just for the heck of it. Soon that single cigarette will grow into many. Before the guy realizes it, smoking has turned into an addiction; almost always lasting for life. Tobacco may be replaced in some cases by marijuana; god help the guy then. Need we mention the even more deadly kinds of addiction like heroin? (God forbid. *Absit omen.*)

*Long ago, it was a hamlet containing a few huts and a few people. (The word population would have felt bashful if used in that context.)

Gradually, the headcount of the hamlet increased—as decreed by Nature, and described by Malthus. The climate was congenial, the people were diligent, the environment too was congenial toward prosperity. The headcount attained four figures, more huts and a few decent dwellings came up. Fate and Nature kept on smiling on the hamlet. New natural resources were found nearby. New traders came and settled. A couple of factories were set up. The hamlet grew into a big village, and soon qualified to be classified as a town. Much happened. Much became more. More kept on growing into more and more… Today, that hamlet is the largest megacity in the world, bursting at the seams—as the newspapers and magazines are fond of saying—teeming with a human population of 20 million. (Along with population, pollution, disease, corruption, and crime too have increased proportionately, proving that much can become more along many venues.)

This is not only beautiful, but also breathtaking. In physics, there is a word called acceleration. There is a slight chance that a few uninitiated laypersons may misunderstand this word, taking it to mean a very high speed. (The car accelerated, the thief accelerated away on his bike, etc.) But in science, it is truly an awesome phenomenon. (We are indebted to the great Newton again.) If the speed of an object keeps on increasing *continuously*, that is called acceleration. Continuously is the operating word. Sorry, a bit more explanation: do not think that the object's speed increases regularly, say, every minute (awesome), or every second (much awesome). It keeps on increasing every blessed minute fraction of a second you can imagine! To speak in kids' language, the increase in speed happens before the increase itself is complete! This phenomenon occurs wherever an object is under the influence of a force. (Once more, a salute to Newton.) An additional small illustration here is justified. Imagine that an object is at zero speed in the beginning. Under the relentless influence of acceleration, its speed goes up to say 3 miles per hour. 3 then becomes 10 before you ask its name, and 10 grows into 50 before you ask from where it came, and 50 has risen up to 200 by the time it replies, 200 having shot up to 1000 to 5000, unerringly to 10,000 zooming up to or past has become already past perfect when the object is ripping past fast at 20,000 miles per hour, which is nothing when compared to 100,000 miles per hour, which is…(stop it, grammar and punctuation are unable to keep up with it!). As you can see, *there is no stopping the bloody blessed object as long as the force is riding on it.* (Salute, Sir Newton.) You may wonder if there is no limit to this. There is. The object (or any object) cannot travel faster than the speed of light. (Salute, Einstein.) Those are incredible speeds. Under such a situation, almost every object on earth should have by now collided and shattered with other objects and everything (including humans) should have been dust particles by now. You have to thank the air (atmosphere) surrounding the earth for that, because it offers resistance to moving objects. In outer space, the object *keeps on moving forever*, until or unless it is attracted by the gravitational force of another object, like the Moon, Mars, Saturn, the Sun, etc. *Keeps on moving forever*. That is why we are able to send vehicles to other planets, or else all the fuel on Earth will not be enough to send a rocket to Mars. (To fill up much fuel, we need bigger rockets and to propel them we need more fuel, and to stock that fuel we need even bigger rockets; the vicious cycle grows on.)

*(LOL trivia) Lichen: The ship, freshly painted and decked sails, out on its maiden voyage. After about six months, you look at it from outside. You can see green lichen sticking to it, ah, like leeches. Lichen does not go away so easily. (Brat, "If you can also derive the adjective, lichen from leech, it looks better.") It accumulates and goes on accumulating. Yes, much easily becomes more. Scraping it off and repainting is a big job indeed.

*The sun is shining on the land. The sky is a clear blue. The atmosphere is calm and quiet, though a tad on the hot side. But the veteran farmer knows, and sniffs the air eagerly and expectantly. Sure enough, after some time, a single molecule of water evaporates and rises into the sky and is metamorphosized into a small unnoticeable cloudlet. (It was Brat's decision to bring in that risible one molecule of water into the scene. He wants to be dramatic.) The speck of cloud grows rapidly; more and more and bigger clouds gather across the sky. The atmospheric temperature drops down dramatically. Humidity increases. The whole sky is covered by dark clouds. There is a flash of lightning. The rain descends in the form of welcome showers. Then it pours and pours.

The quantity of water raining down is unimaginable. Where was all that hidden, you wonder like a kid. It all started with that one drop of (Brat's ridiculous molecule) water, and now there must be trillions and trillions of molecules running down there on the surface of the earth. If this is not much becoming more, what else can be? 'Fact, more can become more and more, even more dramatically. If you have witnessed cloudbursts and cyclones and typhoons, you will nod your head in wondrous acquiescence.

Up there (in both ways) we saw lightning flashing across the sky. That is another result of much becoming more. The movement of clouds across the sky slowly builds up an electric charge in them. (Recall Benjamin Franklin's experiment with a kite.) Gradually the charge builds up to such an extent that the electricity (an enormous amount of it) streaks down to earth, ending in fearsome flashes and thunder.

Up there once more, and far deeper and vaster. Cosmic dust is cosmic dust. But if it accumulates (much), its grabbing power too increases and it begins to grab more and more dust and becomes a star one day. Did we say that much becomes more? This is a case of more becoming most; the most. One star is nothing less than a speck indeed. The number of stars that exist now is uncountable. (And the number keeps on growing as the scope of our power of observation keeps on increasing!) All thanks are due to the one and only Big Bang. (We touched that base once again, and probably not for the last time.) See the wonder of it. This act of accumulation, accretion, much becoming more is occurring at so many levels and on so many varied scales. Once again, we are reminded of that fantastic saying, 'What happens here is happening there also.'

(Diversion tailpiece: We saw above that much becomes more in so many ways. The funny question naturally arises as to how long more it can go on growing into more and more. The process has to stop somewhere, you feel instinctively. "How much is too much?" You are right. Please follow the signpost Limits and Thresholds. Stroll along that road leisurely and come back. It looks as if only time and its cousin, Big Bang, do not have limits.)

12. Contours

As you all know, in the Beginning, Nature was one. And it became many by begetting many from its own (infinite) body. It pondered, "How to distinguish one from the other?"

And it gave shapes and forms to each. Unsatisfied, it pondered.

And gave borders to every object. Thus was the universe filled with contours. (*Thus was Man able to name them.*) Contours flourished everywhere.

The contours of creatures became different from the contours of inert objects. The contours of humans became different from those of other creatures. And the contour of woman (wondrous) became different from that of man. Nature smiled in satisfaction and said, "As long as Creation lasts, contours shall last." Thus, even the contours of dress differed, and proliferated and keep on proliferating.

The contours of rivers differ, the contours of seas differ, of hills and mountains and plains differ. (So do the contours of countries too!)

Languages, bedecked with glorious words and stern grammar but colorful proverbs and expressive idioms, begat their own contours.

The contour of a poem is apart from that of prose. (Of a sonnet from a haiku.)

The contours of sorrow are apart from those of happiness. Of cruelty, apart from kindness. (Of heroin, apart from *amrut,* nectar.)

The contours of activity are apart from those of repose. (Of thinking, apart from meditation.)

The contours of Ignorance are apart from those of Knowledge.

Tailpiece – Seeing all this, our Brat is inspired to speculate instinctively that even the contour of one individual electron differs from that of another electron! Likewise in the case of all other fundamental particles. You and I may be baffled by that brash blasphemy, but who knows, persons with deeper knowledge like quantum geeks may approve or prove it!

(Footnote to tailpiece: There is an impossible professor called Bagdenborg who struts through the pages of the books, Jestus on Rampage and Fentoscience. In Fentoscience, he posits the exact same conjecture as in the tailpiece.)

13. Irreversible

The egg became a larva. The larva became a (not-so-beautiful) caterpillar. The caterpillar converted itself into a beautiful butterfly. Irreversible. Nothing can convert the (same) butterfly now into the caterpillar.

While we are at it, we may as well prepare a cup of coffee–the variety with milk and sugar added. Drink it by all means, but make sure you leave at least four or five spoons behind in the cup. Then, contemplate on the remaining coffee and contemplate where the milk and sugar and water have gone. Try to get back the original ingredients in their pristine condition; coffee powder, milk, sugar, and water, all separately in their separate containers. Do you recall the proverb, "No use crying over spilled milk?" Prepare an omelet and conduct a similar philosophical enquiry over it–about getting back your egg. Our sympathies are with you.

14. Creation

Procreation is the re-creation of Nature on a minor scale.

Note the hyphen; it means that creation is being repeated.

The original Creation is the creation of the universe. Nature was not satisfied. It wanted recreation (joy). So, it began creating a second tier, a parallel. Then what is that re-plus-creation? Procreation!

Patience. Tarry, this is not indecency, by any means. See the beauty of it, dear readers. The first, primordial act was the birth of inert matter, so to say. The second stroke of genius was the birth of life. *And*, there is another stroke within that stroke.

After birthing life, Nature allowed life to birth life again, out of itself; that is procreation!

Poet, if you are, go into raptures over it. For, there is one more subtle stroke within that second stroke. Pure genius.

Wondering what is left after matter became life and life began to beget life? Think again.

Think – that is it! Nature's third stage of creation was the creation of *mind*. (That includes the subtle function of emotions and the subtler function of thinking itself.)

Mystic, if you are, go into raptures again. For, you will now notice one more act of creation within creation; consciousness and self-awareness!

Once the mind takes over, it naturally diversifies the acts of creation. (Refer back to what was said about Nature's insatiable thirst for diversification.)

Mind plays with words and creates a parallel to emotions; you get poetry.

Mind plays with words and re-creates life's activities; you get drama.

Mind wants to elaborate the drama and decorate it with imagination and detail; you get epics and literature.

Mind wants to recreate and improvise a parallel on the sounds of the world; you get music.

Mind wants to re-produce and improvise a parallel on the visible world; you get art and sculpture.

Mind wants to re-produce and improvise a parallel of the world in terms of movement; you get dance.

Mind wants to imitate Nature's act of creation itself. Quite easy and more flexible and inventive. Mind can simply dive into sleep and create myriad worlds in dreams untrammeled by the rigid rules of physics!

And, ah, finally having arrived at the portals of the 21st century, mind wants to re-produce and improvise a parallel of the mind itself! (Selfie, thou art ubiquitous!) You get computers and mobiles and uncountable numbers of software.

[That was one heck of a haiku. Couldn't be helped given the nature of the topic. If you want, you may call it a hi-jacked haiku. Or, you can refer it back to the chapter on anomalies!]

15. Opposites (continued from one of the signposts)

Creation created from itself.

And contemplated. And concluded:

More joy in two than in one; thus arose opposites in Nature. Creation flourished. Man and woman, male and female, played endlessly entwined. Nature smiled blissfully.

Creatures ate creatures to become carnivores. Opposite to that, creatures ate plants to become herbivores. (Nature thought over that and made man eat both kinds to become omnivorous.)

Nature moved slow and made the snail. It oppositted that (as Yankees could very well say) and made the cheetah.

Nature made the smallest thing like an electron (and amoeba). It oppositted that (as Yankees could very well say) and made a mountain (and the whale).

Smallest things lived for the briefest time of a microsecond; It oppositted that (as Yankees could very well say) and made creatures which could live for a hundred years, and trees, for a thousand and more years. And the universe has been living for many billions of years.

And finally, it created both good and evil (delighting itself at the perplexity of the human moralists).

Postscript haiku: Are you speculating that creation needs a womb and not quite sure what it is? Fret not, modern physics itself comes to your aid. If you are still wondering where or what the womb in science is, the answer is that it is everywhere. Yes, it is space that is truly the womb of everything; the whole universe is ensconced in it! There is no arguing it, but if you feel we are talking poetically or romantically, fret not again. See below:

In the study of subatomic particles, especially from the angle of quantum physics, the scientists go deep (real deep) into the nature of space. It seems that there is no such thing as vacuum or empty space. The maths is very highQ (sorry IQ and sorry for the awry grammar), but it shows that the emptiness of space is being maintained in a strange way. Every blessed second, they say that numerous micro-particles are being born and destroyed instantly in "empty" space. The net result is that space manages to keep up an empty face! That space where all those eerie beings are being born truly deserves to be called the primordial womb! Amen.

16. States

In the Beginning, Nature was in a single state.

It desired to be in more states and begat itself mind and matter. (Does the order matter? Never mind.)

Nature wanted more; it was in a state of thirst. So, matter begat the state of liquidness. (And fun in pun to bargain.) Liquid desired one more heir. So, Nature gave her air.

Nature looked at Mind. Mind conceived and begat many states. It could then be awake and alert. It could fall into sleep and be semi-aware, desiring and dreaming. It could dive deeper and fall into slumber. It could fall into unconsciousness. If still not satisfied, it could almost journey up to the border of no-return, being in that mysterious state of coma.

Still not satisfied, mind can be in a state of dreaming while awake! (Ah, Nature, I salute Thee.) It could be in a reverie, it could be hallucinating. It could be also (alas) in a state of existing neither here nor there–in that terrible world of addiction where the drug junkies live (if such an existence can be called living).

The irony lies thus. Though matter appears to be more solid, mind seems to be more facile in attaining and existing in innumerable states!

17. Gaps – a brief history

"Without gaps, creation is invalid," quoth Nature.

And forthwith inserted billions of gaps of millions of miles between planets, stars, and galaxies. And gaps descended from heaven and penetrated matter on earth; molecules and atoms. Gaps, enormous, formed between the revolving electrons and the tiny nucleus.

And gaps searched everywhere and filled-filed themselves on every opportunity they could find and every excuse they could invent.

In human affairs, in affairs of matter, they laid their eggs and proliferated.

They became indispensable to and part of Creation.

If you are on a long journey in your car, hey, you definitely need gaps; gaps to fill your jalopy's gas tank. And for food and rest.

Moron's joke. Yes, gaps are necessary. Our class teacher told us that electrons have a definite mass, say, e. If two electrons come together, and if there is no gap, then a new mass of two electrons will be formed! Nobody has seen an electron of twice the ordinary mass. You can extend the logic and wait for the discovery of an electron ball of six inches diameter! Here, our Brat comes to the aid of Moron. Mon, you forgot that electrons carry a negative charge. Remember that like charges *repel*, as that same teacher told you yesterday. So, when an electron comes near another electron, they *repel* each other. Therefore, you cannot merge two electrons together. But neutrons do not have any charge; they are neutral. You can carry your experiment with neutrons. Forget that six-inch ball of yours. Moron may be a morn, but he has the politician's streak. He retorts with a blank face. Whatever. I leave such petty details for you guys to work out. That is why Nature does not prepare an electron ball of six inches size. Deep down that is what I meant. (And deep down, I have this conviction that that is good for democracy.) Brat aroints himself, as the great Bard would recommend.

18. Waste disposal

A most mundane but equally essential activity for the human organism to stay alive is the system of waste disposal. The human organism produces copious amounts and many kinds of waste products in its daily functioning. Poop, piss, phlegm, sweat, gas, dead cells, and so on. Certainly, your family doctor would add many more fearsome medical words to the list. That apart, the essential part is that Nature manages to flush out all these waste products from the body through various channels; *else waste would turn into toxin.* (Variety, diversity again. Ah, Nature!) Here, our Brat would grumble, "Why should Nature produce waste at all in the first place, and enact the elaborate charade of cleaning it, eh? Since your Nature is so puissant, it could as well have designed human beings and other living creatures such that waste products would not be formed at all. Seems highly inefficient, and *waste* of effort; pun, ha ha." At first glance, The Bratful objection may sound quite logical. But deeper perusal would take us along the mystical-cum-philosophical-cum-theological roads, like death, impermanence, illusion, and so on. An inspired engineer may whisper in awe something about a Carnot engine and the theorem that there cannot be any machine working at an efficiency of 100 percent. Duh. Brat knows this. So, let us smile and avoid the topic tactfully.

The mention of the machine suggests us the other kinds of parallels. Take the case of the most prolific and ubiquitous machine of the modern age, the automobile. Can you calculate the amount of exhaust (waste, toxin) gasses that the automobiles in the world are producing every hour, every day? The amount is staggering–spine chilling in fact, if you are serious about it.

And, the body of the city too carries out a parallel operation to that of the human body. The streets of city are the arteries of the body. The various buildings are like the internal organs of the body. Take the houses where people live. Every day each house generates a good deal of waste products, just the way the bodily organs do! Recall the variety of waste products that the body produces; the garbage from the houses is a parallel to that. Examine the garbage being dumped and you can see all kinds of materials in it. The waste is taken out of the buildings and then further carried off to areas away from the main body of the city. A remarkable simile indeed. Earlier, it was mentioned that waste, if not disposed, becomes toxic to the body. Even the government (or other) offices are no exception. Besides the regular garbage/wastage accruing from physical use of the building (cleaning, sweeping, toilet related garbage), the administrative functioning of such offices produces wastage in the form of stationery, outdated files, secret data that has been fed to the shredder, and so on.

The above metaphor about the toxicity of waste can be extended to the body of the city. There are more than a dozen megacities in the world now that are choking themselves into asphyxia with uncontrollable pollution.

The metaphor can further be stretched to include society also. Without diverting off into moral and religious-dogma issues, we can observe that almost all human societies produce waste products–of a sort. (Again, repeat, no moral issues intended in this statement. This is from a purely administrative point of view, as if running a complex machine; *and keep it running.*) Criminals, murderers, serial killers, psychopaths, anti-social elements, parasites, junkies, and so on. If the administrative machine of the society has to run smoothly ("greatest good of the greatest number"), such toxic elements have to be eliminated. Segregated is a more civilized word. That is why we have jails, penitentiaries. That is why there are elaborate penal codes and the judiciary and arms of the law.

A humorous speculation. When you see that such examples are aplenty in all fields of activity, *you will begin to be gradually convinced that any system that works is bound to produce wastage*—a very ironical deduction. Most probably it could be true and most probably a mathematical nerd would prove it to you through manipulations of head-spinning equations. Or, as simple souls, you and I may believe that Nature wants it so. If such is the case, then a doubt may arise. The whole of the universe, Creation, is a one heck of a working machine. Then, what, pray, is the wastage? Where is it stacked? The answer is so simple as to be obvious, laughs our friend The Brat. The planet earth, ladies and gentlemen, our earth is the danged place where wastage, pollution, and toxins are all being diligently produced at a hectic pace! Correct? Most cynics, misanthropes, and intellectual thinkers would agree.

The idea can be applied to the mind too. In the course of its incessant functioning, the human mind accumulates plenty of unwanted, unproductive, and self-damaging, tension-impregnated impressions. How does Nature clean this dirt-filled (often, dirty too!) warehouse? Well, Nature has devised a simple and elegant solution. It orders the mind-cum-body to go to sleep! *And dream.* (You and I may not hold degrees in shrinkology, but as arm chair psychologists, you and I must admit that sleep is the best medicine.)

19. Thresholds

Only Nature is limitless. Everything else has limits—Nature has seen to it. ("Except human folly," adds our wag.)

Threshold: Certain events will wait patiently for a certain value of a variable parameter to reach a certain size. Then the event occurs. Water, when heated, will wait patiently till the temperature (variable parameter) reaches 100 degrees centigrade (threshold). Then the event occurs—water will *boil.* There is a beautiful parallel in the human (animal) world here, as you guessed. A person will tolerate a certain situation till his personal threshold is reached. Then the person will boil with rage. There is even a further simile. The boiling water produces plenty of steam. If a tight lid is placed over the boiling container, the pressure of steam builds up and *blows off the lid*. That is the idiom we use to describe a person whose emotions are held down too tightly for too long. Finally, he will, well, blow the lid off.

Carry over the same metaphor to a different area. There is enormous heat accumulated deep inside the bowels of Earth, melting minerals and rock into red-hot liquid. Waits patiently, building up enormous pressure. Waits for a suitable outlet on the outer crust of Earth. Once it gets such an opportunity, a volcano shoots up, spewing hot lava high into the air. After that, it may lie dormant, again patiently waiting for the heat and pressure to build up. The volcano will once again begin its dramatic act of spewing liquid fire all around.

Sickness: You are careless about your body. You are voracious, you overeat, you do not care about what kind of foods you eat (okay, they, not you). The body tolerates the insults and injuries up to a level. Then it breaks down. The body falls sick. You are careless about your body (okay, they, not you). You overwork. You do not sleep enough. You overstrain your muscles, you get the Charley's horse. This applies to every organ of the body. You overthink, you get neurosis besides losing weight. (Yeah, chess players playing at high level tournaments are known to lose surprising amounts of weight.) Nature has set up both the upper and lower thresholds. (That is why Buddhism recommends the famous Middle Path. In Sanskrit there is a saying, "*atimsarvatravarjayet.*" Excess should be avoided in all affairs.)

The despot imposes too much restrictions on his subjects; sooner or later he will fall.

Everywhere, in every field, you will meet thresholds and limits…

The Olympic sprint records are being broken, no doubt. But if you study the data over a long period, you will see that breaking of records is not frequent. Besides, a study of the human body will show that there must be a certain limit to the speed beyond which the body–even the most perfect and super-trained–cannot move. The idea, surprisingly, can be extended and made into an absolute statement, thus. Consider speed per se. An automobile moves faster than a human being. A jet plane can travel faster than the automobile. An ICBM can travel even faster than a jet plane. Go on in this fashion and you will be surprised to hear that there is a limit to speed also. Almost a century ago, Einstein showed that no object can travel faster than light!

20. Condensed

It may not be so rampant now, but till about two decades ago if you mentioned that phrase 'condensed version,' people would automatically think of the Reader's Digest! It was (and is) a very appealing idea. Well, long before the Digest thought of that, Nature and Life had already brought the idea into execution in many fields. There are two versions: the direct and the indirect.

The direct version is the bonsai version, so to say. For reasons best known to Nature only, a body (of any kind), instead of growing into the fully accepted size of its species, grows into a stunted form. All the required, relevant organs are there, but their sizes become abnormally small. (Nevertheless, the body can be clearly identified as belonging to a particular species.) Dwarfs, midgets fall under this category. The Japanese have created an art form of this type in growing trees and plants, as witnessed by the worldwide enthusiasm for bonsai plants. Humans, once they get an idea from Nature, are experts at inventing their own versions in as many aspects of life as is possible. The idea of miniaturizing caught on and we have miniature painting, miniature writing (that includes your famous and ingenious technique of the microdots), miniature poems (haikus), millions of miniature toys to amuse children. (A relevant aside: If you are of the present, latest kid generation sporting that mobile phone, you may not be aware that the first, original *forefather computer occupied a whole building of three stories, size-wise*, that they used to pump water through tubes to cool down the whole system to prevent it from getting overheated!)

Nature performs another kind of condensation, that done in the medium of time if we really see it from a certain angle. Every camera buff is familiar with slow-motion videos. The bud may take a whole day or more to blossom into a flower. The photographer takes its photos at certain intervals of time and prepares a video of the clips. The video shows in a few minutes what took place during many hours and so on. Well, Nature does the same thing for our (no, its pleasure) benefit, but in a reverse way. Look at it this way. A tree may take many *years* to grow up into full bloom. The tree has grown to that size from the initial state of a seed. In this sense, the seed contains the whole of the tree; *it is a condensed version of the tree!* The same kind of reasoning applies to development of living creatures also. An embryo is the condensed version of the future, going to be six-foot hulk. Letting go of extreme scientific quibbling, we can view this scenario from a poetic-romantic angle and be able to appreciate the nuances of Nature with more pleasure and satisfaction. (Brat, "The future is in the present.") Do recall the famous adage, "Child is the father of man."

*Words: Words and books are great instruments for condensing time into fantastic proportions. A simple illustration is enough to bring home the point. Mister Arrivecendi, your friend wanted to meet with you and hold a dear heart-to-heart talk. He was far away in another town. It took him a good part of six hours of driving. Finally he arrives, greets you with a handshake, and smiles and says, "I have arrived at last." Note this; *it has taken him only one second to make that statement, but that statement has condensed six hours of time (and plenty of action) into one second!* This surely is a special gift that Nature has bestowed on man. All verbs denoting action have this tremendous potential for compression of time. Books also, being a printed form of words, have the ability to accomplish the same compression. But humans are quite fond of words, and so books do it at a leisurely and ornate pace what the spoken word does urgently. (Naturally, that urgency only induced humans to evolve into *Homo loquacious*.) A war, which lasted for six years (say, WWII), can be condensed into a nice, thick paperback containing a few hundred pages. (The expert Reader's Digest editorial board can get it further condensed into 40 or 50 pages. If your book is lucky enough to have become a bestseller, that is.) Even the whole history of the universe can be packed down into a book. Read 'A Brief History of Time' if you want to get inspired scientifically, or 'In Search of Lost Times' if literature is your cuppa.

*Thoughts are the compressed or embryonic forms of action. This is true of those actions which require plenty of preplanning. (Do not deny it. Remember all the sweat that had poured out of you when you brought forth your first bestseller.) Also true of all things that require initial planning— either short term or long term. Remember the 'Five-year-plan' that some countries adopt to improve themselves. That idea again points toward another physical activity, namely, the construction of buildings. You have to have a blueprint of the building before you start its construction. In that sense, the blueprint is the condensed form of the skyscraper. That again points toward the manufacturing industry. Any product (and there are millions of them) going to be manufactured needs a drawing of its shape, size, and specifications. Recall that "In the beginning was the word," beautifully illustrates what we are discussing here.

That naturally leads us to look at mathematics. All the mathematical formulas and equations are nothing but highly condensed (and special) forms of complicated words and sentences. (A small, amusing digression to illustrate it. Every school student knows that the most famous equation in mathematics, the Pythagoras theorem, can be expressed mathematically just by using three variables a, b, and c. A very short and simple equation. If you try to put it into words, the explanation runs somewhat along the following lines. "Please construct a right-angled triangle. Then construct three squares on each of its sides, using the length of such a side as the side of the square you are going to construct on. Now, measure the area of each square thus constructed. You will see that the area of the square constructed on the hypotenuse of the triangle will be equal to the sum of the areas of the other two squares constructed on the other two sides of the triangle (right-angled, to stress). What you just discovered is not a freak coincidence. You may draw any number of right-angled triangles of all sizes and in every case, the elegant property you discovered holds true." Whew! That was quite long winded! Further, we have left out the enthralling descriptions of other physical aspects such as drawing triangles and squares on a piece of paper.) Repeat; the formula containing a, b, and c unerringly describes all the verbiage used before.

Sutras: By the bye, the formulas need not be in terms of mathematical formulas only. Language can also be terse and condensed. The Eastern, ancient language of Sanskrit has developed quite a unique and fantastic system of words tightly knit as formulas. Further, especially in texts on grammar, a group of letters themselves have been woven together. Such a condensate is called a '*sutra*.' *Sutras* exist in other fields of study also, as in yoga. (Panini's grammar *sutras*, Patanjali's yoga *sutras*, and Buddhist *sutras* are well-known examples.) A prolonged, full explanation is implied in that *sutra;* the explanations can run into many pages! Most probably, the *sutras* were developed as mnemonic aids.

A small digression (not really) as usual. Along the lines of *sutras*, there are what are called 'mantras' also. While *sutras* can be said to contain tightly compressed meanings, mantras are believed to contain far more highly compressed forms of energy and power.

Language, being language, we can expect a similar condensation in other languages too. In English, you have the familiar (almost endless) acronyms. No explanation is needed to understand what US and UK and UNO mean. (Light humor, since the Reader's Digest assures us that he who laughs, lasts. When an alphabetical list of the countries of the world was being prepared, those in England wanted to get the precedence over their cousins overseas. So, they wrote England first and USA to follow it leisurely almost at the end. The Yankees retaliated by writing America first, with Great Britain following it leisurely up the line.)

The Yankees did not stop there. They began to systematically compress any decent looking word of the Queen's language, apart from the above acronyms that is. If a Yankee talks of a deli, he is not being delirious for god's sake. A deli is a delicatessen, a heli is a helicopter just as a condo is a condominium, a cat is a catamaran, bio could be a biography and POTUS could be the President of the United States.

The future that is to unwind systematically (for a considerable period of time) can also be condensed. It is being done by many governments. They call it a five-year-plan or some such thing. A more decent and common name would be 'budget proposal'–watched anxiously by millions of citizens in every country.

Bottom line, as everybody is fond of saying: Somewhere in these mental peregrinations we have predicted that you cannot help touching the Big Bang again and again. Here we go. Condensation, we said. Then, what is (sorry, was) the mother of all condensations? Big Bang (noun), of course! It is the Mother of all mothers. The whole, the full Monty of Creation–which even today you are unable to measure in its totality–was once all compressed into a micro-speck just before the Big Bang (verbal).

21. Geography of earth in body II

Humans have got a body. Earth has got a body of its own. There are rivers long and short and big and small and streams of all sizes on the body of earth. So what? Nature made them in our bodies, with suitable adoptions, naturally (Brat – "Pun is fun, when find one don't shun.") Those rivers and streams became arteries and veins inside our bodies. All the river waters disembogue into the sea. Mimicking that, all blood in the vessels of our bodies discharges into the heart! Sea water rises into the sky (space and air), getting purified. Mimicking that, our blood courses in the lungs (space and air) getting purified. There are hills and dales on earth. They are reflected in our bodies too. (These lines from the beautiful, romantic poem by the Great Bard express the imagery beautifully. Venus and Adonis:-

"I'll be a park, and thou shalt be my deer;

Feed where thou wilt, on mountain or in dale:

Graze on my lips; and if those hills be dry,

Stray lower, where the pleasant fountains lie.")

The earth is enveloped by an outer crust. So what? We humans have skin. (Brat's inspiration – Grass grows on the crust. Hair grows on the skin. There are areas on the crust where grass does not grow, like deserts. On skin too, there are many areas where hair does not grow. Oh, there are tectonic plates on the earth's crust. We got that too, on our skull, yeah!) Life forms grow on the surface of the earth. Go ask your family doctor; he will enlighten you on the millions of living things that exist on your skin. And inside your body, to boot.

Brat haiku – Does your stomach grumble and growl? No great shakes. Earth too shakes (fun in pun) and boy, when it rumbles, you tremble and stumble for your life.

The sea is deep and dark. The subconscious mind reflects that. In the ocean, unseen by naked eyes, underwater currents flow, perfectly mirroring the flow of subconscious thought-streams and dreams. To travel under the surface waters, you employ special techniques and equipment. So does the psychologist when he has to map routes in the subconscious mind, using techniques like hypnosis, truth serums, etc.

Now and then volcanoes spew out hot lava from their innards. Similarly does the human mind erupt when the pressure of suppressed emotions becomes too much to hold down.

Last but not least: life. (Freewheeling of ideas.) Let us rise up to a bit higher level than geography. The earth is surrounded by an atmosphere. It glows spectacularly at the poles. The lights are called aurora Borealis and aurora Australis. Apart from that, earth glows like the moon, lit by the sun's rays. (There are oodles of NASA photos of this.) The human body too glows! Call it bioluminescence or aura according to your preference.

Tailpiece. Stretching similes a wee bit under poetical license. The earth spins on its axis. The human mind spins on its axis constantly; the axis is the ego. Apart from spinning on its own axis, the earth travels in space around the sun. Humans too, apart from spinning on the ego-axis, travel around–other lives on the social level. There exist caves and tunnels on earth. The hearts of human beings are compared to caves in ancient religions. As for the tunnels, you can enter through the ears and travel, or you can choose the nostrils. An interesting tidbit. Long back, Jules Verne wrote a book (Journey to the Center of the Earth) wherein was described the journey of the protagonists *inside* the earth, to its center. Later, Isaac Asimov described a fantastic voyage of humans inside a human body. (Yes, humans, yes, inside a human body. Read the book A Fantastic Voyage by him to know how it was accomplished.) The two books are excellent witnesses to our study of parallels.

One more stretching exercise please. You (and I) may point out that the similarities between the earth and the human body end at the border of life. Human bodies are living beings, the earth is a non-living entity. But go back to the old thinkers. Many of them revered the earth so much that they called it the mother. Many mystics and theosophists believe that the earth is a throbbing, sensitive living being. Their reverence is indeed justified when you consider that humans cannot live without "mother" earth. (Interstellar travel and colonization are quite far off concepts still. And then, even if you land on Mars and live there, it becomes your mother! The old affection to Earth may carry over and you may end up calling Mars your new Earth; the way the term New England was coined.)

22. Nature does it better

Water (sea) is at ground level. There are plenty of areas on land which need to be supplied with water–otherwise, plants and life forms cannot survive.

So what does Nature do? It carries out a marvelous engineering feat. (*Which even to this day man cannot imitate in terms of sheer size.*) Nature leverages the powers of gravity and the sun and wind. Water evaporates and rises up. Genius, if you think of it. Water by itself is heavy and it requires an unconceivable amount of energy to lift it up into the sky. Try to carry only one bucket of water up a tiny-puny three flights of stairs and you can truly appreciate how much energy is required to carry just that one bucket of water up into the sky. Think of all the water contained in all the rivers and streams and lakes on earth and try for a second time to imagine (without swooning) how much energy is required to carry all that water up. Well, clouds are formed by Nature. Wind blows. Clouds move. Then, on land, the clouds discharge water in a controlled, harmless way in the form of rain. Imagine the havoc that will occur if all that water comes down in one go as a solid torrent. Hats off to Nature! Marvel at it and say your thanksgiving—theist, atheist, scientist, politician, and layman alike. Repeat, even in the present day, man, with all the technology at his command, cannot mimic that engineering feat.

But man, clever man, does mimic that act in a different way, on a tiny scale. He has now invented pumps which can pump water to great heights of a city's overhead reservoir and then, in a controlled way, let it out to where ever it is needed.

Electricity: They send electricity through a gas (mercury vapor, sodium vapor, halogens, etc.) and generate *illumination.* They make electricity jump across two points (electrodes) and produce high *arcs* sufficient to melt metals and weld them too. Oh, Nature does that too, in a far greater (and grander) scale. When the sky is overcast with clouds, there is lightning between clouds and frightening lightning that jumps from clouds to the ground below, striking any object that dares to stand tall. *The electricity therein is thousands and thousands of times more than that produced in the tiny-puny welding machines.* Mind you, that awesome electricity is in *one* flash of lightning. During one evening of a summer's thunder shower, the flashes occur innumerable times; go, try to calculate the mindboggling amount of electricity that is generated in that period! (Again, try bravely not to swoon.)

Blast furnace: They put metal ores in that blasted thing. (Sorry, the temptation could not be resisted – Brat.) The temperatures generated inside the blast furnace are enough to melt the metal. Great, no? Not much, if you ask mom Nature. You only have to look at a blasted (sorry, again, by Brat) volcano, and you will laugh if somebody mentions a blast furnace in that context. In comparison with the seething thermal energy of a volcano, yon blast furnace is like a candle (cheap one at that).

23. Seeds

Nature creates some things instantaneously. Most of the time it wants to enjoy its act leisurely, unfolding over time spans that can vary enormously. (Road-sign reads Variations, Ranges. Want to go back there? You are warmly welcome. All things in Nature are interconnected, we said.) Seeds are the entities (physical, non-physical, or conceptual) which Nature has created for this purpose. That in itself is a wonder to contemplate. As usual, you can peruse a couple of examples and ask your friends to go and build a cornucopia (pun-loving Brat smiles) of them.

*A seed itself is one such grand example. The tree takes a long time to develop to its full shape and capacity; years and patient years. *All that is already hidden and joyfully unfolds out of the tiny acorn!* Rivaling that drama is that of the human seed(s), if not in terms of size, but certainly unrivaled in terms of sheer complexity, variety, and artistry. Then there are eggs.

*Seeds come in many parallel types. You look at a huge skyscraper and wonder at its size and beauty and complexity of parts. *All that is already hidden and joyfully unfolds out of the tiny pieces of paper called blueprints.* Seeds or blueprints, it is the same thing. They are entwined, one inside another. You are not ranting when you say that. Take the seed of life and peer, peer deep inside it. You see the spiraled entwined twain. Yes, you correctly identified it as the DNA. (Nature likes to play on words too.) Play on words, but seriously, in deep physics too. Quantum Mechanics (see, as we said back there, there is no escaping from Quantum Mechanics of the Great Triad) gleefully assures us that a particle is in a state of hibernation, enceinte with an infinite number of possibilities and that at the time of being observed, the pregnant womb of space delivers only one particular result. Discard the scientific jargon and focus on the words womb and delivery. There is seed for you; a highly sophisticated, technical one.

*You stand in front of an enchanting work of art for hours savoring its beauty. *All that is already hidden and joyfully unfolds out of the seed in the artist's mind.* Thus also it is, in the case of a poem, a classic in literature, or a haunting musical score. Thus it is in the case of an inventor. Thus it is in the case of a great reformer. Most grand actions of humans unfold out of the seeds of thoughts sown in their minds.

*That is how creation also unfolded; "In the beginning was the word." If you want an up-to-date scientific flavor, well, in the beginning was the Big Bang! *Creation is even now unfolding out of that tiny weeny Big Seed, rightfully the mother of all seeds!* (See, as we said back there, there is no escaping from the Big Bang.)

24. Filled with mutual reactions

In La Universe, everything is eager to mix with, act, react, and leave its impression.

The striking meteor leaves its impression on the surface of the earth it meets. El gringo enters the new land, leaving behind his impressions—on the love-stricken hearts he has reacted with. The gringo could be a Spaniard, an Englishman, an Italian, a Japanese, a Frenchman, or an Indian driven by wanderlust.

Sunlight falls on leaves, reacts with them, stimulating them to grow. The light of the knowledge of the teacher impinges on the pupils, reacts with them, stimulating them to grow and expand.

Hydrogen, carbon, and oxygen come together, react and produce food that caters to the human bodies. The food meets appropriate acids in their stomachs, reacts with the acids, and gets digested; the way knowledge is digested in the minds.

The same light strikes many objects inducing many reactions. Light falls on the human bodies, stimulating the growth of vitamin D. If it is of the ultraviolet kind, it induces severe sunburn. It kills off bacteria. The light falls on some metals and produces enough electricity to burn street lights.

Sound waves too cannot keep quiet. They impinge on your tympanum and make you hear words and music.

Distance is no barrier. Charged particles travel across millions of miles in space, strike the two poles of the earth and light up the skies in fantastic splendor.

Yeah, even so, deadly nuclear radiation can enter the human bodies and finish them off or produce the ugliest mutations.

Yeah, distance is no barrier for two particles (matter) to interact. The wonder of it is that no matter what kind of particle it is among the thousands that exist, it has to, and will act on any other kind of particle in the universe (caste, color, region, religion no bar!). We are talking of the gravitational field here. There is no bloody blessed bit of matter that does not possess gravity. Gravitational force, however minute it may be, is the most universal force. And theoretically its field stretches up to infinity. It may well be said that gravity is Nature's unique stamp of creation. It has been said earlier that gravity is always attractive; all things are attracted toward one another under its influence. As a parallel among humans and living creatures, love claims that spot—like gravitation, it brings and binds persons together. What happens there, surely, happens here and everywhere too. As the wise scientist-cum-philosopher says, the universe is holographic.

25. Impressions

Along the lines as above, things leave their mark, leave an impression on other things they come into contact with… (Oh, our Brat insists that we begin with the tell-tale signs of lipstick that the lass forgot to wipe away before entering her home. Guess, you-we have to agree with him there!)

You meet a great human being and depart, carrying away the many impressions he has left on your mind.

Wherever the dedicated traveler moves, the places and wonderful natural sceneries make unforgettable impressions on his mind. Brat points out another subtle and beautiful analogy here. Forget about the traveler and the beautiful scenery, or even the writer and the poet. All objects, in spite of being dubbed 'inert,' make an impression on you merely by existing. How? Yeah, says Brat, *they leave impressions on the cornea of the eyes of the person who sees them*, irrespective of his likes or dislikes! True.

That is nothing if you look deeper into physics. *An object, just by existing, leaves an impression on the space surrounding it.* That space gets curved! True. Ask Einstein if you doubt it. (There we go again.)

Ask the hunter. He will rave ecstatically about the spoor of animals in the forest.

Tidbit. Achtung! Actions and reactions and impressions are okay–so far. Leaving impressions behind, and repulsions are comparatively harmless, but the attractive kind of reactions can have a deadly effect on both the parties involved. Under the influence of attractive forces, Romeo and Juliet may get involved in tight embraces and resounding smackeroos and you may argue that there is no harm done there. Right, but physiology and physics are different matters. Recall Newton and gravitation and the falling apple. (The apple and earth are attracting each other.) Imagine what may happen if a stone is there instead of the apple and it has decided to descend on you. Worse still, a meteor is attracted to the earth, and if it strikes the earth without getting completely ablated, the impact will be tremendous.

An asteroid of sufficient size can even blast away the whole of a megacity in one fell strike. All this happens due to the power of the attractive force; be careful! (A poetic parallel demonstrating the immense destructive power of attraction—read the Iliad!)

Objects hurtling toward each other need not necessarily be big. If two micro-particles of opposite charges meet each other, they will annihilate each other! Don't blame us; the boffins say so. They have been smashing particles for so many decades in their laboratory tunnels. (One such tunnel is some 27 kilometers in circumference, constructed 100 feet below ground—LHC of the CERN or some such thing, near the Geneva-France border.)

Bottom line: Actions and reactions and impressions are the very stuff the universe and life are made of. Nothing exists without showing one or more of the above characteristics.

26. Power of congregation

"There is strength in numbers." This, one of the oldest aphorisms, was probably uttered either by an army general or a vote-seeking politician. There is no arguing about this practically wise saying. It holds true in almost all affairs of the worlds of humans and matter. (Back to our familiar Brat's parentheses. The signpost at this juncture reads Anomalies. Can go back there and return leisurely. (Brat – "For Google's sake, this is not a game of Snakes and Ladders. We are serious, of course. This is Life, more immense than a Disney Park. There is no fixed itinerary. You can skip, jump, hop, twist and turn, go and come, and sidestep as you like.") Amen. The anomaly is that numbers need not mean strength—or victory. See you at that chapter!)

First comes the old fable about the bundle of sticks. There, the father's sons were able to break a single, isolated stick, but when enough sticks were bundled together, the sons were unable to break the bundle; strength in numbers, surely. A single thread of cotton can be snapped without blinking, whereas when many such threads are twisted together to form a rope, the rope will withstand the full weight of the snapper on it and can even be used to bind him into immobility.

Consider sunlight falling on an area of one four-inch circle on a piece of paper. It is normal and nothing special happens to the paper. If you place a lens of the same size at a proper height above the paper, all the light rays will come together (at the focal point) and the paper soon gets burned! A telling example of the power of congregation.

27. Combinations

The universe itself is the result (play is a better word) of uncountable combinations of multitudes of elements, entities, activities, and effects.

Elements are very limited in number–about 118. They combine in all sorts of permutations (which includes combinations of combinations) to produce all the matter in the world. That includes food and poison and medicine and shelter and clothing.

Not only matter, but even the frames (you call them bodies) in which and through which life acts, are the result of combinations of preferred elements.

At the deeper levels of the elements, fundamental micro-particles combine and create individual atoms of the elements.

Bricks combine, changing their appearance and behavior to become walls.

Pages combine and give you books to read. (Inside parallel: Letters combine and give birth to words. Words repeat the act and yield sentences, which carry out the tradition and give us literature.)

Threads combine and change, and give you yarn and clothes. And transform themselves into bags and beds and sheets and curtains, let alone the indispensable dress (though some call them rags).

As a beautiful parallel, even persons exhibit changes in behavior when they are in a group. (Remember the words group behavior, group psychology.) Societies and nations too exhibit similar properties.)

28. One for many, many for one

Some similar sentiment bound the four musketeers together. We are not orating on the famous Musketeers here. Similar, and parallel, are the operating *words* for us. The intention of pun on words was to draw your attention to words themselves. Words too possess some peculiar properties. A single word may have different meanings. (If you demand an example fast, you have the word 'fast' itself as an excellent example.) On the other hand, there could be many words connoting a same (or similar) meaning. They are called homonyms and synonyms, respectively. This phenomenon is common to many languages of the world. (The ancient language Sanskrit excels in the usage of such words.) It has been often repeated here that Nature has a flair for diversity. Humans too exhibit that propinquity in abundance. ("Be not proud, man. For it is Me, Nature only that is working on and through you!")

Small talk: À propos the above paragraph a slightly humorous situation also arises with words. That a common object would have different names in different languages is obvious. Then, a word in one language may serendipitously mean many things in other languages; it is quite a common occurrence. Then again, the same object, idea may have almost the same—or similar sounding words in other languages. (Many Latin and Sanskrit words fall into this category. The similarity in the words for numbers in the two languages is especially striking. *Tres, thria, trois, teen*—all mean the number three.)

*Poor man; number-wise, (quantity) he thinks he is one only. But everyone around him, who is much intimate with him, specifies him by different words! Yeah, father, son, brother, grandpa, brother-in-law, son-in-law, uncle, nephew, cousin; by many names is he called. Even mute objects identify him differently. His driver's license, his credit card, his bank account, his social security number, his mobile phone, all identify him with different numbers! Poor guy. But he can have his revenge when all those guys who called him by different words are in turn dubbed with a single word—citizens. (If he wants a scholarly sounding name, he can use *Homo sapiens*.)

*Among plenty of parallels to the above, pick up the case of human beings. A single person (especially if he is well known) will be judged and evaluated by different persons all around him in different ways. Absolutely normal in this world of ours. [One word, many meanings; one person, many evaluations, eh?] Wondering about the obverse—many persons, one name? All collective nouns perform that service! There could be many persons with different names and different in every way. Lincoln, Kennedy, Roosevelt, Eisenhower; all different personalities with different names etc. But they all share one common word—President!

*Happens with inanimate objects too. There is one single book. 10 professional readers give it 10 different reviews. The obverse? Macbeth, King Lear, Faust, Waiting for Godot, The Barber of Seville, The Importance of Being Earnest—all are different books with different names. They all share a single word—drama.

*Happens with words too. "The quick brown fox jumped over the lazy dog." This can be classified as a sample of the English language. If printed, it can be viewed as black (or colored) ink over white paper. It is a group of words arranged in a particular way. If written on a blackboard (do those ancient artifacts still exist?), it is an arranged distribution of chalk powder on a black surface.) From the angle of calligraphy, it is a piece of art. It goes on and on… In the end, to sum it up in a sentence, it is a sentence! (Recall the old fable of the elephant and the blind men.)

29. Birds Haiku

What happens in one field has parallels in other fields, as we have been seeing all along. Besides this, man creates different parallels by copying or adapting what he observes in nature. Just take the case of other living creatures. Man has created plenty of things that imitate what other creatures do.

Birds *fly*. Ah, man created balloons that can float, and zeppelins that could travel. Ah, man further created metallic birds that fly! What happens here can happen there too. Flying machines? That is nothing, says our Brat. Thoughts can soar higher and farther *and faster*. No arguing that, Mister Brat. What happens there can happen elsewhere too. Elsewhere too, as in dreams. If birds can fly, so can human beings too, in their dreams. Almost everything that occurs in the objective world out there can be facilely accomplished in dreams; and most often even things that *cannot* occur out there. If you want to speculate romantically, you can say that dreams are the experimental laboratories for Nature before approved products are outputted out here. "Dreams are the seeds of reality," so runs a one-line Haiku. Brat thought over it and added a second line, "Many are sown, few do sprout," shamelessly imitating a famous saying. And when they sprout, how they sprout! For, while the birds could fly only paltry distances and at paltry heights, and could never, never go above the air-filled atmosphere of the earth, humans soared above the air layer and journeyed clean out of the pulling clutches of planet earth itself. (Dream big, dream wild, that is the mantra.)

Looks like man can learn a lot from birds. Bats are blind. They navigate in the world by emitting high frequency sound waves which strike the objects in their path and return to their sensitive ears. Man copied the idea and invented the radar, a most wonderful invention.

Birds build nests. Humans copy them (oh, sorry, no insult meant to humans there, even though humans insult birds' brains) and build cozy nests. They call them homes; the superior kind are called castles.

Looks like man can learn a lot from birds. Some migrating birds travel thousands of miles in the skies without the aid of navigation charts. They are able to sense the magnetic field (and its subtle variations) of the earth.

Humans copied them (oh, sorry, no insult meant to humans there, even though humans insult birds' brains) and built the magnetic compass.

Some birds like eagles have sharp eyesight, being able to spot small objects on the ground while floating at great heights. Humans copied them and invented the telescope (and its sibling, the microscope); that is all.

LOL moments as a foil to serious reading. Birds lays eggs, and the eggs hatch, giving rise to new chicks. Humans copy them. No, we are not suggesting that humans lay eggs. Humans copy them mentally and regularly. New and interesting idea-shells incubate inside the warm brains of humans, and at the proper moment come out of the hatchery with full-fledged wings. Come to think of it, Man copies from plants too. The *seeds* of an idea lie dormant in a person's mind for a certain period. At the right moment, they sprout. More copying from flowers. Emotions (beautiful) and ideas flower in a person's heart and brain. Copying from the tree continues. The tree or plant has many branches. Oftentimes, a major idea gives rise to further branching-out ideas. In the fields of mathematics, science, and technology, this phenomenon is more pronounced. Arts too are no exception to such occurrences.

Birds and insects too. There is the drone (bee) out there in the natural world. There are drones here now, merrily delivering groceries and books at your doorstep (or engaged in some secret military venture, or being busy hovering over vast agricultural fields).

The weaver bird weaves beautiful nests. Early man was fascinated by it. Human weavers were born. More things are being imitated in mind and by words. The poet began to weave poems using words. The storyteller did the same on a larger scale, weaving fantastic tales. The computer nerds do similar things in another, different medium. They weave logical syllogisms and algorithms to produce awesome software.

The other kind of birds, ducks, can move both in water and on land. Nature made Man think it over and over and finally inspired him to imitate them successfully. Now we have hovercraft which can move in water, and on reaching the shore, move on land as if it was no great deal.

Humans do not stay in one place. Wanderlust has been haunting them from the beginning. They *migrate*, you say? Yeah, but they learned it from the birds, which have been doing it in the skies long, long before crawling humans learned to fly.

In water, the fish swim and float. Nature made Man dream in a different medium. Man recreated that scene and made boats that could also float and move in water; the paddles became the wings of the boat. Bigger than fish were the whales that could traverse the seas. Man dreamed and built ships that could sail across seas. The fish could not only float, but could also move under, inside water. The metaphor was haunting humans for ages. Then, one day, even nature could not hold down Man. Man himself could hold down himself under the depths of water and move freely inside water—he had invented the submarines.

Animals and birds are experts in merging their bodies into their surroundings. Man copied the idea (without saying even so much as a thank you). The military, the guerrillas, hunters, anybody intent on stealthy operations, regularly employ camouflage in their activities.

The cuckoo, the nightingale, and other birds sing beautifully. Our Brat avers that humans were inspired to sing by observing those angelic birds. The parallel extends further. The donkey brays, the toad croaks. There are quite a few humans who can enthusiastically out-sing them. The sounds they produce are enough to make you close your ears, and leave the scene both tactfully and hastily.

Among the animals, there are herbivores, carnivores, and omnivores. That is correct; among humans too there exist all the three types. Humans devour not only food, they devour books too; especially the omnivores are very good at it. Humans need food for the mind also. ("Man does not live by bread alone.") Music is another type of food which most humans relish. Its votaries affirm that music is food for the soul. Indeed.

Birds, animals, insects; the parallel activities and characteristics abound in Nature's folds. (Brat, "Naturally, since everything is Nature only. Nature being Nature, the nature of one species is reflected in another–suitably morphed.") Bees build honeycombs and diligently deposit honey therein. Someone else comes along, takes out their honey and merrily goes away. Not only humans, but the ursine marauders too do that to them. Among humans, there are enough souls that suffer a similar fate as that of the bees. What they patiently build up, save up, is often taken away by the cheats, robbers, thieves, and clever businessmen in a perfectly respectable fashion. (Brat comments, "Here, the active/proactive role is represented by the bears and the passive role by the bees.")

Bees again. When they are enraged they attack, not singly, but all of them as a group. That is called an army in other words. Humans imitate that perfectly. They have well organized and better equipped armies.

Ants too. Ants know how to collect and stock up food for a rainy day. We have copied it beautifully and we stock up plenty of food and grains and seeds and fruits and what-not in all those varied kinds of air-conditioned storehouses.

There is that bird of Australia which, when confronted by a threatening situation, hides its head in the sand, pretending to believe that the danger does not exist. Or wishing for the enemy to go away. The similarity of this behavior among many of us humans is so striking that the name of that bird is given to such a behavior. In other parts of the world (especially India), cats are notable for a similar habit but under a different context. It is said that cats close their eyes when lapping up milk on the sly. The popular belief is that the cats are pretending that no one is observing them when they close *their* eyes! Any dabbling psychologist worth his salt will be eager to inform you that there is a strong parallel of this behavior among humans (maybe not all, not all, sir). It is instinctive; just close your eyes and pretend that nobody is observing you. But our Brat opines that dreaming, or even daydreaming, is a closer simile. You close your eyes to the surroundings and do what gives you great pleasure, without caring a hoot about what others–or your censor ego as papa Freud would say–think of it. There are plenty of parallels among the various kinds of life-forms. Let us round off the topic with a couple of similes.

Brave. You already got it. A person is brave as a *lion*. ("Curious," says The Brat, "nobody says a lion is brave like a human!" Um...) Cunning. Cunning like a *fox*, see? (Though the fox remonstrates that it is no match for the human beings.) Busy? You are, as a *bee* then. Are you examining something from all possible angles? Oh, you are having a *bird's eye view*, there. Faithfulness? A dog is there to show what it means. Is that person slow and tardy in everything he does? Maybe the person caught it from the *sloth*. Do you sing well? You are a *nightingale*. Do your friends remark that you are a very hardworking person? What they meant was that you are a *workhorse*. (Brat, "Even machines also are compared to horses. The power of machines is designated in terms of hp, which stands for horsepower!") After a long bout of hard work, you want to take a (well deserved) long rest. Then you are *hibernating*, that is all. If you are a fast runner, you are compared to a *cheetah*. If you are steady and sure-footed in climbing a steep, narrow rock, you are like a mountain goat. Your neighbor is very good at copying others; he is aping the *ape*. Another neighbor is noted for his wisdom; he got it from the *owl* on the nearby tree. The third one is always insatiably hungry. Then he has a wolverine appetite. The bone-breaking hug of a wrestler is a *bear* hug. If a person is thick-skinned, he got that quality from all those pachyderms. If one is tall and showing it off, he is ineffectually trying to reach the heights of a giraffe. Those of the extroverts who cannot help chattering on any and all occasions obviously inherited the propinquity from baboons and monkeys. The dancers? They were inspired and learned the art from the peacocks. Think that man is the only animal that laughs? No, *hyenas* do it better; ask them. In the Indian system of yoga, many body postures are named after animals.

There was a problem that arose a few days back evading solution. You have been constantly thinking about it, you have been turning it around in your mind. In this instance, you have copied the activity of your bovine pals. You have been turning it around, they have been chewing the cud. If you have been thinking and thinking about it, you have been *ruminating*–a favorite pastime of the cows.

Our Brat wishes to close these ruminations on a whimsically ironical note. Brat conjectures that Nature is either mocking at directly, or insulting indirectly the humans it has taken so much pain to create! To appreciate what he says, let us examine the nature of a simile. In a simile something, say A, is compared to another thing, B. In all such instances of comparison, that which is compared (A) is on a lower ground than that to which it is being compared (B), speaking figuratively. When you compare the bravery of a person to that of a lion, the lion is on a higher ground. Obviously. Now, look at all the examples studied above. Man has been compared to birds and animals in terms of specific qualities, abilities, etc. So (therefore, hence, thus), Man is on a lower level than the other living creatures! *Quod erat demonstrandum.* Maybe, Nature wants Man not to be unduly proud.

Infinity and eternity: The Brat's haiku master once said, "Do not be unduly awed by infinity and eternity. They are already contained in the number one. Keep on repeating one forever, that is all." That analysis is simple, straightforward and irrefutable! Looking at it from another angle, we can appreciate the fact that Nature itself intended and designed us such that all our experiences are doled out to us in tiny, microscopic bits–just to keep us all trudging along the field of infinity, through a narrow road along eternity.

30. Bits and bytes and doles

As said earlier, you do not ingest the water in that jug in one go, even if you chugalug.

Surely, you do not and cannot ingest all that tempting food on your plate in one go–even if you have an abnormally big mouth. (No insinuation or innuendos are meant there, dear.)

Surely, the great orator there on the podium cannot disembogue all that he wants to perorate upon instantly, all in one go. He has enough words to mesmerize you for hours. Yet he has to discharge the words one at a time. One at a time, again, see? The concatenated irony is that even if the listener is eager to hear all that at one go, he too has to hear out the words one at a time.

The poet's heart is brimming with powerful emotions and ideas and visions. Yet, he has to put them down on paper, one word at a time. So it is in the case of the avid reader. He may be eager to browse through all the pages of that bestselling whodunit in one gulp. Naw, he has to turn page after patient page, read line by line (word by word if it is poetry).

Even dying. As every thinker or preacher is apt to say, Death is the one Mighty force which nobody can defy. All living creatures die. Yet–hold on–yet, all the people, animals, birds, and living creatures do not die at one stroke. (Even the mass-destruction dealing techno-nerds have a long, long way to go before inventing the All Out weapon.) Living creatures die one at a time (and place). The most perfect Haiku too cannot do justice to this wonderful drama of Nature. The reverse event–that of birth–too is true.

Bottom line: Being the smart reader that you are, you have already arrived at the bottom of the issue. There is nothing like instantaneous. Even an explosion. Brat insists that the greatest irony is that the greatest explosion of them all, the Big Bang, is still continuing after 14 billion years. A bit of Zenoesque logical manipulation deserves a place in this context. The whole universe, creation, is being patiently cooked in the cosmic maw of Time. Time, by definition is a process, a concatenation of sequences, however small or big their duration may be.

Tailpiece. A small bit of entertainment–but a pertinent one. The Classical Greek thinkers of yore were really cute when it came to dissecting a concept. Above, we saw that Zeno argued that there is nothing like instantaneity. After convincing you thoroughly through a series of logically sequacious statements, he would greet you the next day with a totally

contrary affirmation and show you that everything is instantaneous! (Brat
– Better say, at once.)

The logic is seductive. Firstly, consider any action, preferably of the
shortest duration. Say, it begins at time zero (for notation purposes)
and ends after a hundredth of a second passes. The duration could be
of a thousandth of a second, or even a millionth; it does not affect the
extrapolation of Zeno's logic. In this case, you have no hesitation to
call the action as being instantaneous—*well, empirically, since it is almost
impossible to recognize a duration of a hundredth of a second by relying on
our senses of perception alone.* The subtle point is that even though the
action has a time duration, the important nodes are the *beginning and
the end only.* Repeat that. The duration can be neglected, since, well, uh,
it is negligible. We dubbed such an action as being instantaneous. (Zeno
does not blush here, and we can condone him.) In the next step of his
seductive (subversive?) logic, he asks us to consider a second event longer
than the first by only a millionth of a second in duration. Empirically,
again, the two events are instantaneous. Then, the third event differs from
the second by being a millionth of a second longer. All the three events
are evidently instantaneous actions, as per our logical sequence. The main
point, repeat again, is that there is a beginning and an end to the events.
The time in between is of no concern to us. (Zeno blushes, but his blush
is below the threshold level.) Now for the final *coup de grace*, so to say. We
observe that events have a beginning and an ending. So, all such events are
instantaneous! Finally, make a broad further generalization and claim that
ergo, *all* events are instantaneous. (Before you ask, "Eh, what was that?!"
Zeno has scarpered from the scene.) You may slowly begin to wonder
whether the act of creation and destruction of the universe can fall under
the same classification. Zeno may have departed, but our Brat is still very
much present, and he whispers in an awestruck voice "Why not? If it
has a beginning and an ending, Zeno proved just now that it could be
classified as being an instantaneous event. Well, modern science itself says
the universe is going to end some day; a few more billion years do not

matter. I, for one, vote for the cagey Zeno." We are out of breath here at the enormity of the revelation…

One thing at a time, bit by bit, byte by byte, that is how Nature intends to dictate our lives. No arguments allowed; nor petitions.

31. Orbits and spins – spill over

Planets orbit their suns, we saw. Galaxies spiral. Twin stars, like neutron stars, rotate around each other at mindboggling speeds. Back home, on Earth, delving into the heart of matter, we see that electrons orbit around their nuclei.

Gyroscopes spin and spin, ensuring solid, stable axes for many gadgets and instruments.

And, yes, we spin yarns (of both kinds) zealously.

While kids enjoy a gut-chewing ride in a giant Ferris wheel or in a merry-go-round.

Analogy in a different field: Around a powerful leader, the lesser profiles seem to orbit always.

Virtually, a person afflicted with vertigo feels his brain spinning uncontrollably while looking down from the top of a tall building.

32. Cyclical acts

They have been mentioned a couple of times earlier. They come here once again. (This is like a huge park. As you go on wandering, you will certainly come across familiar trees and flowers now and then.) The universe and our existence therein is filled with infinite acts and events. There is plenty of scope for new events to stage themselves at random. But logic shows us that since time is of infinite extension, there is a far greater scope for events to repeat. Here too, some events may repeat at random, some will occur at regular intervals–cycles, as we can define them.

Simple cycles can keep on repeating, filling up the whole of the infinite expanse of time. (As if their minuteness was challenging, taunting the infiniteness of space-time!) Here we go.

Planets keep on going around and around their stars.

Some planets and stars keep on turning around themselves.

That kind of thing here on earth is the cause of the cycles of days and nights; and months and years. The seasons keep up with them.

That reminds us of the eternal cycles of sleep and wakefulness, of births and deaths. The regular cycles of heartbeats are there, resonating (as if empathizing with) those cycles. (Both the philosophical and practical, existential kinds are included.)

Civilizations come and go. Stars are born and die.

This is a broad picture. Countless kinds of cyclical acts can be found in all the branches of human knowledge, which can fill up a whole book if written down.

33. Embryos

Let us keep aside strict science for a second. Then, you can see the beautiful (exhilarating, uplifting, soul-filling, and all that), general statement that all things which are manifested, come out of an embryo. The embryo can be of many genres and refinements; does not matter. This seemingly sweeping statement will become clearer if we start looking at examples of things of big size first. A gigantic tree, in spite of its immense size, came out of *one tiny seed millions of times smaller in volume!* From a poetic or mystical perspective (highly justified), it can be said that the tree was already contained in the seed, the embryo. This is true in the case of animals, birds, and humans too.

Following the theme of this book, we can extend the analogy even to inanimate matter. All objects of all kinds and sizes and shapes are, in the final analysis, the 'result' of atoms of elements. Atoms are the embryo of matter. ("No science, please. We are poets and imaginators; please vote for that word if you think that originator is derived from origin.")

Mind's embryos: Plants of different species sprout from as many different, specific seeds/embryos. Seeds sprout in earth. So, earth can be said to be a common embryo! (Why not? Recall the ancient reverent phrase, Mother Earth.)

Jump to outer space, draw inspiration from the Goddess of Haiku and intuit that space is an embryo from which stars and galaxies sprout. (Science is put inside the deep freezer for the present.) In fact, there is a Sanskrit word, *Brahmanda*, meaning the Cosmic Egg, which beautifully expresses this idea.

Then, jump and dive deep from there into the inner recess of the mind. The Goddess of Haiku will again make you understand that the mind is the common embryo for all dreams, ideas, empires, great books, industries, and inventions and buildings and bridges and roads and dams, art, music, and dance and entertainment, every blessed activity that human beings indulge in. A wonderful and fitting parallel to the soil, the earth. (The signpost reads Seeds here. If you want to explore further flora and fauna of the park, you can walk along that road and come back. Parallels, we insist. These ubiquitous signposts are like so many webpage links that are thrust under your nose in every favorite website you care to browse. The crosslinks constitute an unavoidable fact of life.)

34. Creation

It started with the capital C, in the beginning, when our universe came into being. Nature wants us to remember it and is constantly throwing the broadest of hints at us (as if it doubted our mental brightness). But, of course, we are all not that dumb. Day in and day out we witness the birth of thousands and thousands of new human beings–and more of other life-forms. The original act of Creation is being mimicked every imaginable second in a different way. Parallels, analogies, again and again. That is what occurs when there is a birth of a brilliant idea in a person's mind. Brat adds–unnecessarily–that it need not necessarily be a brilliant idea. All thoughts are like new births. That is also a pale mimicry of creation, you got to admit.

To link back to what was said earlier, empty space is not truly empty, modern science says. Every second, strange particles are being birthed, and other stranger particles having been birthed too, go chasing the first ones and devour them. Ah, and strangely (perplexingly?) they are also being destroyed at the same time; leaving the space to its emptiness! It is as if the space was a stage, and a superfast micro-drama was conducted, and the actors (those particles) exited in a mighty hurry, leaving the stage empty! The Great Bard indeed observed that all the world was a stage. How he would be thrilled if he were here today and know what the Great Boffins have discovered! Your point here is creation, creation, how it occurs across so many platforms.

An alluring postscript. Creation, we saw, is occurring both in the realm of life and in that of matter. There is another tempting way of looking at the play of Nature. Any change in a given state can also be justifiably interpreted as an act of creation. For example, a flash of lightning in the sky is an act of creation. If you accept this interpretation, then the universe is being breathtakingly creative every blessed second. Billions and billions of events are taking place throughout vast regions. *That ungraspable grandeur is beyond all descriptions.*

35. Awareness

Awareness is the primary function. The act of seeing physically is a parallel reflection of that. Nature has designed us such that we can see only from the front; the back is normally hidden. The same condition is reflected in our mental awareness. The mind functions in the conscious state during normal wakefulness. The subconscious is hidden from it. Just as you can see what is behind you using a mirror, so too you can peep into the subconscious using hypnosis or other psychotherapy techniques.

36. Action here, result there

There is a hilarious local language (Indian) saying which succinctly translates thus: blow on the ass, teeth fell out. That is to say, pressure or action occurred at one area, but the effect was expressed in a different area! It may be a humorous saying, but is coined after observing Nature's acts here and there, now and then. You have an air bag in your hands, fully blown and uniformly smooth all over. If you now press it on a spot, the pressure shows up on other areas of the bag and they get ungainly bulges.

Similar act occurs in the case of the mind. If there is undue pressure on the mind of a person, its effect often shows up in some other context. All those jokes about the nasty boss, who was butt-kicked at home by his Xanthippe, bear witness to that phenomenon. Even a simple lever illustrates this effect. You apply pressure at one end, and lo, its effect shows up *on the opposite* end! This kind of effect is seen everywhere in the present day after the arrival of electricity and *push-buttons!* You push the button here, and the real action shows up somewhere else; could be even hundreds of thousands of miles away, in the case of space gadgets. Pulling strings is a similar act that happens all the time in our world–especially in politics.

37. Expanding things

When things expand, their nature and structure, actions, reactions change. A water droplet by itself is just that only. When it expands–yes, by way of joining millions of its own kind–it becomes a cloud. Its color and shape and size change. That is, when it rises up into the sky. When it is in the ground, it becomes a stream, a river, the sea. So huge a change.

Science tidbit. When a gas expands suddenly, with force, *it cools down!* That is how the fridges in your kitchen work.

Okay, you have to admit that when your mind expands, its nature changes. You will know it directly, and nobody need tell you about it. Even if the others doubt it, you know it, and that is enough.

Lastly, we touch the Big Bang for the umpteenth time (as promised). Initially, just before the Bang, the universe was less than the size of a pin head. (Do not argue that; the boffins will not be amused.) It expanded. And see what has happened to the universe that we see and live in now. Nothing can be more mindboggling.

38. Leverage

Archimedes is the man who made the lever memorable with his famous saying, "Give me a lever of sufficient length and a place to stand on, and I will move the earth!"

He is famed to have formulated the principle of leverage. You apply force at one end of the lever (usually on the longer arm) and that force will be effective at the other end of the shorter arm. The point to notice is that the force experienced at the end of the shorter arm will be multiplied many times, without your having to sweat over it! This is how we are able to move heavy objects in daily life. The amount of increase of your force depends on the ratio between the short arm and the long arm. That is why Archimedes boasted he could move the earth.

In a humorous way, you can say that the more distant the applied force is located, the greater is its effectiveness! Parallels in real life can be seen in human affairs, as in politics and other huge organizations. The power or the authority is far removed from the small circles of ordinary citizens. But the effect is tremendous.

Extrapolate that idea to the maximum distance possible. What do you get? God is quite invisible and far from our mundane affairs. His power is infinite!

39. Birth and Death

This is the eternal theme of Nature. In fact, if you look at it from the philosophical and mystical point, you may even be tempted to say that that is the only theme of Nature's Intent. Nothing is permanent, as every philosopher is fond of saying. (And, sigh, it seems to be true! Except death and taxes, as the great American wit said.) Our Brat wants not to dilate on this topic since, as he says (correctly, of course), we are all witnessing it in umpteen forms all the time. Things come, things go.

40. Morsels

Imagine this scene. The famous gourmet chef, Guzzler, is staring (and salivating) at a large plate of food prepared especially for him. (Brat – "Is he groaking?") The plate is loaded with all the food he likes to eat. The quantity of food is five times more than what normal guys like you and me can ingest–and hazardous to digest. Okay, enough of petty details. Let us come to the serious, practical, and scientific matters. Our query is, how does Guzzler manage to eat the stuff on the plate? The question may seem pointless at first glance, but please observe the purely physical/mechanical process of the Guzzler's act. Okay, again, enough of teasing. The main point of interest here is that Guzzler does not eat the whole or all of the food on the plate in one go. Human mouths are not designed to swallow all the food on the plate in one fell sweep.

Not only eating, even seeing. The whole world lies in front of you, quite open for inspection, and for free. But you can see only the equivalent of one visual morsel at a time.

Mon, you have about 36,500 days to live on this earth. (Amen. If you want to bargain for more, we heartily approve it.) But you can only experience the equivalent of one diurnal-morsel a day.

41. CPU

In the computers and other electronic gadgets, there is what is what is called a CPU; central processing unit. This unit scans all input and decides what is to be done, and allocates the various routines to other units and working parts. What else is it but a pale copy of the marvelous CPU that Nature has already created millions of years back—the brain!

42. Humor

And finally, you cannot avoid noticing Nature's elaborate sense of humor. Leaving aside the infinite instances of humor in human lives, it is like this. For thousands of years, humans, especially the thinking specialists, have been continuously busy to delve out the ultimate secret of the universe. In every century, the geeks were much sanguine that they would find out the secret. In fact, around the beginning of the last century, a few scientists are said to have declared that very soon science would know all that is to be known about the universe! More than a century has passed since then. Alas, the Final Theory still seems to lurk below the discernible horizon. The subtle joke is that it always seems to recede as we progress! The parallel imagery of The Mirage naturally raises up in this context.

CHAPTER 34

ANOMALIES (PARADOXES, EXCEPTIONS)

The paradox here is that Nature itself is one heck of an anomaly! There is a solid reason for making this seemingly peculiar statement. In the earlier pages, there is a chapter on opposites. That opposites exist should surprise nobody. But we will adopt the way of the old sophists and argue as follows. Once again, we wish to take you back to your high-school days and make you remember how your teacher on logic would declaim in a stentorian voice, "Every rule has an exception." All you students would smile appreciatively, since by then you would have come across a number of anomalies in your science classes. Physics, chemistry, biology, geology, any law in any branch of science is sure to contain at least one anomaly. And real life (of us, supposedly reasonable, thinking human beings) abounds in anomalies and paradoxes. Add it all up and you will then certainly see Nature itself as abounding in anomalies. Just to satisfy your curiosity, here is a point to ponder. The universe contains uncountable trillions of objects like galaxies, stars, planets, and so on. Uncountable, repeat that. Yet, in such a vast place, there is life on only one planet, our Earth!!! Now, please do not give that spiel about SETI, Carl Sagan, Alien sightings, and things of that ilk. Let us take up that sophist thread. Respected science itself accepts that the contents of the universe are uniformly distributed and from there derives great mathematical conclusions. (Pardon a small diversion. Another great scientist, Avogadro, assumed a startlingly similar proposition about gasses filled in a container—that the gas molecules under normal conditions are uniformly distributed in any given space inside the container—and from there derived exquisite insights about the nature of the gas molecules. If you are a student of physics and if you have studied that particular methodology of mathematical investigation in your college days, you will remember how fantastic, mind-blowing it was. Well…) To lay stress again on that uniformity of matter in the universe, think again of the existence—and glorious proliferation—of human life on a particular patch of space. Got it? If space is the same everywhere in the universe, then the universe must have been teeming with untold number of human civilizations. Well, at least a thousand? A dozen? Come, a minimum of two? Nada. Nil. That, by any standard, is an immense anomaly. That is why we called Nature itself The Great Anomaly…

It is not over yet. (We are condensing a huge amount of data into a few paragraphs.) A little joke (or paradox, if you are of serious disposition) is in order. Recall that your teacher in the above introductory paragraph declaimed that every rule has an exception. You gotta accept what the teacher said; it is a rule. If it is a rule then there must be an exception to that rule also! Reminds you once more of the college joke on logic. Honest Alex declares that he always tells lies. Then what he said must be a lie. That means he told the truth—that he is a liar. So, if he is a liar, his statement must be false…a jolly ride in a merry-go-round.

*Heat expands objects and cold contracts, was the general rule in physics: verifiable by plenty of simple, direct experiments. But then, your teacher told you that water is an anomaly. When water *cools* down and becomes ice, its *volume increases!* Not only that; there is by now what is called the famous Mpemba effect. It seems that hot water freezes faster than normal water! (Aristotle had suspected it, and now Mpemba has confirmed it by scientific experimentation; thus.) And so on, and so many examples. In fact, the joke is on normalcy. If you go on making a list of all kinds of anomalies in every field, then anomalies will soon seem to outnumber the normalcies! (If you are addicted to epigrams, then you may declare that normalcy itself is an anomaly; and attribute it to Oscar Wilde or Bernard Shaw.)

Water. That is a liquid. Normally, solids are heavier than liquids: stone is heavier than water, a piece of brick is heavier than petrol. These are obvious examples, no? No. A piece of wood is solid, but it floats on water. Even the human body, though solid, floats on water (unless the body panics and takes in water). A ship, made of more solid and heavier material, floats on water. You will be quick to point out that weight and density are different. Okay, agreed. But you have to concede that an anomaly, even if apparently only, is an anomaly. Well, our Brat asks, "How about a cauldron of *liquid* like beer, say? Surely, it is lighter than a good deal of solid objects." He has a point there. He was keeping the final card up his sleeve. *Mercury is a liquid. It is heavier than all other solid objects below it in the Clarke's Periodic Table!* Can't beat that, we suppose. *Besides being a liquid, the damn thing is a metal.* That Nature has got a finely tuned sense of humor coming out in many flavors cannot be overstressed.

*Cells–division, mutation: Cells in a living body multiply by division. One cell divides itself into two similar parts, and we have now two cells. These second-generation cells again divide themselves into four cells. Not immediately, of course. Because, this is an astonishingly fast rate of multiplication, as anybody with a basic knowledge of mathematics will tell you. This is how, in fact, a chain reaction in a nuclear bomb occurs; and you know what happens. With growing cells (exponentially, as the phrase goes), there won't be a nuclear explosion, of course (smile), but the rate of growth is so unbelievable that soon the cells will increase into such a size that the living body will burst, if the growth is left unchecked. Normally, Nature sees to it that the first generation of cells die. Or, the reproducing capacity of the cells will dwindle down after a designated generation of cell-multiplication takes place. That makes perfect sense and exquisite control.

Otherwise, imagine what would happen if the liver or a gland in the body goes on increasing in size non-stop! Life would end before it grows fully! One exquisite paradox here is that for life in one form (body as a unit) to sustain, lives in another form (cells) die. Sacrificed by Nature would be a more befitting description. (Diversion, as before: Sacrifice, you see. Small units of life are sacrificed for the sake of the bigger overall unit. The poignant parallel scenery of soldiers sacrificing their lives for the sake of the country passes before your eyes, does it not?)

So much about normalcy. Beautiful and awe-inspiring indeed. Then comes the equally awe-inspiring quality of anomaly. Now and then, the cells in a particular organ or area of the body go on and on multiplying. The tragic result is that the higher unit (body) dies. A tragedy perhaps best comprehensible to Nature only. As you all know, this deadly anomaly goes by the innuendo, big C.

There is another kind of anomaly also in this affair of cell reproduction. Usually, a cell with a particular group of characteristics, say A, divides itself into more cells of the same characteristics, A. There is a whole branch of genetics dealing with this. Then again, at random, something happens and the reproduced cell acquires characteristics other than that of the parental cell. (A becomes B, so to say.) This phenomenon is called mutation.

*Tidbit: Mention of human bodies goads our attention to this scenery. Normal humans have 10 digits on their feet, and 10 fingers on their hands. Nature is fond of anomalies, we said. Sure enough, you will find people with more than 10 fingers. The normal human foot has five digits on each foot. But in Africa, there is a tribe in which the people are born with what is called ostrich foot; there are *only two digits*, similar to that of an ostrich! The heart is located on left side of the chest. Anomaly again; some rare persons have hearts on the right side. There are even people with just one lung (yeah, you read it right.) Another anomaly that is fairly common—related with sex. Among humans, male and female sexes are the norm. But (as with everything in nature), anomaly peeps its head, and eunuchs, transgenders are born. The list of anomalies can be quite long indeed.

*A humorous note, but true, nevertheless. Go and inspect any office anywhere in the world and this scene will greet your eyes. The employees are busy, each engaged in the duties assigned. "Hold on, that is natural," you would say. Normal, we agree. But tarry, and look around more intently. You will surely descry at least one idle person! (If he is not exactly idle but engaged, most probably he will be engaged in reading or checking his personal emails, or even slyly watching porn on his latest phone.) If the number is two, then those two could be busy exchanging gossip. That is quite a different kind of anomaly in our list, but still deserving of an inclusion. Recall that somewhere in these pages we said that everything has an opposite. It is so, in this instance too. On an off day for the office, normally, nobody bothers to work–unless there is an incentive like "overtime pay." Every employee will be holidaying, probably somewhere far away in a different town. But you will surely find our "anomaly" guy who will be deeply immersed in work, heroically rejecting all temptations of leisure and entertainment.

*Tidbit: Normally, when mention is made of hills and mountains, we visualize them as rising above the surface of the earth, either suddenly rising up as many hills and hillocks do, or gradually rising tier after tier into great ranges. That is normal–for mountains to grow on *land*. Hold there. There are mountains *inside the sea* too! Some rivaling the Himalayas and Andes in height! (In Hawaii, the volcanic mountain Mauna Kea is in the sea, rising 13,976 feet above the water level. When its height is taken from the base, which is at that bottom of the sea, its height comes to 33,465 feet, whereas the height of Everest is at 29,035 feet!) That is the beauty of anomalies for you. (Otherwise, "Life would be dull without you," as a guy told 007, once upon a time.)

Up there, the wit in you wryly observed that normalcy itself was an anomaly. The obviously intended meaning was that there are so many anomalies everywhere. That could possibly be true. (But very difficult to prove practically.) Still, if you want to defend your case like a tenacious lawyer, you can maliciously advocate a Google search for anomalies–on all imaginable topics. Your opponents will then throw in the towel! Then, Google indeed will justify its unquestionable reputation. An infinitesimal sample follows, to give you an idea of the vast scope of anomalies. (Do not be deterred by the scientific jargon. You can always memorize them and throw them at your opponents in an argument.) You forgot your purpose? Your purpose was to reverse the epigram and declare (superciliously) that in Nature, anomaly itself is normal. Go ahead, you have our assured support.

*Yes, take any subject on earth, you will surely find a case exemplifying an anomaly. Nature, science, biology, physics, maths, logic (!), chemistry, geology, archaeology, anthropology, *any* field of knowledge will serve our purpose. You can fill a whole book with examples. (The temptation is very exciting; we mean, writing a book within a book! That could also be an example of an anomaly…)

Biology, humans, animals, etc: The following interesting items have been culled from a web page. Humans have two hands, left and right. (Please don't frown. It is only an obvious statement; there is no hidden meaning in it.) Since Nature has equipped them with two hands, it is natural to expect that humans would be equally proficient in using both hands. There lies the anomaly. Almost all of us prefer to use the right hand for most activities–writing being one such example. But Nature enjoys playing the game of anomalies (as we said earlier) and has created persons who use the left hand, the way the rest of us use the right one–southpaws, as they are dubbed. There are also some very rare persons who are equally dexterous in both hands. But by and large, right is right! As a parallel in language, recall the phrases 'left-handed' compliment, 'leftist party,' and so on. (A funny tidbit. Do not jump to the conclusion that right is right. The southpaws will point out–with justifiable pride–that Nature has placed the most important organ of the human body, the heart, on the *left* side! Can't argue that. And again, Nature plays the double game of double anomaly, by equipping some rare people with hearts on the right side! Refer back to our statement that every rule has an exception and savor it.)

And here is another funny, but interesting piece of information dealing with the left-right pairs of the body. Again, we start with the obvious, that we have two nostrils, the left and the right. In this case, Nature plays a different tune than the previous one. In contrast to the case of hands, here, there is no preference. We breathe through both the nostrils. That seems to be quite natural, you must agree. But there is a quirky twist. Some innocent readers may think that we are breathing through both the nostrils at the same time. It is not so; the researchers assure us. The human body uses one nostril at a time for a brief period and then changes over to the other one! It goes on alternating throughout the day. You may be tempted to argue that the body is giving rest to the unused nostril for that brief period. But then, our Inner Child-cum-Brat will point out that we have two eyes. Why don't we alternately close one eye for a short time, giving it a deserving rest? He has a point there, especially when he (he is a brat, we said) relentlessly points his fingers to your ears and frames a question following the previous line of enquiry. He has a point there too. The human body exhibits many more kinds of anomalies. The mention of breathing reminds us that we normally have two lungs. Some rare guys are there who are born with a single lung and go on leading a normal life! There is what is called anesthesia awareness. Some people are aware when anesthesia is administered to them in the operating room. When surgery is going on, they are aware of the surrounding sounds and conversations among the operating team! Some people develop a kind of skin blemish on the lower ankle, called the Mongolian spot. Usually it goes off by itself.

*The mention of organs brings us to another surprising (highly indeed, from the human point of view) anomaly. The eyes are surely the most important of the sense organs of living creatures. But look at bats–Nature has created them without eyes! First of all, eyes are most important for movement of the body. But look at wily Nature. As if challenging itself, it created the bat which moves ('navigates') using its ears! That is not enough for Nature. It has also created a few kinds of fish which do not have eyes. One wonders how such a handicap can be looked at as an instrument for survival.

Tidbit: This is a funny item but deserves much serious thinking. Most of us are aware that there are plenty of bacteria inside our bodies. The guy who hears this mentioned may nod his head knowingly and add, yes, quite a lot. But the final joke is on him. The fact of the matter is that if you count all the *cells* in the human body and sift them, you will be aghast to see that *there are more bacteria cells in the body than human cells!* A website seriously affirms this. That is one heck of an anomaly for you.

Biology to physics: A human being normally possesses five fingers on a hand. On rare occasions, we come across someone having six fingers. It may be a minor anomaly, but that does not disqualify that person from being identified as a human being. Nature does parallel tricks in physics also. Normally, the various elements in physics (or chemistry, if you want to be choosy in terminology) are distinguishable from one another by the number of electrons, protons, and neutrons that their atoms carry. That is, each element is characterized by the number of protons and neutrons its atom contains. Surprisingly, (not by Nature's point of view) often a same element comes with atoms having more than its usual number of neutrons. (Protons and electrons do not vary.) Yet, the nature of the element does not change. Such elements are called isotopes. Hydrogen and carbon are the most famous examples. (Recall the terms carbon 14 dating and deuterium.) Most often, the isotopes become radioactive. Oh, again, the signpost reads anomaly at this point, and we have to draw your attention to the vagaries of Nature. You see, all 'matter' in the world is made of around 118 elements only, as already stated elsewhere. The joke is that out of them, around 81 elements come in the form of isotopes, the number of isotopes being around 275. And the radioactive varieties are about 800 in number!

Repeat, the total elements are 118 only. The isotopes of an element carry the same name as that of the element. That means the 'abnormal' elements outnumber the normal ones. That is why we said that anomaly itself is normal for Nature. It is Nature's way (one, out of many, Naturally) of having fun.

*An anomaly which is one its kind (good pun from the pundit). Hapaxlegomenon: It connotes just a one-time occurrence of a word. That phrase is a subtle anomaly. Because, as you can see immediately, that such a word must be in the dictionary—if it is to be officially recognized. Such a word does not drop by itself from the sky into the revered page of the lexicon. Somebody has used it once. Then the somber lexist has culled it and lovingly placed it on the page where you descried the word. (Lexicographer is too cumbersome a word. So, in the best tradition of the Yankees, you have compressed the word. After all, if a condominium becomes a condo, if a catamaran becomes a cat, why not our lexico…?) You got the photo? *Matter o"act, nothing happens only once!* Think it is a tall claim?

There is a lot of scope for debate (light-hearted) on this point. Only once? There is no such thing. You thump the table and shout, "Bull, what about creation of the universe? It happens, we mean, it is still happening. That is a one-time act."

Pundit – "My dear friend, go to any Eastern theosophist. He will assure you that this particular creation which your scientists calculate to have begun 14 or some billion years ago, is but one among the countless numbers of cycles of Creation and Dissolution."

You snort and are about to remonstrate, but pundit calmly wags his index finger at you (almost tapping you on your chest, if you permit such an act) and continues, "Your science says that this particular creation began with the Big Bang. The same science confidently prophesies that there is going to be a Big Crunch. (*pause*) That Big Crunch is the goose which will lay the egg of another Big Bang! Quite logical, see? (*pause*) That Bang is going to fizzle out in a whimper and result in—you said it, another Big Crunch! Endless cycles, see?"

Pundit has got a point there. We are sifting through all things for our parallels and lo, a highly artistically satisfying instance is here. He talked of cycles of creation and dissolution. We witness them every day in the form of sunrise and sunset, beautifully symbolizing creation and dissolution. This again is intimately connected with the other cycle. We will start it with a second objection going to be raised by you. You will remonstrate a second time that death happens only once. Back to pundit for an answer. He will ecstatically lecture you on the same Eastern philosophies which expatiate eloquently on *samsara*, karma, and endless cycles of births and deaths. We will snatch the thread from pundit at this point and link back to the point raised a few sentences earlier. The parallel is being mirrored in miniature daily in our lives. Sleep and wakefulness—what else? Those two states beautifully mirror death and birth. (You can say that Nature has been throwing broad hints at us.)

Nothing happens only once. You do not put one step forward, be satisfied, and keep quiet forever afterwards; do you? If such is the case, can you expect Nature to be satisfied by doing something for once and shut down forever? (!) (Er, excuse us, the Inner Child-cum-Brat whom you had encountered back there, is back here now. He has a brilliant, breath-stopping angle on this only once happenstance. He fancies himself to be Plato this time, and is addressing Aristotle thus, "Now, dear Aristotle, consider this much cogent line of enquiry. You throw a stone up once and it falls down. Naturally, we attribute this power to Nature using the earth as its agent. Then, I urge you to give serious thought to what I am going to put forward. The stone went up and earth wanted to hold on to what belonged to it, and pulled it back with vehemence unto its bosom. Is Nature satisfied and does it feel smug for having demonstrated its power on things that belong to it, and so does it keep quiet the next time you throw one more stone? No, dear Aristotle, it will again pull back the stone. And do so every time you throw a stone up. I have received reports that Archimedes was recently exploring the very same idea. You know how much he loves experimenting. They say that near the temple of Gaia, he threw the stone a myriad-myriad number of times to ascertain the patience of earth. That is why I said that nothing happens only once." That is our Inner Child for you. The child, as you might have noticed, is also a brat and a braggart. He shoots off at a tangent in the name of what he calls a 'negative anomaly.' "I think," he continues, beaming a crooked smile at you, "old Plato and Archimedes were in a hurry to forge forceful conclusions. The odd myriads of experiments of stone-throwing were not enough. Though they were acceptable to Plato, they are not (so) to me. We are now in the 21st century. Poor Plato did not have the advantages we now have of Science and Google and Microsoft and Android. I am especially referring to the weirdest kind of thinking in all of human existence, yeah, the thinking that goes by the name of Quantum Physics. To put it simply, or very plainly, in Quantum Physics, anything goes. *Anything may happen to any thing any time anywhere.* Yeah, that is science, take it or leave it. If you begin to even so much as argue, the boffins will throw tons and tons of mathematics at you, so that you are floored and will never be able to get up under the weight of all those equations. Ah, leave it at that. Let us come back to our poor stone thrown into the air and lingering there at the height of its upward journey, at which point it got entangled into quantum mathematics. Having journeyed so far without a hitch, the poor thing is now in a state of quandary. That is, it is in The Quantum State ('Anything may happen to any thing any time anywhere.') Whatdoes it mean? What does it portend? The official jargon says that the stone is in a superposed state. In plain terms, there are many pregnant *possibilities* (infinite, mon), from which there will be a single outcome. One such possibility is that the stone may decide to continue moving upward forever! It may decide to stay where it is. (It is called static floating, in case you are not sure what to call it.) You can forget that stone forever. Do not watch it—it is never going to come down." Whew, that was quite a lecture by brat.

Since he went off at a tangent, we will add another tangential note to that. What he called a negative anomaly may as well be christened as quantum anomaly. It is an anomaly for those of us living in the mundane world. For those boffin-geeks living in the quantum field, it is perfectly normal. "Quantum is quantum." (Those nerds not only live in the quantum empire, but also, they eat quantum, they drink quantum, they talk quantum, they sleep quantum, dream quantum, and wake up in a quantum state.) A further clarification on the once and only once logo. When the Inner Brat contemplated the situation of the stone in suspended animation, he meant that such a situation can justifiably be cited as an example of the 'once and only once' speculation. There is a peculiar, unclassifiable logic in his justification. Because, you see (he expounds), once you have thrown the stone and it does not come down, you cannot repeat the experiment. No, by Zeus, you cannot. How can you be sure that the stone does not descend forever? You can only be sure by *watching over the stone forever*. (And Quantum being Quantum is more enigmatic than the Sphinx.) That 'forever' is never going to end. Ergo, no more stone throwing. Hapax phenomenon. QED.

Final remark. In theosophical circles, the day when the stone goes off or floats in air is called The Day of Dissolution of Creation; *pralaya*, as the Indian system calls it. Brat the Terrible interlopes here and says, for Quantum's sake (á la, for god's sake), do not bring in your maddening cycles of creation and dissolution. 50 billion years are quite sufficient for all of us who are living now and all who are going to live in future.

*A short bout of word-wrestling regarding a thing happening only once. After listening to that quaint harangue on stone throwing, you may suddenly remember the fact of death. You may jut your jaw aggressively and taunt confidently that death happens only once! To that, pundit and brat would pounce on you simultaneously barking at you alternately. Brat would mischievously point out that every second, millions of lives are dying on the planet earth–just to confuse the issue. You will naturally respond that you are talking of death of an individual. To that, pundit would reply sharply that as per the wisest ancient wisdom, a soul goes through many, many cycles of death and rebirth. Brat nods his head excitedly and says the subject of rebirth is being studied diligently in recent days, that there are plenty of books describing elaborate researches done by eminent doctors and psychologists on incidents of rebirth, and therefore that means that death is not a one-time phenomenon, and nor is rebirth, whew! After a brief pause, brat being brat shoots off at another angle (but roughly in the general previous direction). He asks you to remember an old proverb whose equivalent you will find in almost all the languages of the world; that a coward dies a thousand deaths. Brat wants to win his argument at any rate, but we feel he has a solid case and need not overdo it. He will not stop there. He extends the argument to the case of *living* also. Yes, he seriously asks you to remember the famous book and film of the incomparable 007, You Only Live Twice. The whole world knows 007. Birth too happens twice! (As per the ancient Indian system, persons belonging to certain sects are dubbed as being born a second time when they undergo particular religious rituals.)

If you are really honest, you cannot reject that excellent reasoning…

*Surface appearances: It has been suggested often (especially by our dear friend, The Brat) in these pages not to stick to serious scientific facts and figures always. We would be missing a lot of joy that way. In keeping with that spirit, we can examine a suggested anomaly as follows. Take a bottle of dirty, polluted water. It obviously contains a lot of bacteria and other kinds of living cells. Next, discard that moniker bacteria, and think of them as living cells. Say, life, in short; there is nothing logically wrong with that. Next, imagine that the bottle is as big as the earth. Then, your bacteria–life–extends to all parts of the bottle: top, bottom, inside, center, surface, and so on. Still, we are on logical and scientific grounds. In the next step, think of the earth itself instead of the bottle. The surface of the earth contains an enormous and astonishing amount of life in myriads of forms.

Surface. Surface only, that is what we want to stress. Compared to the volume of the earth (roughly a bottle of 9000 miles diameter), the *surface on which life exists is negligible.* The anomaly is that whereas in the case of the bottle, life exists uniformly throughout the bottle, it *exists only on the surface of the earth!* Discard those odd bits of 'living' cells that geologists dig out sometimes. Compared to 9000 miles, the depth to which humans have managed to dig down is negligible. This is something to be wondered at seriously. The readers will at once point out that the temperature of the earth goes on increasing as we move inside, that there is no air, no water, and so on. All that does not count for our essential argument. Moreover, Brat points out—just as the reader pointed out—that mighty, much-honored evolution had had millions of years to evolve and adopt and improvise, and could have easily created life forms in those depths too. Brat has a point there. (Unfortunately, we cannot summon evolution to the witness stand.)

*Strength in numbers: Welcome from the pages of 'congregation.' Brat said there he has an *anomaly* in his sights. Well, what he meant is simple. There is a big board with 64 squares, black and white. There are 16 white pieces at one end and blacks at the other end. At one end, the famous world champion, Vishy Anand (or any world champion of your choice) sits, beaming benevolent smiles at his opponents. Plural, yes, because *one thousand beginners* are crowded at the other end. It is a battle of one against 1000. Any bet on who is going to win? Numbers, ha, ha, ha, Brat laughs.

Strength in concentration? Take liquids, especially of the medicinal kind. Then, say a litany and invoke the venerable gent who invented Homeopathy. Then, take one part in ten of your original medicine and add water to dilute it by a ratio of ten to one. Then take one part out of that solution and dilute it again. The resultant liquid is now so dilute (thin) that you can say there is practically no medicine left in it. Careful. Doctor Hahnemann will chide you in chagrin. He swears that the thin liquid is more powerful than the original medicine. Proof? All the millions of practitioners of Homeopathy, since then, are proof (and more than proof) enough.

One soldier possesses quite sufficient physical power. A thousand of them together do certainly possess far more power. Think so? As the delightful Yankee slang says, you have got another think coming. Imagine all those thousand soldiers arrayed, standing rigidly at attention before a general–*one single person.* It is unnecessary to comment further, but Brat cannot help asking, "Who is more powerful morally, mentally, legally?" And he chuckles, murmuring, "Ah, numbers."

There are roughly more than a million malevolent dangerous bacteria seething inside the guts of that patient there. The doctor gives him one single small tablet. Within hours, all the bacteria are wiped out. Numbers? What numbers? (For the discerning/smart reader that you are: You have become aware that Brat is deliberately concealing some data and concentrating on numbers. Suppose you could condone him, though the Queen of Logic may not be amused.) Following the same vein of argument, you can replace the bacteria with a *million* men, and the capsule with *one* nuke. That one nuke will wipe out one million humans. (God forbid–may such an event never happen.) Such kinds of analogies are aplenty. Let us close this with one last sample. The black hole is only *one* in *number.* A *million* earths approach it with ignorant curiosity. The black hole simply gobbles all of them for breakfast without batting its metaphorical eyelid.

Lastly, Brat asks us to look at a new administrative act that is going to come into effect. It runs into some pages, comprising of a considerable amount of words. All those words are quite ineffective *without one small signature!* (Does not that also remind you of the famous saying that one picture is worth a thousand words?) That again should remind you that oftentimes simple gestures could be as powerful as the signatures. The power of the gesture depends on the person doing it. Compare the popular 'thumbs down' gesture. If you and I do it, it may not wield much power. But when, in the days of yore, when the Caesar did it, necks rolled.

CHAPTER 35

NATURE LIKES TO PLAY BOTH WAYS

This is another offshoot from the subject of opposites. (In the chapter dealing with that, we saw that Nature often likes to keep opposites together.) A slight variation on the theme also offers us an entertaining perspective. In big urban cities, there will be streets where vehicular traffic is permitted to flow both ways and some streets where the vehicles can move only in one direction. Likewise, there are certain acts in Nature which can be played forward and backward and some acts which can only be played in one direction, that is, forward.

The words forward and backward imply the flow of time. Time, as we all know, can only flow in the forward direction. What we are talking about in this instance is not to be mixed up with that. There are some actions that can be retraced or taken back. An old popular Sanskrit verse says that the arrow shot from the bow and words shot through the mouth cannot be taken back. Very much true. But here and there, in these pages, we have repeatedly said that Nature likes to show you examples opposite to what you observe and make a rule out of. (Writer's license utilized to end a sentence with a preposition. Besides, it perfectly illustrates what we said just now about rules.)

First case; one-way street

*One-way street itself is a good example of where things move in one direction only, and not the other way. There are plenty of parallels in other fields, apart from the arrow we mentioned above.

You set fire to a can of gasoline. It explodes. There is no turning back the event. (Process is a more apt term.)

The candle burns itself out. You cannot trace back the process and have the candle back. (The proverb about the egg and omelet says it perfectly.) Most chemical reactions are of this type.

A glass bottle, once shattered, cannot be remade into its original shape and *state*. In a different context, poets from all over the world have compared the case of a broken heart to this catastrophe–a very touching simile indeed. (A bit of chinwag: Like our Inner Brat, you may argue adamantly (are you a mumpsimus or sumpsimus?) that if all the broken shards of the glass are collected, it is possible, theoretically, to apply glue or some thingummy and assemble the pieces into the original shape. If so, please refer to the word in italics in the previous sentence, *state*.) The shape may perchance conform to the original, but the state of the glass container is an entirely different matter; a repair is a repair.

The scene is back from the past, a few decades back. You are banging away on your venerable typewriter. Egad, you misspelled a word, and lo, you notice that you have left out another word that was in the original manuscript. Drat! You cannot undo the error. (True, there is that liquid something with which you can paint a white strip across the misspelled word, but what about the word left untyped?)

P.S. That was then. Now you do what you do in the second case, as enumerated further below.

*Fall. If a person falls, the person gets up, gathers himself up, and proceeds without looking back. You think so? Well, go and ask Humpty Dumpty. Even all the King's men couldn't set him back.

*Cat and bag. There is a top secret which an organization is guarding carefully with, beg your pardon, utmost secrecy. Somehow, the secret leaks. (Fate of a good percentage of them, especially in these days of diligent hackers.) The cat is out of the bag as they used to say in the old days. Like in the case of Humpty Dumpty, nothing can make the cat go back into the bag; pity.

LOL – Food: Food may travel from the local store or mall to your doorstep and (theoretically) back again. But its real destiny is to go down (yup, *down*) the one-way street. Yes, it is 'the;' you will see it clearly when you realize at the dining table that you have swallowed the food. Thereafter, it (the food) travels *down* along a one-way street, impelled by gravity and propelled by peristalsis as compelled by nature. Hope nobody will contradict it! Apart from physically traveling along a one-way street, the food that you consume undergoes a chemical change so much that the final product in no way resembles the initial object of entry.

*The final word – entropy. Entropy is a very vague but highly scientific term! (Even a few science buffs agree that it is a vague word. Therefore, please do not ask us to define it precisely! In a general way, entropy is described as the amount of disorder in a system as opposed to order deliberately arranged with intent. (Thermodynamics and plenty of mathematics creep in at this stage.) Okay, just concentrate on the word disorder. It is something like the way the molecules move about in a closed container. Scientists have calculated that the entropy of a system without external interference always increases. More importantly, they show that the entropy of our universe (system) is steadily increasing. Even if you do not understand that statement (do not worry; you have my sympathy and company), do not say that it does not concern you. It concerns all of us, because *the increase in entropy means that our universe is going to shut down.* Do not worry, again; it may take some billions of years for that final closing down. The bottom line is that entropy cannot be reversed; one-way street, as we said.

*Evolution: Nature too has prepared a long and grand one-way street for all its beings to tread upon, at a leisurely but sure pace. It is evolution. Starting from the simplest of forms, life has been gradually, bit by bit, over thousands and thousands of years evolving into more and more complex and varied forms. Only a dedicated natural scientist can appreciate the enormous mindboggling varieties and astonishing complexities and intricate patterns of life that exists now as a result of all those million years of patient steps. The apex of this process is the molding of man. This is clearly a one-way process. There is no way a human being can go back down the road of evolution and become an ape! (It can happen only metaphorically when you want to insult your enemy. Or, in a sci-fi fantasy novel.)

*Death is the final word as far as we, living beings, are concerned, and we have already tagged it. In that purview, we have to include aging too. Not only do living beings die, but they age too. (Terrible and sad.) This is not only a one-way street but also a street of no return. An irreversible process. Science–apart from many quack shamans on the Internet–is seriously trying to find ways to retard the process. But slowing it down is quite different from reversing and we may rest assured that reversing the aging process will not be possible. Legends and myths mention persons who have lived for unimaginably long years. The Indian mythology especially lists a few persons–not gods–who have been living eternally; *chiranjeevi* is the Sanskrit word. But that is the business of myths. Aswaththama of the Mahabharata fame is one such, believed to be still roaming in the Himalayas. Quite a few persons of the recent past have mentioned that they have seen him! In China, a person is recorded to have lived for 260 years. In India, Sri Tapaswiji Maharaj, a king turned yogi, has been recorded to have lived for 184 years, being alive till the 1950s.

Second case; two-way street

*As above, you can start this series of examples with a two-way street. If you want to begin the list auspiciously, begin with the politicians. In all countries, they are (deservedly) famous (and experts too) for taking back their words. Not only words, but also promises. (This may be a joke only, or a true occurrence. The journalist met with the politician famous for his unctuous utterances, reminding that he had pledged to give his promise. Uncle Unctuous went in, came back and placed a tube of toothpaste of a well-known brand. The brand name of the paste was Promise. Must be a true anecdote; politicians are capable of anything.)

Still in that lighter vein. You can walk five steps forward and trace them back easily.

Physics – The swinging pendulum of yonder grandfather clock swings one way and back; It does this both in the left and right directions.

Chemistry – In chemistry, there are what are called reversible reactions. Some form of reaction occurs between two chemicals. A visible change in the system occurs. Later on, the process can be reversed and the system can revert to its original state. Without bothering you with scientific jargon, we can offer the example of the famous 'lead acid battery,' the battery invented more than a century ago. They are still in vogue and most equipment needing heavy electricity use them. While being used, the chemicals inside the battery (lead plates and dilute sulfuric acid) undergo certain chemical processes. Later, when the battery is being 'charged' the reverse process occurs. Almost all chargeable batteries of all sizes follow a similar principle; the materials used are different.

Engineering – The piston inside the cylinder of a gasoline engine moves up and then moves back.

Biology – The most important organ of your body, the heart, contracts, pushing the blood along the arteries. It traces back the movement by expanding. The blood in your veins etc, now return to the heart. Under normal conditions of the body, the heart beats 72 times per minute as your doctor must have informed you long back. (Do not worry if it is more or less. Go, read the section on anomaly and come back. You will belong to the group of guys tagged with the name of bradycardia or tachycardia, that is all.) Similarly, the eyes, the neck, the arms, the back, hips, and legs trace back their movements.

Your lungs too keep rhythm with your heart, expanding and contracting as you inhale and exhale. (The one difference here is that you have control over the rate of your breathing, but not on that of your heart beating. There are tales of certain yogis who can control their pulse rate to an abnormal extent. Well, push them into that anomaly section of this book and relax.)

Maths. LOL – Why not? Just simple arithmetical operations. Start from the number zero. Add a dozen numbers and note down the total. Then go on deducting those numbers one by one. You are back at zero! (A similar thing happens when you play Snakes and Ladders. You keep on moving up rung by rung and reach number 99, only one number short of the final goal. Alas, you forgot the snake patiently lying in wait at that house. Suddenly, you are back towhere you started–at the bottom.

*LOL – You are back from those old decades. This time, you are seriously banging away on the keyboard of your laptop. Again, you mistype a word. (You call it a typo. Those guys in those yesteryears didn't know the word. With seriously knit brows they would declare they had committed a typographical error.) As you did then, you notice that you have left out one word. (Things have changed drastically now. MS Word draws your attention to the misspelled word by underlining it in red color. The word you had omitted is a verb, and so Word underlines it with a different color.) Going back is easy now, in contrast with then. The computer has got a nice word for that–undo. You press the Ctrl and z keys and you have undone what you had done. How about the word omitted? No problem; you just 'insert' that word at the proper place. The cursor is ready to oblige your navigation up and down and across the paper. (In the new lingo, it is called a document.)

*Socially: Two persons are initially attracted to each other and they want marriage. They enter into wedlock. Alas (Brat clarifies, "The alas is addressed to the word only as something which existed in a dictionary of bygone days. No socio-political connotations are hinted at."), that lock does not function, or is irrelevant in these enlightened days. The couple soon realize they are not made for each other. They separate. Life has plenty of two-way streets; what has been done, can be undone, thank the law… It is a two-way street. They happen to bump into each other a few years later. Both are wiser now. What was undone, can again be redone; thank the law. Rebound marriage. Ah, life.

Law, we said in the preceding paragraph. The government enacts some law purportedly for the betterment of its citizens. Alas, the citizens (people, as some political ideologies call them) do not see it that way. Widespread, vociferous, violent, wild protests arise spontaneously. Finally, the government repeals the law. A government may even fall and break if it does not take back the imposed law. (Brat, "A country which boasted that it ruled the world broke into two just because of some law enacted over a mundane tea leaf!")

*The ensuing lines can be included as exemplifying both the one-way and two-way streets. Religion is a sensitive word. Since it is an unavoidable (some may say fundamental) fact of life, we will just have a cursory look. A person is born in a particular religion, say A. Later, either being self-propelled, or being persuaded, he converts and joins another religion B. He may stay attached to the second religion for life, or he may have second thoughts and want to come back into the folds of his first religion. If he is accepted back, it illustrates a two-way street. There could be some religions which do not accept a person back once he has crossed over. Well, it is a one-way street for that person.

Nature abounds in cyclical processes. All such processes are examples of two-way streets. Water resides in the vast stretches of the sea. The water is converted as vapor, rises up, reaches the sky, and becomes a cloud–plenty of changes in state. The clouds travel all over the earth. They shed down rain. The rain waters become rivers (plenty of them). The rivers in turn carry back the waters into the sea! If you think of this process in a bald, abstract way, you may feel that it is all very basic and as per scientific laws. But imagine as an exercise, the entire surface of the earth (and the skies above them) and try to visualize in how many kinds of dramatic and breathtaking ways rains descend on earth, and the equally dramatic and breathtaking ways that the rivers flow across hundreds and thousands of miles on land. Further realize that without that water in the form of rivers, lakes, and wells and underground reservoirs, neither humans nor living creatures can survive. Verily, water is life itself; we must all be thankful to mother Nature for creating this grand cycle of sea-rain-river-sea.

*LOL moments: Considering humans to be a part of the Great Nature, we can say that Nature has found a way to take back or correct its mistakes through humans. Very facile–we just have to say 'sorry' and the error is remedied! We can take back what we uttered also, as the politicians all over the world have been demonstrating.

CHAPTER 36

LIMITS, CONSTRAINTS

Creation, or the universe, appears to be infinite. (Better add the caveat "Well, almost," or else some science nerd will begin nitpicking on that word infinite. They may show by a kind of jugglery that what appears to be infinite is a special kind of finite!) The universe as we know now is only limited by the capacity of our instruments and equipments of exploration. With the construction of more and more powerful telescopes in the coming days, we will definitely be able to see farther into the universe. The interesting point is that even though Nature is limitless, all objects and activities inside it invariably have limits (either upper or lower or both) and constraints. A list of all such instances will fill up a whole book. Since this book is not about lists but parallels and metaphors, we will limit (damn, another pun again) the scope of our search.

Begin with the book itself, then. There are books and books of all sizes. In modern times, there are some (not many, sure) books that run to a thousand pages or more. They are big books, no doubt. The funny part is that it is more difficult to write poetry than prose, and yet epics written in the poetic form are bigger than books of prose. Recent epics like Savitri, older ones like the Iliad and Odyssey come to mind. The great Indian epic, Mahabharata, by the incomparable VedaVyasa, contains more than a hundred thousand couplets! Yet, even a hundred thousand is not unlimited, or infinite. From books, the connection leads us to languages.

For one, the vocabularies of all languages are limited. A language like English may contain one million words (!), but yet it is a limited number when compared with infinity. Secondly, when it comes to writing down those words, a most severe form of constraint is placed on the alphabet. This is so in the case of all languages. (Damn practical and intelligent, no doubt.)

Size: Entering the practical world of objects, we see that the same rule reigns, both in the case of inert matter and living creatures. Objects created by nature like mountains and hills–though they be the Himalayas or Andes or Rockies–are yet limited in size. The same observation holds good in the case of the oceans like the Pacific or Atlantic. The lengths of the rivers are limited. (Brat, "Show me a river that goes around the globe.") Giant trees in America and Africa like the sequoia and the baobabs have definite (though big) sizes. Yeah, even planets and stars have definite sizes. (Brat, "I cannot comment. Chandrasekhar has already set a limit on the size of stars!") And the continents and countries in those planets–only one planet qualifies for this statement as of now. (Brat, "Show me a continent as big as the earth.")

The dinosaurs were the largest creatures of a bygone era and at present, whales and elephants hold the record. Still, their sizes are limited. (Brat says that he has yet to come across a whale that is one kilometer in length, or an elephant that is 50 feet tall.) We humans too are no exception. (Brat, "Have you seen a human being 20 feet tall? Giants and Cyclops of mythologies do not count. Nor do yetis.") Going down a rung further, if you take a living organism like a human, there is a limit to the size of the limbs and organs it contains. It goes on and on.

Since you mentioned biology, well, the lifespans of all creatures are limited. (Brat, with tongue in cheek, "That includes human beings also.")

Brat is not being deliberately facetious when he says that sex is limited. No, he is not talking about the act, but about the genders–only three as far as he knows. (Nature decided that for propagation of life, two genders were enough. The third one was probably an experiment in variation.)

There is a limit to the number of hours you can keep yourself awake, forgoing sleep. (Now and then, an article appears in a paper about somebody not having slept for so many months etc. If that is true, well, we have a good suggestion. You can include such an item in our chapter on anomalies!)

There is a limit to the number of things you can do simultaneously, just as there is a limit to the number of things you can be aware of at a time. (Nature is great, we say again and again. Your body is engaged in a number of actions simultaneously, most of which you need not be aware of: breathing, beating of the heart, digestive process, filtering actions of organs like kidneys, lungs, liver, secretions from glands, traveling of signals along your nerves, inputs to the body from the five sensory organs, etc. If you were to pay attention to all of them at once, you will go mad, you will not be able to function properly.)

Numbers, nature's and manmade: In creating limits, man is not lagging behind Nature. (Brat, "He need not brag, Nature made him so.") Nature created infinite objects. If you go on giving unique, individually different numbers to each of them, well, you cannot. It needs a whole lifespan and more. (Brat, sadly, "Nobody will be able to remember all those *names* of individual numbers.") Here lies the greatest genius of Man (the capital M represents woMan also). Objects and their numbers may be infinite, but representing them symbolically is easy when a name is given to a group of them, like say, 10. By employing the numerals 1 to 9 and 0. (Greater than the greatest invention. Brat is convinced that the symbol 0 was not invented by Man, but that Nature itself took mercy on him and breathed inspiration into him. Brat, "See that beautiful play on words, breathe and inspiration.") Infinity is contained in just 10 numerals! Digital man has gone one up on that and now he needs even less. Just 0 and 1 are enough for him to represent any number. Those damned beautiful binaries, 0 and

1, can not only represent numbers, but almost anything in the universe, with the help of another equally damned beautiful entity called a CPU. ("The world in my pocket.")

*National borders are the best known (and most unavoidable, given the practical realities of the world of humanity) examples of manmade limits. Visas and passports exemplify the constraints.

Voice: Elsewhere, we saw that there is a threshold to our sense of hearing. The flipside also holds good. Our voice produces sound waves of many frequencies. If you are a devotee of music, you will appreciate the statement all the more. Yet (as Nature decreed), there are lower and upper limits to the variations in the audio frequencies of the human voice. This is natural since our instrument of producing sound is made of flesh and bones. Animals and birds, of course, have a different and higher range. But still, there is no need to say that all these sounds have limits.

Colors: Sound tips us to look at colors. There may be millions of colors all around, but at the basic level they all boil down to three. RYB: red, yellow, blue (or CYMK). Over.

Shapes: There may be millions and millions of shapes all around, but at the fundamental level they all boil down to two: a straight line and a curve.

*Ruling: There is a limit to the number of persons who can rule (or run the machinery of) a country. In the olden days it was the king. Now it is the prime minister or the president. They have, of course, ministers or senators under them to manage various portfolios. Usually, there is a single person at the top. (Troikas and oligarchies do not last long.) The nation may be quite big with a huge population, but still, the governing members are limited. Naturally. If all the billion persons of a country are engaged to administer its governance, utter chaos and utmost failure will ensue at once. (Brat, "If a bus is carrying 50 passengers, ask all of them to drive it and see what happens.")

Forces: The universe is unimaginably big, and our earth is immensely varied. Thus, at first glance, you may think that there must be plenty of 'forces' acting in the universe. The surprise is that there are only four kinds of fundamental forces in the universe. The whole of the working mechanism of the universe comprises of these four forces only. Four—just four. (Elsewhere in these pages, their names and properties have been enumerated.)

Dimensions: The spirit of the forces is reflected in the good old familiar (most solid and reassuring) three dimensions of the world we live in: length, breadth, height. Forget time and the theory of relativity for the present; we are talking of solid, palpable objects. The less said about the 10 or 11 dimensions of the String Theory, the better. (Brat – "They are just mathematical conveniences.")

An LOL observation á propos dimensions and space. The greatest limit or constraint on an object or person imposed by Nature is expressed in this old textbook law in physics, "Two things cannot occupy the same place at the same time." Wonderful theorems and physical laws have been derived using this simple law. A human being cannot be at two places at the same time, obviously. All the legal cases with alibis are based on this.

A small tailpiece to that LOL. Previously, we have shown how we cannot avoid going back and touching Big Bang and Einstein once we go on elaborating on any topic. Add Quantum Theory to the list, and we have The Great Trinity. The reference to Quantum god comes here on that old law of alibi. You and I (and the judge) may be quite certain that an object cannot be at two places at the same time. But with Quantum Physics, anything is possible, since it solemnly states (and believes, believe me) that that object is in an infinite number of states, until…oh, forget it. You can argue on any subject, but not on Quantum god.

Speed: Looks like we cannot escape from the embraces of The Big Bang and Albert Einstein in these pages. Let us say the inevitable and end the topic. There is an upper limit to the speed of any object on earth—it is the speed of light. Zeno has already set the lower limit–it is the speed of the Tortoise. (Brat – T, is in caps because that tortoise was kept by Zeno.) Amen.

Sight: The faculty of sight exhibits dual properties; it is both limitless and has limits. Starting from the focal point in the eyes, the field of vision expands into a cone of ever-increasing size. (Leonardo da Vinci has noted down many interesting observations on this cone of vision in his famous notebooks.) In that sense, if the cone keeps on expanding, it will encompass the whole of the universe! Not yet, in another sense, because the human side-angle of vision of the eyes is limited; you have to turn your neck in order to see what is to your left or right. Secondly, you cannot see what is to your back. Thirdly, we have the famous limitations of short sight and long sight. If an object is too near our eyes, we cannot see it clearly. If the object is far away also, we cannot distinguish it clearly. (Brat – "Please do not tell me you can see yonder hill clearly, for god's sake. Ask your kid to hold that newspaper on your lap at a distance of 20 feet and try to read the small print. You can see yon hill clearly, can you? Fine. Point out the object Ultima Thule to me on da sky up thaar.")

Perhaps Nature designed us like that for our own comfort and peace. If we were able to see everything all around us, left and right, front and back, and up and down at the same time, and near and far objects equally clearly, we would probably go mad, or swoon due to the immensity of sensory input. Nature has been kind to us. One small sip at a time, one small step at a time. That is how infinity and eternity are built up.

A FAREWELL NOTE

I t is in the dictionary too!

The phenomenon of what we have examined extensively in this book can be found elsewhere too, not to mention everywhere. Everywhere, yes; it can be found in the dictionary too. No, we do not mean the word 'parallel' (smile). Just go on searching words in the dictionary at random, and chances are that most of the times, you will come across a word that can be linked to our subject here; and you can go on expanding from there. It is a fascinating exploration apart from being an entertaining word game. To illustrate the point, we will give here a brief list of words. Accidental, Brick, Colorful, Depth, Effect, First, Ghost, Heart: Hope that is enough to illustrate what we mean.

The end, but not quite the end. The ideas that have been discussed above are ever-fresh and it can become a thrilling hobby for the readers to go on observing these parallels cropping up at every turn, throughout their lives.